NIXON'S ENEMIES

ALSO BY KENNETH FRANKLIN KURZ:

The Reagan Years A to Z

NIXON'S ENEMIES

BY
KENNETH FRANKLIN KURZ

LOWELL HOUSE

LOS ANGELES

NTC/Contemporary Publishing Group

Library of Congress Cataloging-in-Publication Data

Kurz, Kenneth Franklin.
    Nixon's enemies / by Kenneth Franklin Kurz.
       p.   cm.
    Includes bibliographical references (p.   ) and index.
    ISBN 0-7373-0000-0
    1. Nixon, Richard M. (Richard Milhous), 1913-   —Adversaries.
    2. United States—Politics and government—1945-1989.   I. Title.
E856.K87   1998
973.924—dc21   98-31490
                                              CIP

Published by Lowell House, a division of NTC/Contemporary Publishing Group, Inc., 4255 West Touhy Avenue, Lincolnwood, Illinois 60646-1975 U.S.A.

Design by Laurie Young

Printed and bound in the United States of America
International Standard Book Number: 0-7373-0000-0
10 9 8 7 6 5 4 3 2 1

CONTENTS

ACKNOWLEDGMENTS

Even under the best conditions, an author needs encouragement, advice, companionship, and all sorts of things he never thinks about until he needs them. My family, friends, and associates have supplied all those necessities many times over. My parents, Egon and Elsie Kurz, were unfailingly encouraging and, besides, I owe them my interest in history in the first place. In 1952, I probably knew more about Eisenhower, Nixon, and Stevenson than most other three-year-olds, thanks to Mom and Dad.

My sister and brother, Meredith Kurz and Anthony Kurz, always showed great interest and gave a lot of encouragement during the past year, as did my nieces and nephews, Laura, Jennifer, Daniel, and Theodore.

My nieces' young children put me in mind of why history is important. I dedicate this book to them: Emilia, Yvette, Sarah, and the newcomer who will join our ranks in February 1999.

Many friends deserve thanks, particularly Bruce LaForse, Jacqueline Long, and Paul Goyne for their companionship and moral support during the course of this project. Jim and Ann Lee lent their trailer, their land, their decades of friendship and ines-timable generosity to the project's initial stages, and to my entire adult life. Their children—Kaeton, Travis, and Elizabeth—lent their spirit. My old mentors, Robert Dallek and Paul Boyer, as always, were ready to advise and encourage whenever called upon.

I could not have written this book without the coffee, bagels, and atmosphere of Juice-N-Joe, corner of Reseda and Prairie in Northridge, California. Everyone should go there.

This is my second book for Lowell House, and I again thank them for their diligence and patience, especially Bud Sperry and Maria Magallanes. Also for the second time, I thank Barbara Bernstein, at UCLA, for her help in getting the show on the road.

AUTHOR'S NOTE

Space limitations and editorial policy prevent the inclusion of formal citations in footnote or endnote form in this volume. Therefore, attributions are made in the body of the text, except when the same information appears in three or more published sources.

INTRODUCTION

"Opponents are savage destroyers, haters."

So wrote President Richard Nixon in a note to himself on New Year's Day 1974, in the thick of the Watergate scandal that resulted in history's first and—so far—only presidential resignation the following August. In January, there was talk of impeachment in Congress as congressional committees held highly publicized televised hearings. The news media's extensive Watergate coverage, Nixon believed, turned it into the national obsession it had become. Congressional Democrats and the news media—these were his longtime enemies. They were, he maintained, part of the "liberal" establishment that he despised and which despised him. The powerful establishment, the Goliath, now mobilized its forces to end his presidency, and the Nixon administration died by inches in the merciless glare of publicity and persecution.

Nixon felt that the enemies besetting him had for two decades resented his past victories over them. The most unforgivable victory was his successful pursuit of Alger Hiss, an alleged Soviet agent. Hiss's eventual perjury conviction and imprisonment stuck in the liberal establishment's craw, Nixon believed. There was more, because the liberals who never forgave him for getting Hiss also hated him for winning the war in Vietnam. Nixon insisted that his negotiated peace left South

Vietnam ready and able to defend itself. In that sense, according to Nixon, it was a victory. He held that the liberal establishment originally got the United States into the war, then, during Lyndon Johnson's presidency, those same liberals turned against it. Nixon, their archenemy, managed to end America's involvement honorably, and they could not forgive that. At least, that is how he saw it. With Nixon weakened by Watergate, the liberal establishment now stood ready to exact its revenge.

Nixon later wrote that various commentators said of him that "long before Watergate, I had more intractable enemies than any postwar president." He brought into the White House two decades of accumulated hatred and resentment, but that was just as much from his viewpoint as from his enemies'. When he finally faltered, when he and his administration fell under the siege of Watergate, many of his older enemies emerged from obscurity to join in the drive to impeach him. Jerry Voorhis and Helen Gahagan Douglas, both of whom were Red-baited in election campaigns many years earlier, emerged to make speeches to anti-Nixon audiences. Even Alger Hiss hit the lecture circuit, insisting on his innocence and calling for Nixon's impeachment. While these three had no political power and did not substantially contribute to Nixon's fall, their resurrections from obscurity were symptomatic of the president's decline. Ultimately, Nixon's more current and active enemies had their victory, as the scandal brought down his administration.

After his resignation, in the desolation of political exile in California, Nixon told a friend that he got up in the morning simply to confound his enemies. Combat kept him going; it was central to his character, his career. He was a man of enmity.

Richard Nixon had many enemies. He did not imagine them, they were not figments of paranoia. Politics is a business of enmity, and enemies come with the territory. Nixon faced bitter and insistent opposition throughout his career, and he himself was a bitterly adversarial politician who fought hard and carried grudges. As a member of the opposition party in the middle and late 1940s, he stood for turning back the lingering forces of the

New Deal and defending the nation against those who, he and other Republicans and some conservative Democrats claimed, would virtually sell out America to the Soviet Communists. His campaign style was to attack and hit hard. He showed no mercy to Voorhis and Douglas. He accused the Truman administration of cowardice and appeasement in the face of the international Communist threat. Later, as vice president he attacked the Democrats on behalf of the Eisenhower administration, enabling the president to remain above the partisan battles. Later still, as president himself, Nixon tried to use federal agencies, including the Internal Revenue Service, to punish and sabotage his political enemies.

Nixon defined himself in terms of his enmities more than most other American politicians do. His closely considered and complicated schemes to defeat and ruin his political enemies were not in and of themselves unusual, but he allowed his enmities to shape his thoughts, actions, and policies, often to the point of dominating them. His obsession with his enemies sometimes seemed excessive even to the hardened and committed combatants who worked for him.

That is one of the many reasons Nixon continues to fascinate, bewilder, and haunt his fellow Americans. The tensions and conflicts of his life and career make for compelling drama, and this odd, enigmatic man performed at center stage for a significant portion of our recent history. Was he a remarkable statesman or a common ward heeler? Was he, in journalist's Tom Wicker's phrase, one of us, or one of "them"? Did he epitomize the "Establishment," or did he loathe it and oppose it in ways that would astonish even his harshest critics? That he spent so much of his public life locked in deadly battles against his adversaries highlights many aspects of the man even as it obscures so much about him. We are continually trying to figure him out, to separate myth from history. With Nixon, as with many other historical figures, there is plenty of both.

Even before Richard Nixon resigned his presidency in August 1974, figuring him out became something of a national pastime.

On the international stage, the Watergate scandal brought forth efforts by foreigners to understand why Americans found Nixon so difficult to understand. Various commentators, both foreign and domestic, came up with numerous glib, catchall solutions: Nixon embodied America's dark side; he was the little man who rose to great heights and then fell to equally great depths. Nixon was the David who became Goliath and was then hit by his own slingshot. In a recent dramatic film on Nixon's life, the screen president drunkenly gazes upon a portrait of John F. Kennedy and says, "When they look at you, they see what they want to be. When they look at me, they see what they are." The list could go on; this is sloganeering, not analysis.

Sloganeering often passes for profundity in public discourse, and American popular culture, much of which Nixon loathed, is prone to perky summations and easy shorthand that hint at dark truths lurking below our awareness. Nixon, many pundits emphasize, emerged from the common workaday world of his time and no more understood his own phantoms and demons than we do ours. The assumption, or presumption, is that Hollywood filmmakers and other self-appointed pundits *do* understand the hidden forces of power that the rest of us, in our willful innocence, fail to detect. Those of us who are professional historians are doubly duped, of course. In our academic befuddlement, we lack Hollywood's definitive insights into how things really work.

According to this view, which is popular in post-Vietnam and post-Watergate America, Nixon too never understood how things really work. It is amazing that a man who spent so much of his adult life in and around the highest levels of government should know so much less of the truth than do film directors and any number of actors and comedians. Among the ironies here is how closely Nixon actually agreed in some ways with this viewpoint, at least to the extent that he saw himself opposing what he called the Establishment—except that the establishment Nixon saw as sinister and powerful was what he termed "the Goliath of the liberal and media establishment." Nixon and many of his critics considered themselves the Establishment's enemies, but they had different establishments in mind.

On the other end of the analytical spectrum, some excellent historians have done some fine work on Nixon. Scholars such as Stephen E. Ambrose, Stanley Kutler, Herbert Parmet, and others have created a responsible basis for future Nixon scholarship. Their intellectual integrity precludes indulging in easy judgments and sloganeering, or in post-sixties cleverness. They have arrived at no single answer to the Nixon puzzle because, as intelligent individuals, they have sought none. No one's life comes down to a single answer. "Rosebud" did not summarize the fictitious Charles Foster Kane; "Checkers" or some other single word or succinct phrase ("I am not a crook," or "Let others wallow in Watergate") will not summarize the entirely real Richard Milhous Nixon.

Likewise, this book attempts no answer to some single, essential riddle of Nixon. Ideally, scholarship should be inquiry and analysis, not the promotion of political or other kinds of ideological agendas. Scholarship is flawed because scholars, being human, are flawed. Honest scholarship is an ongoing attempt at objective inquiry. That we cannot fully succeed in attaining objectivity does not mean that we should not try. To abandon the attempt is to fall back into the convenient, complacent, and pleasing refuge of conventional wisdom. To do that is to surrender to mythmaking. Whether the myths are worshipful or iconoclastic, both are equally ideological and idealistic. The myths serve to reinforce political orthodoxy for the left and right; they serve to reassure and comfort partisans in preconceptions. The Nixon of the movies and the Nixon of the polarized legends and illusions is the easy way out.

Another irony is that the actual Richard Nixon is so much more fascinating than the hazy, shambling drunk of Hollywood's imagination. Even for purposes of cinematic drama, the easy way out is unnecessary, for Nixon was not dull. He was a sharp, alert politician with an analytical mind. He had considerable historical and literary knowledge and perspective and a keen instinct for what he could sell to the public. But with all this, Nixon defined himself in deeply personal terms; his views of his crises and enemies figure prominently in that definition. His siege mentality and sense of beleaguerment were at his core. His intensely personal animus distinguishes him from other major political figures who must have had as many enemies as Nixon had. Whereas Lyndon Johnson's story—to the extent that any individual's story can be boiled down to a tidy theme—speaks of backroom politicking and wild electioneering; John F. Kennedy's chronicles a family's dynastic ambitions; and the two Roosevelts' stories detail the Progressive tradition, Nixon's story resounds with his combat against his enemies (though one must take care not to look for Rosebud).

Of his presidential predecessors, Nixon is in many respects much like Woodrow Wilson, whom he admired, even though Wilson was a Democrat. Both Wilson and Nixon stood for internationalism and a strong, central role for America in the world. Both professed a commitment to world peace, but both showed a willingness, even eagerness, to use American military power. Wilson considered himself a pacifist and justified taking military action in Mexico and leading the United States into World War I by defining higher purposes for his policies. Wilson told a British diplomat that he intended to teach Mexicans to "elect good men," and he went to war with Germany, after first proclaiming that Americans were "too proud to fight," in order to make the world safe for democracy.

Nixon, like Wilson, spoke of hating war, and he considered himself a believing Quaker all his life. He served in the Pacific during World War II and, though not a combat officer, he directly experienced war's horror. He lived through a number of Japanese air attacks, but on his way to San Francisco from overseas duty in 1944, he had what he considered his signal experience of war. His cargo plane stopped to refuel at Wake Island and, getting out for a stretch, Nixon for the first time saw a war cemetery. "I shall never forget those white crosses, row after row of them . . . ," he later wrote. ". . . I was overcome with the ultimate futility of war and the terrible reality of the loss that lies behind it." Like his admired predecessor, Nixon was a president who hated war but became inextricably associated with it. Like Wilson, Nixon professed to see war as a means to an end, a necessary evil given the state of the world, but one that had to be eradicated all the same.

Wilson was a self-confessed idealist who worked for a new world order. By contrast, Nixon considered himself a proponent of what he called "hardheaded" programs for ensuring America's advantage in the strategic balance of the cold war. Each man entertained grand ambitions for world peace, though of the two, Nixon was the more realistic and effective. Each man was stubbornly adversarial and apparently believed that his enemies were the principal obstacles to effectuating his political agenda. Each man never seemed to consider that anything about himself may have contributed to his problems, although Nixon, at least, wrote that he "did some stupid things during the Watergate period." In their respective final crises—for Wilson, the fight over the League of Nations, and for Nixon, Watergate—each man misread public opinion and his enemies' resolution.

Nixon said of his enemies: "I don't hate them." One who studies his history, however, may find that difficult to believe. Much of his writing absolutely drips with venomous resentment of his enemies. He admitted various mistakes and misconceptions, but nowhere in his writings does there appear any sign that he understood the extremism and hostility he brought to his political conflicts. To Nixon, his attacks, no matter how unwarranted or brutal, were "politics as usual."

Nixon's emphasis on enmity is part of the sometimes alarming (though selective) personal honesty that partly characterizes his postpresidential writings. Other politicians try to appear statesmanlike. Nixon tried too but was unusual in his willingness to talk "down and dirty" about politics and politicians and to air his many resentments against the enemies he fought all his life: the "Eastern liberal Establishment," the political left, the press, the Kennedys, and Congress, among others. In his writings, the former president sometimes seems possessed by his demons, or at least obsessed *with* them. When one reads the corpus of Nixon's writings, one cannot escape the feeling that his expressions of hatred and resentment are deep and intractable, and are by no means rhetorical. There is nothing academic about Nixon's ruminations, autobiographical and otherwise, and most appear ultimately autobiographical.

Nixon wrote with astonishing frankness about his ambition and drive for higher office. His accounts of his political career are refreshingly free of the cant and disclaimers that characterize other statesmen's memoirs. Nixon's writings plainly show his hardness; though when necessary or expedient, Nixon waxed as sanctimonious as any other politician. Like everyone, he had paradoxical elements in his personality, but his were especially incongruous and displayed themselves in bold relief. He was tolerant and prejudiced, empathic and ruthless, grandiose and hard-headed, brilliant in some ways and limited in others. He could be brutally frank, scheming, and deceitful. He was often shockingly revealing and obsessively secretive. He was an intellectual who resented intellectuals; he was a self-proclaimed outsider who spent much of his career in the citadels of power. He was a man of extremes of temperament, yet he sought the political center.

William Rusher, publisher of the conservative *National Review*, told historians Gerald S. Strober and Deborah Hart Strober that "Nixon has the soul of an alley cat; he travels alone at night, stealthfully." Witness after witness has described Richard Nixon as distant, unreachable, ruthless, and cold. Other witnesses attest to his warmth and concern. Nearly all agree that he was essentially solitary and that he was extraordinarily combative.

Nixon wrote, "In politics, most people are your friends only as long as you can do something for them or something to them." In one of his last books, *Seize the Moment*, he wrote that Russian president Boris Yeltsin "certainly aspires to power—all politicians do . . ." We know that, of course, but we hardly expect politicians and statesmen actually to say so. On more than one occasion, Nixon described himself as an introvert in an extrovert's profession. His propensity for honesty and openness coexists with his equal propensity for secrecy and deceit.

At times, Nixon's writings take on a tone of special pleading while simultaneously telling us hard truths about political leadership. "When we choose our leaders," Nixon wrote in *1999: Victory Without War*, "we must remember that they are not candidates for sainthood." Personal character surely is an issue, the former president noted, "but it is far more important to know whether a candidate has the strength and intelligence to hold his own across the table from Gorbachev than whether he might have smoked marijuana in college." Here Nixon addressed the "character issue" of politicians' private lives, and added that, for instance, Grover Cleveland fathered an illegitimate child, Ulysses Grant was an alcoholic, and Abraham Lincoln suffered from depression. All of them were able leaders, but today, Nixon continued, "... any man who cherishes his private life has to think twice before stepping into public life and submitting himself and his family to murderous vendettas by sensation-crazed reporters and inquisitions by senators posturing for television cameras."

That one passage contains several of Nixon's favorite themes, and smacks of special pleading both for the 1952 fund crisis that nearly resulted in the end of his career and the Watergate scandal that did end his active political career. The 1952 crisis occasioned the famous "Checkers speech," and Watergate drove Nixon to resign his presidency. The passage is at once wise, generous, self-serving, and hostile, and the concluding sentence clearly shows Nixon's enduring resentment for the news media and his old congressional tormentors. The phrase "inquisitions by senators" obviously harks back to Senator Samuel Ervin's special Watergate committee and to the House Judiciary Committee's impeachment inquiry, which, to the end of his life, Nixon regarded as a spiteful show trial and virtual lynching.

The passage indirectly allows that Nixon had some character flaws; in effect, he declares, "I am not a saint." There is even some generosity toward Bill Clinton, who had to contend with the marijuana controversy during the 1992 presidential campaign, as well as charges of marital infidelity. One wonders what else the scandal-ridden former president would have had to say about the scandal-ridden current president, had Nixon lived past 1994 and seen Clinton become the target of an impeachment inquiry.

"I don't think he genuinely liked people," William Ruckelshaus, the former deputy attorney general famous as one of the casualties of the Saturday Night Massacre, told the Strobers years after Nixon's resignation. The former president lent this notion considerable credence. If he tried to conceal the long-standing resentments he harbored, he did not altogether succeed. In his best-selling books, Nixon wrote page after page excoriating his favorite enemies, all the while insisting that he did not really hate anybody. He even devoted an entire chapter to the subject of enemies in politics for his book *In the Arena*, which he published as a sort of supplementary volume to his memoirs. The "enemies" chapter is a curious exercise, as it contradicts a good deal of the excoriating Nixon committed to paper before and after *In the Arena*'s publication.

In other words, Nixon wrote that chapter in his elder statesman's mode rather than his down and dirty mode. Early on, his analysis notes that Franklin Roosevelt once commented that "if a leader didn't have enemies, he had better create them." Nixon thus struck the pose of distinguishing between political and personal enmity, and explained that many political enemies maintain personal friendships. For example, President Reagan and Democratic House Speaker Thomas "Tip" O'Neill waged deadly combat in the political arena, but the president often had the speaker to the White House's residential quarters after-hours to have a few drinks and swap Irish stories. During his own presidency, Nixon wrote, he remained on friendly terms with Democratic congressional leaders Michael Mansfield, Carl Albert, and John McCormick, although those three led some of the stiffest opposition to Nixon's policies.

Still, he conceded, some political enmities cannot help but spill over into personal areas, particularly if the enmity is deeply ideological in nature. "I would like to believe," Nixon wrote in conclusion, "that an enemy is a friend you haven't met. Unfortunately, it is seldom true." Perhaps Nixon believed those words when he wrote them, but he was himself such a relentless enemy that it is difficult not to doubt his convictions on the subject, especially in light of his other writings, some of which this book will examine in due course.

Privately, as the White House tapes reveal, Nixon frequently aired his hatreds and resentments, often in brutal language. That brings us to an especially intriguing part of the Nixon puzzle: his accidental self-revelations. When reading his voluminous writings, particularly the books he authored after leaving the White House, one gets the impression that Nixon is revealing far more than he intends to or realizes. The same is true of some of his interviews. On the subject of Watergate, for instance, Nixon as writer and interviewee fulminated endlessly on the unfairness of it all, the double standards, the exaggerations, the circuslike atmosphere of the congressional hearings and media coverage. No one, he pointed out on countless occasions, ever personally profited from Watergate. He was, he insisted to his dying day, treated with abominable injustice.

Yet, he told David Frost in his first television interview after the resignation, had he been in his enemies' position, he probably would have done the same thing. He said that more or less in passing, tossing off the thought in the middle of more major reflections, but it is one of the most revealing things he ever said. Review the history of the Alger Hiss case and the inflammatory rhetoric Nixon used in his campaigns for congressman, senator, and California governor, and you will find the Nixon who would have called for the president's head had he stood on the opposite bank of the Watergate moat.

From *In the Arena*: "I always find it amusing when psychohistorians I have never met conclude that I have what they consider to be a warped personality. Usually they trace it to my poor, lower-middle-class family. In fact, these pseudo-biographers are telling you more about themselves than about me, because it is obvious that in their books, *lower* class signals a *lack* of class" (italics in the original).

Nixon was not in the least amused, and his class resentment glares through this passage. Many of his associates, including chief of staff H.R. Haldeman and John Ehrlichman, assistant to the president for Domestic Affairs, have commented that Nixon never let anyone forget his "poor boy" beginnings. Nixon identified many of his adversaries—particularly the liberal Establishment, the liberal news media, and liberal professors—with the upper-class world of power and privilege. He believed the elite held him in contempt, and in turn he detested them. He was not wrong; many of his enemies indulged an effete snobbery in their hatred of him.

Richard Nixon held grudges. He overreacted. He could dish it out but had trouble taking it. He harbored an underdog mentality and believed himself constantly besieged by powerful, entrenched enemies; he reacted to the slings and arrows of political conflict with great personal resentment. He felt that he was the victim of double standards. He often affected the stance of wounded victim, which it seems he pretty much believed. He attributed his lifelong striving for achievement to the enmities of his youth. "What starts the process, really, are laughs and slights and snubs when you are a kid," he told former aide Kenneth Clawson. If you are smart and "if your anger is deep enough," you can change how people regard you through "excellence, personal gut performance while those who have everything are sitting on their fat butts."

Former Attorney General Richard Kleindienst told the Strobers that bearing grudges "might have been [Nixon's] great, limiting factor ... [H]e permitted himself to develop thoughts of retribution and revenge." Kleindienst called Nixon's grudges "the small, dark side of his character"; and he believed it "might have led to his downfall."

Nixon never knew when to stop; the factor that powered

his ambition to rise also powered the grudges that resulted in Watergate and his ruin. Nearly every Nixon biographer and chronicler has commented on this flaw. It may stand out as the quintessential Nixonism, the Shakespearean tragic flaw. If Nixon had lacked that "factor," he may never have risen so that he could fall.

Nixon's grudges and vindictiveness were legendary. Former White House speechwriter William Safire described the president as "magnificent in defeat and vindictive in victory." When he lost, he made a graceful statement and moved on. When he won, he schemed to avenge himself by defeating his enemies. No victory was complete; there were always enemies to be crushed. During campaigns, his attacks were vicious and devastating, as when he ran for the House of Representatives in 1946 and the Senate in 1950 against Jerry Voorhis and Helen Gahagan Douglas, respectively. The nation still remembers Nixon's mudslinging and Red-baiting in those campaigns. Nixon called such things "politics as usual," yet he was outraged by attacks of similar intensity against him, and his attackers had to be vanquished utterly. It was politics as usual only when he did it.

Yet Nixon complained endlessly of the double standards applied to him. The press, he said, condemned his political tactics but ignored worse misdeeds committed by the Democrats, especially the Kennedys. His enemies condemned him for bugging opponents and taping Oval Office conversations, while, Nixon maintained, opponents had bugged his offices over the years and he was not the first president to place recording devices in his office. Franklin Roosevelt recorded conversations and so did Lyndon Johnson. But when Nixon did it, it was a crime. When Democrats did it, it was ignored, he said.

Yet another in the long series of Nixonian ironies is that some commentators, despite Nixon's self-revelations, often describe him as inhibited, painfully restrained in his dealings with others, and thoroughly unwilling to show his emotions. There certainly is a large measure of truth in these descriptions, but, as is so often the case with Nixon, he was a paradox in this matter.

In an interview with journalist Barbara Walters some years ago, he reacted irritably when she asked him a personal question and suggested that they stick to "something serious." Walters, in a later interview with talk show host Oprah Winfrey, agreed with Winfrey that it was unfortunate Nixon was so unwilling to open up. They spoke of it as a problem rather than allowing for the possibility that a bit of personal reserve may be no bad thing.

The irony is that if anything Nixon was much more publicly emotional than many of his contemporary politicians. He laid bare his financial history in the famous Checkers speech in 1952 and then, when Republican presidential nominee Dwight Eisenhower confirmed that he would remain on the ticket as the vice presidential candidate, Nixon publicly burst into tears.

In his memoirs, Nixon told millions of readers that at his mother's funeral Billy Graham comforted him as he wept. Nixon often acted emotionally in public during the Watergate crisis. He physically shoved his press secretary, Ronald Ziegler, in full view of reporters and cameramen. Nixon sobbed openly and discon-solately at his wife Pat's funeral in 1993. Oddly—paradoxically—he, too, described himself as restrained and inhibited. But the public record is full of instances when Richard Nixon displayed a considerable range of emotions in public view. Further, the raw and powerful emotions that permeate much of his writings, par-ticularly his memoirs, are unmatched in other American states-men's writings.

This enormously complex man was in many ways at war with the world he lived in, even as he rose to positions of lead-ership and dominance. Nixon fought every battle with what he described as "normal partisan instincts," which meant going straight for an opponent's jugular. His own jugular was vulnera-ble, but some of his rivals, such as Voorhis, did not have the instinct to go for it. He lost his congressional seat to Nixon in 1946 and Nixon's enemies remember Voorhis as the future pres-ident's first victim. Voorhis was curiously passive during that campaign, as the Nixon camp branded him a Communist in one of the most famous episodes of Red-baiting in American history.

Helen Gahagan Douglas, on the other hand, tried to give as good as she got, but proved inept. She faced Nixon in the 1950 senatorial election; both were members of the House. That campaign left both combatants with memorable epithets attached to them: Douglas became the Pink Lady and Nixon became, for all time to come, Tricky Dick. Neither invented the other's nickname, but each enthusiastically employed them in the campaign's orgy of mudslinging. Nixon called Douglas "pink down to her underwear," referring to her alleged sympathy for Communists. Douglas referred to Nixon in such choice terms as peewee and pip-squeak, besides the memorable and permanent Tricky Dick.

It was between those two memorable campaigns of 1946 and 1950 that Richard Nixon became a national figure, well known to the American public. In 1947, the freshman congressman took a seat on the House Committee on Un-American Activities, known inaccurately as HUAC—where the defeated Voorhis once sat. Nixon involved himself and the committee in the pursuit of Alger Hiss, a former Department of State official alleged to have been a Soviet agent. That case made Nixon one of the most famous members of the new generation of American politicians to emerge from World War II. Nixon had won his seat in the House largely by Red-baiting, so the pursuit of an accused Communist traitor solidified his reputation as a champion of anticommunism in the early days of the cold war, when fear of communism and the Soviet Union ran rampant among Americans. Nixon was sharply attuned to the times and he knew how to pitch his product—his product, of course, was himself.

Nixon's adversarial nature was his great asset, even as it would prove to be his greatest liability. His capacity for enmity fit the times like a glove and one might make a reasonable argument that Nixon, not the most adaptable of men, may not have risen politically had the times been calmer. World War II ended in 1945 and within a short time the cold war took hold of the voting public's fearful consciousness. The atomic age imposed novel terrors on a nation and world still reeling from the effects of both the

Great Depression and the most terrible war ever fought. Now, with Germany, Japan, and Italy defeated, the American people found in the dark bear of Soviet communism a new foreign enemy at least as frightening as the beaten Axis powers. Fear of the Soviets overseas engendered fear of leftist subversion at home.

In the elections of the immediate post–World War II era, Nixon and other Republicans were only too happy to attack the Democrats for having delivered the United States into the new nightmare. The fears were exacerbated by two key events in 1949: The Communists won the civil war in China and established the People's Republic, and the Soviet Union detonated its own atomic bomb. These events, which occurred with a Democratic administration in the White House, added fuel to Republican charges that Harry Truman and his associates were at best dangerously incompetent and at worst harboring Communist sympathizers and Soviet agents in the executive branch itself—hence the impact of the Hiss case, and its star-making effect for young Richard Nixon.

The Hiss case established Nixon's national reputation as a warrior. That image was already part of his reputation in his home district in California, and now it would define a major part of his political image for the rest of his life. In 1950, the newly famous young congressman won election to the U.S. Senate, having further established his warrior status by savaging Douglas. In 1952, that reputation had a lot to do with his nomination for vice president. Advisers persuaded Eisenhower that he could rely on the young Californian to savage the Democratic ticket as he had Douglas, while the grandfatherly World War II hero comported himself with presidential dignity. Nixon added to his laurels a reputation as Ike's attack dog. That November the Republican ticket won, and Nixon became vice president of the United States.

For the next eight years, the partisan combat assignments fell to Vice President Nixon. He attacked Eisenhower's critics, campaigned for Republican congressional candidates, scorched Democratic opponents, and Red-baited in ways that the elderly,

dignified president could not and would not. Eisenhower periodically had Nixon tone down his rhetoric, since the president
had to work with a powerful Democratic opposition in Congress,
but Nixon's combativeness continued to be useful to the White
House. That Nixon was a young man—he turned forty while vice
president—enhanced his suitability for his vigorously partisan
role. As the Eisenhower era and the 1950s neared their end,
Richard Nixon was probably the most famous Republican, other
than the president himself, and many pundits, analysts, and commentators confidently predicted he would win the presidency
in 1960.

Still young in that election year, Nixon was the first incumbent vice president to run for president since John Breckenridge
lost to Abraham Lincoln in 1860. Democrat Breckenridge's position as President James Buchanan's number two man proved to
be no advantage. Republican Lincoln took the White House and
the Republican party took control of what was left of Congress
after most of the South seceded. No incumbent vice president,
in fact, had managed to be elected president since Martin Van
Buren won the office in 1836 and succeeded Andrew Jackson.
After Breckenridge's defeat, no incumbent vice president even
tried, not for another hundred years.

But none of that seemed to have any bearing on the 1960
race, and it was widely believed that Nixon's incumbency gave
him a distinct advantage over his Democratic opponent,
Massachusetts senator John F. Kennedy. At forty-three, he was
four years younger than Nixon, and he was a Roman Catholic to
boot. Nixon had the advantage of experience, both as a campaigner and as an officeholder, and, despite being a Quaker, was
not regarded as belonging to a religious or ethnic minority.
A Quaker had already been elected president: Herbert Hoover
defeated a Catholic for the office in 1928. The experts said the
smart money should be on the more experienced, more publicly
established vice president.

The experts may not have been wrong, since to this day it is
unclear who actually won the election of 1960. Whatever way

the vote went, and whether or not there was any election fraud in Illinois and Texas, the election was the closest in American history, and approximately half the voters rejected Kennedy in favor of Nixon. As fondly as Americans remember President Kennedy, he won office not by a landslide but in the all-time classic squeaker. The result sent Richard Nixon, not yet fifty years old, into the political wilderness.

It may be fair to say that, as of 1960, not many people saw anything particularly strange about Richard Nixon. His enemies considered him an extremist, but the public apparently did not. In the 1940s and 1950s, he had been a Red-baiter, but that was not unusual, especially for Republicans. He was strident and combative and could not match Kennedy for charisma, but that in itself did not set him apart in any radical way. His national image actually gained stature with his loss to Kennedy. He conceded graciously and at Kennedy's request met with the president-elect to offer his experienced counsel and advice. So, at the end of 1960, Nixon appeared dignified and statesmanlike, the gentleman warrior who fought the good fight and lost.

He had earned a new image, partly because he waged a clean campaign. He did no Red-baiting, made no move to exploit the widespread anti-Catholic bigotry in America, and conducted himself with a maturity and poise he had not shown in previous campaigns. He believed that he may have won, but he did not demand a recount of the disputed votes. He went out looking good, a class act. He carried with him a lot of goodwill from the voters. Two years later, he threw much of that away.

Nixon's disastrous run for governor of California in 1962 changed everything. He Red-baited his opponent, the incumbent governor Edmund "Pat" Brown, and, after he lost, told off the press in the infamous "last press conference," that fateful morning in the Beverly Hilton Hotel in Beverly Hills. That was when he gained his loser image. His 1960 loss had not created the impression that Nixon was finished, but the 1962 fiasco seemed the end of the road. The ABC television network presented a special program called "The Political Obituary of Richard Nixon," and among the talking heads analyzing Nixon's sudden descent into oblivion was none other than Alger Hiss. Reminiscing about the young Nixon of the late 1940s, Hiss said he thought that his adversary was not interested in the facts of the case so much as in "seeking ways of making a preconceived plan seem plausible." Hiss considered Nixon's actions to have been "motivated by ambition, by personal self-serving."

That, in many ways, was the crowning insult: The network had dug up the man whom Nixon helped bury to comment on Nixon's own burial. But Nixon was not buried. The loser image stuck for several years to come, but during his time in the wilderness, he stayed in touch with Republicans around the country, did favors, campaigned for Republicans, and put a lot of politicians in his debt. He quietly stood by as the party's right wing wrecked itself with Arizona senator Barry Goldwater's apocalyptic loss to Lyndon Johnson in 1964, and then emerged as the nation's leading Republican. As 1968 approached, Nixon established himself as the front-runner for his party's presidential nomination.

Through the years 1962 to 1968, Nixon maintained his low profile and did not engage in the combative tactics of his youth. After his relapse into Red-baiting in the California gubernatorial race, Nixon maintained a dignified presence on the scene, and even after he became an active presidential candidate again, he did not revert to his old form. He ran a tough campaign, first against his rivals for the Republican nomination and then against Democrat Hubert Humphrey and American Independent Party candidate George Wallace, but he eschewed "dirty" politics. He really did not need to resort to base tactics, since the wild and traumatic events of 1968 did much of his campaigning for him.

It was a year of riots and assassinations. Martin Luther King, Jr., was gunned down as he stood on the balcony of a Memphis motel, and three months later an assassin shot New York senator Robert Kennedy in the kitchen of the Ambassador Hotel in Los Angeles. Kennedy had just made his victory speech after winning the California primary and appeared to be on his way to winning the Democratic presidential nomination. His two rivals were Vice President Hubert Humphrey and Minnesota senator Eugene McCarthy. President Johnson had decided months earlier not to seek another term and he had announced his decision only days after Robert Kennedy told a press conference that he would challenge Johnson for the nomination. Kennedy's decision came after McCarthy won 40 percent of the vote in the New Hampshire Democratic primary. That 40 percent left Johnson the technical winner of the primary, but McCarthy's strong showing inflicted a crippling humiliation on the president.

McCarthy ran as an antiwar candidate. By 1968 the Vietnam war had radically polarized American politics, and President Johnson's popularity plunged accordingly. A president facing two challengers for his party's nomination is a sorry creature indeed, and Johnson threw in the towel before things could grow much uglier. But things were plenty ugly for the country, as that year saw race riots (especially following King's murder) and riots and demonstrations against the war. To many Americans, particularly the vast conservative middle that Nixon would later name the silent majority, it was clear that the center could not hold and things were falling apart.

In response, another new image emerged for Nixon, or, as some pundits put it, another "new Nixon." Nixon, the onetime extremist, was now Nixon the stabilizer, the bringer of moderation, the restorer of sanity. One of his campaign slogans read, "Nixon's the one." Another read, "This time vote as if your world depended on it." Nixon deplored the "sirens in the night," denounced those who coddled criminals, criticized permissive courts, and preached law and order. Nixon hinted that he knew how to end the war—although he never really said, as many inaccurately remember, that he had a secret plan. Nixon showed voters that the Democrats in the White House and in Congress had delivered America to the brink of chaos. This time, vote as if your world depended on it, for it surely does. The Nixon campaign was sleek, scary, and made masterful use of the available media, especially television.

VICE PRESIDENT HUMPHREY AND FORMER VICE
PRESIDENT RICHARD NIXON, 1965.

It was an effective, at times, brilliant campaign. Nixon's gospel of stability played well against Humphrey's attempts to distance himself from the Johnson administration and Wallace's undisguised racist appeal. But as the autumn wore on, Nixon's lead diminished, and the election resulted in yet another squeaker. It was not as close as 1960, and the vote was not in doubt, but Nixon nearly lost. His reaction to those late developments of the campaign season was purest Nixon. He suspected Lyndon Johnson of manipulating events in Vietnam to attract support for Humphrey. The most glaring instance of this manipulation, by Nixon's lights, was an eleventh-hour bombing halt and American initiatives in negotiating with the North Vietnamese. Years later, as he wrote his memoirs, Nixon still smarted over what he considered Johnson's nearly successful last-minute attempt to snatch away Nixon's impending win.

But Nixon won. His enemies were appalled. At least one Nixon–hater proved almost prescient; the author of this book remembers a friend commenting, "I'll bet Nixon gets caught at something and winds up impeached." Close enough—Nixon resigned just as the House prepared to consider articles of impeachment. As Inauguration Day drew near, NBC news anchor Chet Huntley, about to retire to open a resort in his home state of Montana, told an interviewer that he considered Nixon a shallow man. That Nixon was going to be president, Huntley said, "frightens me." Comedians ridiculed the president-elect on national television. *Esquire* magazine printed an article lampooning Nixon, implying, among other things, that the coming age of Nixon would inflict some sort of extreme middle-class banality on the nation. Snobbery ran rampant, as many of the hip and fashionable derided the uncool poor boy who had won the presidency.

Today's audiences are accustomed to television programs and movies that regularly serve up hostility and paranoia regarding the presidency and other institutions of authority and governance. Much of the widespread cynicism and distrust of government arose after the Vietnam War and the Watergate scandal, and in a very real sense, we are still living out the disillusionment and youthful rebellion of those times. Such attitudes were becoming common even before Nixon won the presidency.

Lyndon Johnson entered the White House upon the death of John F. Kennedy, and had a long honeymoon with the public, press, and entertainment media. He won reelection by a landslide vote in 1964. But, just as many New Dealers could not forgive Harry Truman for not being Franklin Roosevelt, many minions of the new frontier could not forgive LBJ for not being JFK. His Texas drawl suffered in comparison to Kennedy's cultured Harvard accent. Johnson was the earthy Texas cowboy instead of the suave New England aristocrat. The honeymoon ended shortly after Johnson defeated Goldwater, and then began the disdainful attacks on Johnson for his regional accent, for showing his scar on television after he underwent gallbladder surgery, for simply not being cool. With growing dissent and division over the Vietnam War, substantive issues further drained the president's rapidly diminishing support.

Many of those who hated Johnson hated Nixon as much if

not more, and the average television viewer in 1968 might have gotten the distinct impression that Hollywood, aghast at the approaching Nixon presidency, decided to go on a no-holds-barred crusade against it. Nixon's longtime complaints about the hostility of the entertainment media gain credence if one examines Hollywood's reaction to his election. Much of the snobbery that characterized opposition to Johnson found its way into the opposition to Nixon. There was plenty of legitimate, well-considered opposition to Nixon and his ideas and policies, but much of the contempt that some of his enemies had for him did indeed translate into a contempt for the silent majority that elected him.

Again, not all the enmity was unjustified. Nixon had been assiduously making enemies since the day he entered politics, and some observers, such as the author's friend who predicted impeachment, certainly held perceptions of Nixon that proved entirely accurate. It was not long before Nixon's way of seeing things began to color his entire presidency, and so early on, a Nixonian siege mentality took hold in the White House. Numerous members of the Nixon administration have since written that the president, obsessed with his enemies, spent entirely too much time and energy fretting over their moves and dreaming up ways to counter them. He also spent a good deal of time and energy thinking about taking preemptive action—about getting them before they could get him.

Before he was through, Nixon would go so far as to attempt to use federal agencies, especially the Internal Revenue Service, against his enemies. When some of the agencies balked, the furious president insisted that he had been thwarted by entrenched career liberal bureaucrats who had been running their shops since Kennedy's new frontier. Nixon claimed that some of the recalcitrant public servants had been around even since the days of Franklin Roosevelt's New Deal. Nixon's crusade to reorganize the executive branch to concentrate more administrative power specifically in the White House was in large part prompted by his perception of liberal control of the federal bureaucracy.

One does not have to believe in fate, divine will, or historical inevitability to suppose that Watergate had to happen. One need only believe in Nixon. The White House turned into a palace under siege, owing largely to the president's attitudes. The drastically polarized political climate of the time surely aggravated that state of affairs, but it would be difficult to imagine Richard Nixon comfortable or complacent under any circumstances, even—or particularly—at the pinnacle of power.

Crowds of young antiwar demonstrators cursed Nixon in the streets. He viewed the White House press corps as a nest of liberal journalists ready to catch him in any misstep. Liberal Democrats in and out of Congress could be counted on to do all they could, to pull all the strings at their disposal, to defeat him. The new president dug in and prepared for battle.

Nixon thought, or at least wrote, with a good deal of hyperbole; the present study will more directly examine some of his writings in the main body of the book. But even with the Nixonian exaggerations, it is clear that he was not entirely wrong. The times *were* highly polarized, and much of the public discourse had become coarse and abusive. Riots and demonstrations continued to wrack the land. Nixon faced bitter opposition on Capitol Hill, as well as in the streets, as he was the first new president to face a Congress controlled by the opposing party since Zachary Taylor, a Whig, took office in 1849 and found himself squaring off against a Congress dominated by hostile Democrats.

Under these circumstances, Nixon, a man given to enmity and gamesmanship in the best of times, was bound to take aggressive action. He could be counted on to figure that a good offense was the best defense, and so began the various machinations that eventually resulted in the Watergate scandal and the constitutionally premature end of Nixon's presidency. By the time the Watergate burglars were caught in the act in 1972, the Nixon White House had done battle, both openly and in secret, with its enemies on many fronts. The arrests simply heralded the end, although nearly two more years passed before the end came.

Meanwhile, Watergate became the nation's obsession and

fascinated a portion of the rest of the world as well. Younger readers may have some difficulty understanding the extent of the obsession—Watergate in its time was, if anything, more pervasive than, say, the O.J. Simpson case. Cars carried bumper stickers that read HONK IF YOU THINK HE'S GUILTY. As the scandal deepened, some entrepreneur sold another sticker that read DON'T HONK IF YOU THINK HE'S GUILTY. Cartoonist G.B. Trudeau put out a volume of Doonesbury strips entitled *Guilty, Guilty, Guilty!* No one had to ask what the title meant. An ice cream parlor in San Francisco advertised the flavor "im-peach-mint."

Watergate was not just an obsession, it was a pastime. Many of us who lived through it thoroughly enjoyed it. That fact puts the author in mind of Franklin Roosevelt's words, which Nixon paraphrased for *In the Arena*: "If a leader didn't have enemies, he had better create them." Nixon often spoke and wrote about enjoying combat, and biographers have reported that he thrived on it. Some of Nixon's aides, such as Charles Colson, attest to Nixon's enjoyment of planning how to "get" his enemies. It is well to remember, then, that many of Nixon's enemies enjoyed hating him. Just as in the nineties, much of America loved the O.J. Simpson trial (though for different reasons), in the seventies, much of America loved Watergate.

Nixon did not love Watergate. This was not the kind of combat upon which he thrived. During the course of the scandal the president visibly deteriorated, and became testy and defensive as the strain increased. He was grouchy in public, to the point where he shoved his press secretary. He made a memorable and telling Freudian slip during what turned out to be his final State of the Union speech to Congress. While describing plans to reform the welfare system, he asked Congress to join him in overhauling this "discredited president." He probably meant to say "discredited system," or something close to that, but he uttered the deadly words and was obviously shaken by his error. It was one of those moments of palpable tension—in the House chamber and probably in the viewing audience's living rooms. The president recovered as best he could and continued his speech.

Watergate was the challenge Nixon could not meet, the crisis he could not resolve. His presidency destroyed, he resigned in August 1974 and went home to California, there to endure exile, his nation's scorn, and the terrible distinction of being the first president driven from office. Not even Andrew Johnson, the only president actually impeached (although not convicted; the Senate vote fell one short of the two-thirds needed to remove him from office), suffered a disgrace of such magnitude. As Nixon settled in at San Clemente to brood and nurse his wounds, probably the last thing anyone expected, including Nixon, was that he would eventually recover.

Nixon often said that he was not a quitter. That was no hollow sentiment, nor a simple device of self-motivation. It was true. Nixon never gave up. Watergate cost him his presidency and plunged him into a long depression, but he recovered and returned to the public eye. It was a remarkable recovery and public rehabilitation. The first couple of years of his retirement were hellish, but through a singular act of will he established himself as an elder statesman. He wrote important books, made public appearances, and speeches. He had a lot to say, and in his best-selling books, guest columns in newspapers, television appearances, and through other media, he said plenty.

Nixon marshaled his profound expertise on foreign affairs and wrote vital and substantive analyses of the world scene and America's role in it. The former president had a distinct contribution to make, and indeed it would have been a shame had the opprobrium over Watergate deprived us of the benefit of Nixon's experience, regardless of how appropriate the opprobrium was. It is unfortunately true that, as the years wore on, his powers eventually diminished and his age told in his writings. Some of his later material doesn't seem to be as pertinent or perceptive as his earlier contributions, and his old prejudices and resentments somewhat colored his perceptions in all his books. Nevertheless, Nixon played an important role in educating American readers to the hard realities of international politics.

Nixon the elder statesman had much to impart, but Nixon

the fighter had scores to settle. In his sunset years, he extensively and repeatedly revisited his old antagonisms. Like Captain Ahab, from the heart of hell he stabbed at his enemies. He never lost his fire or his sense of grievance. In his first post–White House book, *RN: The Memoirs of Richard Nixon*, he not only told his side of the Watergate story, but he excoriated his adversaries ferociously. As more books followed, so did more excoriating. His writings convey his anger, outrage, and resentment to an extent that the author of this book, for one, doubts Nixon fully understood.

In any case, according to many of the histories, he rehabilitated himself and lived out his life no longer in disgrace. But that is true only to an extent. When, in the early 1980s, Nixon had clearly returned to the public stage and was widely accepted in his new role, one observer commented that Nixon "still couldn't get elected dogcatcher." That undoubtedly was true. The nation gladly accepted Nixon as an elder statesman, but the former president's reputation stayed within certain bounds. No one forgot Watergate, and Nixon was not forgiven for it. He had not transcended his past—or, if he had, then he had done so only in part.

Watergate will never be relegated to the footnotes. It will never be merely incidental to Nixon's career. Watergate will always be central to Nixon's history. He will indeed be remembered as the president who made the opening to China, who initiated détente and visited the Soviet Union. But just as prominent will be the fact that he was the first president of the United States to resign. He was the second president against whom the House Judiciary Committee recommended articles of impeachment. History will always note that Nixon almost became the second president to be impeached. No doubt, future historians will speculate with confidence that, had the House voted impeachment, the Senate would have voted to remove him from office.

Many biographers and commentators have said that there were, in effect, two Nixons. That pronouncement has become a cliché in recent years, and the author confesses to feeling a little trite for repeating it. But it is apt. A striking duality permeates

Nixon's story, both in terms of his life and personality. There is no reason to suppose that this impression will ever change or fall prey to historical revision. Nixon the statesman and Nixon the scoundrel and disgraced political exile will coexist in the histories. Sometimes it seems that the two Nixons were unaware of one another or, as biographer Jonathan Aitken put it, barely knew each other. It is difficult to judge if one was dominant or if both had equal say in running things. Whatever the balance, the results were mixed. Along with his achievements came the bitter enmities that lasted a lifetime, personal torment, and eventual political and personal ruin.

When he returned to public favor, he had climbed up from terrible depths. But he never found total rehabilitation. When Nixon died, there was an understandable outburst of forgiveness from the media and the public, but a few weeks after his funeral, the late H.R. Haldeman's diaries were published. As Haldeman's accounts of the Nixon White House's skulduggery and of the president's own glaring faults claimed public attention, Nixon's posthumous honeymoon abruptly ended.

Central to the study of Richard Nixon is the issue of Nixon and his enemies. Enmity, as a dominant factor in his life, merits examination in and of itself, apart from a general biography of the man or the examination of other critical aspects of his life and career. The present study takes up the question of Nixon's enmities and examines it through several categories. Although most or all of them overlap to varying extents, the author believes that the division serves the cause of clarity.

An entire generation was born and grew up after Richard Nixon resigned the presidency in 1974, nearly two and a half decades prior to this book's publication. Nixon's career and the Watergate scandal are not firsthand memories for them. They knew Nixon the elder statesman, the gray eminence who died only a few years ago. But for many of us, Nixon and his times still are almost current events. So, while this is not a general biography of Nixon nor a general history of his times, the author has included historical information and perspectives about various matters that do not constitute vivid memories or common knowledge for readers of a certain age.

The cold war itself is none too vivid to many young people born since 1974. That is an inevitability of time's passage, and it must be reckoned with by historians. But, if I may drop the authorial voice and adopt the first-person pronoun for a moment, I have noticed that Richard Nixon is among the historical figures who manage to capture the attention and imagination of many of my students. People who do not remember him well, nor his presidency at all, still find him interesting, and many of my students over the past few years have explored the puzzle of Nixon through various research projects of their own. I suspect that Nixon will interest students for a long time to come. His odd mix of statesman and scoundrel exerts a distinct, dramatic appeal.

That said, I will close this introduction with a historian's warning: Many outside the historical field tend to believe that history renders definitive and final judgments. It does not. History judges nothing; those who write and read history do the judging. I offer this because people ask me quite frequently what is the definitive historical judgment of this or that issue or person. There seems to be a basic human urge for finality. Was Nixon a good or bad president? Will Watergate matter to future generations? I am continually asked to reveal the historians' final consensus.

There is no historians' consensus, not in the sense of ultimate judgment. Inquiry never stops. Historical perspectives and interpretations constantly change, as the members of any given generation see history through their own eyes and interpret it on their own terms, based on their own perspectives and experiences. My comments on how future historians may view Nixon are pure speculation. We cannot know how succeeding generations will perceive Nixon or any other historical figure or event. It is also worth noting that Nixon may well be viewed differently at different times. That which seems set in stone to us will not seem so to others—and it is also worth noting that there is no single, definitive view of Nixon, or any other historical figure or event, even in the present. Unanimous judgment never exists about anything.

With all of the above in mind, let us now examine Richard Nixon and his enemies.

PART I

POLITICAL ENEMIES— LEFT, RIGHT, AND CENTER

★ ★ ★ ★ ★ ★ ★ ★

EARLY ANTICOMMUNISM:
NIXON VERSUS VOORHIS

⋆　⋆　⋆

Richard Nixon entered politics in 1946. World War II ended the year before, and the Democrats had been in control of the White House and Congress since 1933. As Nixon prepared to run for the House of Representatives from California's Twelfth Congressional District—where he was born and raised—a long period of reform and a certain kind of government activism ended, as the nation moved in more conservative directions. Nixon and other Republicans would that year end liberalism's long national reign. With the war over and many Americans anxious to return to normal life and set about pursuing prosperity, prospects for Republican candidates for Congress and state offices were favorable throughout the nation. In fact, the Republicans won control of both houses of Congress that year.

When President Franklin Roosevelt took office in 1933, he quickly initiated a series of initiatives to combat the Great Depression. Roosevelt's New Deal, a haphazard collection of programs and projects, aimed to stimulate the economy and impose some amount of regulation of business. Probably the most famous aspect of the New Deal involved using federal funds to create relief programs and jobs. Most scholars agree that, ultimately, the New Deal did not lift America out of the Depression, but Roosevelt greatly expanded both the power of the presidency and federal authority.

America's entry into World War II effectively ended the New Deal, as Roosevelt and the federal government concentrated on the war effort. Roosevelt himself said that he had changed from "Doctor New Deal" to "Doctor Win the War." A side effect of wartime conditions in government was to solidify the expansion of presidential and federal power, a tacit policy that had been in progress during the years of the New Deal. All of this was controversial, and remains so to this day. Many of the New Deal's conservative opponents regarded the program as an assault on the nation's constitutional system of checks and balances, as well as a subversion of American traditions of self-reliance and limited federal power. In the immediate postwar era, Republicans led a national backlash against the government's activism and power of the Depression and war years.

Throughout his political career, Richard Nixon presented himself as a defender of basic American values and a warrior against the left. The leftist enemies of America ranged from the extreme of communism to the relative moderation of the New Deal liberals left over from the days of Roosevelt. Anything that smacked of socialism or communism not only called for vigorous opposition, but also had to be shown to pose a deadly threat to America itself. Nixon's first campaign for political office involved an assault on the New Deal. He ran for Congress in 1946, some years after the New Deal period, but with the war over, President Harry Truman was trying to modify and extend the old New Deal through his own Fair Deal. Nixon and other Republicans leveled charges of communistic subversion at both Truman and his deceased predecessor. In the conflict for America's soul, there was no middle ground. At least, that is how the conservative opposition portrayed matters. Things were not that simple, and the conflict was rife with ironies and contradictions.

In the inflamed political climate of the years just after World War II, Nixon built his original reputation, and his career skyrocketed. He set his sights on an impressive array of targets, lumping together strikingly disparate entities as leftist enemies of America. During the early stages of his career, those he designated as enemies on the left ranged from Truman and twice-nominated Democratic presidential candidate Adlai Stevenson to accused Soviet agent Alger Hiss and leaders of the Soviet Union.

Nixon was by no means the only practitioner of this sort of rhetoric—nor even one of its pioneers. The politics of fear was not new to the American scene in the years after World War II. From the Salem witch trials of 1692 to the Army-McCarthy hearings of 1954 and beyond, what historian Richard Hofstadter called the "paranoid style" has played a major role in American political discourse. The anti-Communist hysteria that held sway from the mid-1940s to the mid-1950s was only one strain of this dubious tradition. Americans always have tended to believe in dark forces conspiring to subvert and destroy the nation, the system, the American way of life. In the post-Watergate period, many Americans believe the federal government itself has subverted the traditional American system and poses the greatest threat to some imagined, basic Americanism.

As noted, this fear of subversion plagued the United States long before anyone thought in terms of left and right. Numerous analysts—James V. Compton and Gary Wills prominently among them—have argued that Americans are particularly prone to the fear of subversion because the United States is an idea as much as it is a nation. We are not what Compton calls an "organic nationality" in the sense that the Germans, English, French, Spanish, and others are. There is no basic American nationality; we are a nation of immigrants in a historically immediate sense. Even the country's oldest inhabitants came from Asia by way of the Bering Strait. Further, we are our own creation. First came our revolution, then, in time, our Constitution. More than most or all other nations, Americans identify their very nationhood with their national system. If you take away the Constitution, remove the Congress and the president, then we are no longer the United States of America and, by extension, we are no longer Americans. Consequently, from the beginning of our history as a nation, there has existed the fear that we might lose our system, our nation, ourselves.

The most likely way to lose what we have would be for someone to take it from us. In the early days, Americans feared monarchist subversion. Thomas Jefferson often accused his political enemies of being "monocrats" who sought to overthrow the Republic in favor of a new monarchical system. In the nineteenth century, Americans feared immigrants and Roman Catholics—and the two groups overlapped during the first waves of Irish immigration. Later in the century, especially after the Civil War, immigrants from Eastern and southern Europe scared settled American residents, including the Irish Catholics who had arrived only decades earlier. Each new immigrant group, be they Catholics from Italy or Jews from Russia and Lithuania, appeared to the older population as potential subverters of Americanism.

Immigration was only one aspect of the threat to American selfhood. Not only foreign peoples, but foreign thinking presented a subversive menace. Economic freedom was central to Americans' ideas of freedom itself. Political and economic freedom were, and are, inseparable in widespread American thinking. But in the nineteenth century, strange, foreign theories arose that struck at American economic traditions, at the heart of the American idea of freedom. Socialism, anarchism, and communism loomed as hazily understood but frightening specters to haunt a recently reunited America still recovering from the shock of the Civil War.

That there is no generally agreed-upon definition of "American" is a separate issue and carries its own problems and conflicts. But that the question even exists in our society has fueled the politics of fear for longer than the United States of America has existed. The Salem witch trials, even though they occurred in colonial times, manifested the Puritans' dark fear of subversion by hidden, satanic forces. In the twentieth century, much of that fear centered around communism, which holds its own special horrors for Americans. Communism forbids private property, and Americans traditionally place private property at the center of their concept of freedom. Consequently, politicians who sought to rouse mass terror of communism had much to work with, since a grassroots fear of communism already existed, as did fears of socialism and anarchism and any number of other foreign doctrines that threatened to destroy free enterprise and abolish private property.

An early outburst of this fear of the left came in 1919 and 1920. The so-called "first Red scare" began with a series of mass arrests and illegal deportations of suspect aliens in response to a series of terrorist bombings. Attorney General A. Mitchell Palmer ordered the roundups after a package bomb exploded in his house. Palmer's primary assistant in administering the raids and roundups was a young Justice Department attorney named John Edgar Hoover. Hoover's fame lay ahead of him, but the attorney general he served unintentionally gave the infamous Palmer raids their historical name. The raids constituted one of the most extensive and massive tramplings of civil liberties and human rights in American history and set the tone for the rest of the 1920s, when a number of civil liberty travesties occurred, probably the most famous of which is the Sacco-Vanzetti case.

Nicola Sacco and Bartolomeo Vanzetti were Italian immigrant Anarchists accused of robbery and murder in Braintree, Massachusetts, in 1920. Convicted on weak evidence before a judge who made his prejudice painfully obvious—he was overheard on at least one occasion to refer to "those Anarchist bastards"—they were executed in 1927 after years of appeals. Their case turned into an international controversy that occasioned mass demonstrations in America and Europe, and drew into focus the basic American fear of subversion by foreign doctrines. The case also radicalized a number of young people in the United States who, disillusioned by what appeared to be the callousness of the American system, turned to leftist solutions to the world's injustices. They were the forerunners of the young radicals of the next decade, when America experienced the Great Depression.

The Great Depression brought on a fairly large leftist upsurge, especially in the cities, and an accompanying upsurge in the fear of subversion. Many conservatives considered the New Deal itself a leftist attack on the American system. But Socialists and Communists did not like the New Deal, either, as they believed it was Roosevelt's nefarious plot to preserve and promote capitalism. Many corporate leaders, meanwhile, denounced the New Deal as socialist or communist and formed a high-powered anti-Roosevelt group called the Liberty League. Among the league's star performers were former president Herbert Hoover, who lost the White House to Roosevelt in 1932 and years later was one of Richard Nixon's political mentors, and former New York governor Alfred Smith. The latter was the 1928 Democratic presidential nominee who lost to Hoover. Four years before that, in 1924, when Smith unsuccessfully sought the Democratic nomination, Franklin Roosevelt made the nominating speech for Smith at the party convention.

The seemingly respectable league joined a shrill and accusatory chorus that opposed the New Deal. Just as Socialists and Communists derided Roosevelt and his New Deal for using reform as a ruse to save capitalism, and called him a Fascist, so the gray-suited Liberty League initiated a scurrilous propaganda campaign that depicted FDR and the New Deal as attacking American traditions and imposing dictatorial government on the American people. Oddly, the league often called Roosevelt a Fascist and a Communist, which is an interesting mixture.

President Roosevelt himself made no secret of the fact that the New Deal was meant to preserve capitalism by reforming it. The New Deal enjoyed strong voter support and Roosevelt was immensely popular, so conservative members of both parties in Congress were reluctant to defy the president by opposing his policies, especially after his landslide reelection victory in 1936. But as the midterm elections of 1938 approached, the New Deal ran into trouble and the Supreme Court ruled some of Roosevelt's programs unconstitutional, so the president embarked on an unpopular crusade to restructure the Court so that he could pack it with sympathetic justices.

That misadventure cost him support in Congress and hurt

him with the voters. Roosevelt's position was further weakened when the economy took a downturn in 1937 and 1938, in what was sometimes called the Second Great Depression or the Roosevelt Recession. Consequently, in the 1938 elections, many conservative Democrats and Republicans won seats in both houses, and Roosevelt thus lost his iron grip on Congress. Conservative Democrats jumped ship and openly turned against Roosevelt and the New Deal. Among them was a representative from southeastern Texas, Martin Dies, Jr. Largely forgotten today, Dies had a far-reaching effect on American history, because he founded the Dies Committee, which eventually became the House Committee on Un-American Activities.

Congressman Dies, along with many other conservative Democrats and Republicans, charged that the New Deal centralized federal authority and gave too much power to the presidency itself. This was an episode in another traditional American conflict, the struggle between federal power and localized power. To Dies and other conservatives, Roosevelt's New Deal was in and of itself a threat to the Constitution and other American traditions; it posed its own subversive danger, because it raised federal power to dizzying heights. But Dies and other enemies of Roosevelt further charged that New Deal programs were full of Communists and Socialists—even Fascists. Dies seized the moment and persuaded the House of Representatives to create a special temporary committee to investigate "un-American propaganda activities" within the United States.

The Dies Committee leveled wild accusations. Usually, Dies and other members accused federal employees of being Communists, although committee investigators also worked to expose activities of Fascist agents in the United States. But Dies and his committee mostly looked for headlines and plagued the Roosevelt administration by hunting for Communists in the executive branch and in New Deal programs. Martin Dies has often been called the immediate predecessor to Senator Joseph McCarthy, and the description has considerable merit. Dies presided over hearings that resembled a combination of circus and inquisition, which would later characterize McCarthy's antics in the 1950s.

President Roosevelt and Congressman Dies, despite belonging to the same party, quickly became archenemies locked in a vicious struggle that itself made headlines. Roosevelt condemned the Dies Committee in public but never actually tried to prevent Congress from renewing its funding year after year. The president claimed that to do so would violate the constitutional separation of powers between the executive and legislative branches, but more likely he held back owing to the committee's strong national support among voters. Possibly, too, the president was still smarting from the shellacking he took when he tried to restructure the Supreme Court.

Even so, the administration aired its displeasure in a number of ways. In 1941, the Justice Department submitted to Congress a report on the effects and results of investigating federal employees for alleged disloyalty. Attorney General Francis Biddle declared that such investigations hurt employee morale and usually resulted in "inquisitorial action alien to our traditions."

During the later war years, the Dies Committee faded from the headlines, although Martin Dies remained a magnet for reporters. The committee actually held no hearings for more than two years, though Dies, on his own, continued to harass the Roosevelt administration with attacks and accusations against usually obscure federal employees. Dies even declared that one government economist might be a Communist because the man's hobby was dancing in an amateur ballet company. He referred to the hapless minor official as an "esoteric dancer" and smirkingly passed around Capitol Hill a snapshot of him in full ballet costume and makeup.

But the committee itself was fairly moribund during this period. Its true glory days lay ahead, after the war's end. When the committee next made headlines, Richard Nixon gained national fame for his role in the Alger Hiss case. Strangely, Dies heard allegations about Hiss several years before the case broke but took no action to net what would have been a considerably bigger fish than he usually went after. It is a wonder that this pre-eminent Red-baiter let that one slip through his fingers.

In 1945, Congress reconstituted Dies's special temporary committee as the permanent House Committee on Un-American Activities. Dies had left Congress by then, choosing not to run for another term under the mistaken impression that he had throat cancer. He returned to Congress in the 1950s with his throat and big mouth intact, though he never again sat on the committee he created. Roosevelt, in 1945, was at the beginning of his fourth term and in the last months of his life, and World War II was approaching its conclusion. The creation of the permanent committee came as a surprise to most observers; the committee had not made headlines for the past couple of years, the war occupied the nation's attention, and the feud between Roosevelt and Dies was effectively shunted aside as the dramatic events of the war's final year took center stage. For the moment, the Red scare was in abeyance. Pundits confidently predicted that the new Congress would kill the Dies Committee when it convened in January 1945. Many people were shocked and surprised when Congress created the permanent committee. Congress may have surprised itself.

The war ended that summer. Roosevelt had died and Harry Truman was now in the White House. Young Richard Nixon returned home from the navy and ran for Congress. Many voters were tired of the trauma and excitement of the Great Depression and World War II and longed to return to the nation's isolationist traditions—in short, business as usual. But with the United States and the Soviet Union now squaring off in the emerging cold war, fear presented itself as a potent and irresistible weapon for Republicans and some conservative Democrats to wield in their drive to steer the country away from New Deal liberal reforms and back to familiar ground. Hence, many congressional candidates in 1946, Nixon among them, resorted to Red-baiting, with great success. After the 1946 elections, the Dies Committee, created by Democrats to interfere with a Democratic president, ultimately turned into a Republican weapon against the entire Democratic party.

Richard Nixon did not spring into the world as a fully formed Red-baiter. In his youth, according to his later reminiscences, he "had no particular anti-Soviet or anti-Communist feelings," even though he felt "disenchanted" with Soviet leader Joseph Stalin for the 1939 Nazi-Soviet pact. In this respect, Nixon was fairly typical of many young adults in the late 1930s. During those years of economic depression, liberal politics attracted a significant portion of the nation's youth, and many went further into Socialism and even Communism. Nixon was not drawn to either one, but he apparently respected Stalin and the Soviets as staunch opponents of Hitler and the Nazis. That was a common sentiment; many Americans saw the Soviet Union as Europe's great anti-Nazi bastion.

In 1939, Stalin shocked the world by allying the Soviet Union with Hitler's Germany. After years of denouncing Hitler and the Nazis as the most dangerous enemies of Communism, Stalin's action caused mass disillusionment among American Communists, and the American Communist party sustained massive desertions. Non-Communists reeled from the shock as well, and many moderates who had respected Stalin, such as Nixon, became, to use his curious term, "disenchanted." Even so, Nixon's attitude toward Communism and the Soviet Union remained "one of general disinterest," although he despised Hitler.

Prior to 1939, Nixon recalled, he had no objection when President Franklin Roosevelt granted diplomatic recognition to the Soviet Union in 1934, and during the Spanish civil war he sympathized with the anti-Fascist loyalists, who were known to be heavily socialist and communist. Then, once the United States entered World War II, Nixon appreciated the fact that the Soviets had allied with America against the Nazis. In 1945, he was "elated" when the Soviets supported the creation of the United Nations. Nixon believed strongly in the international organization since, "as an admirer of Woodrow Wilson," he regretted that America had not joined the League of Nations after World War I.

Like many Americans, Nixon grew alarmed about the Soviets after the war ended and the cold war began in earnest. In March

1946, Winston Churchill, recently ousted as Britain's prime minister, visited Fulton, Missouri, as the guest of President Truman, and delivered a memorable speech, one of the epochal addresses of the twentieth century. "From Stettin in the Baltic to Trieste in the Atlantic," Churchill told his audience at Westminster College, "an iron curtain has descended across the continent." The fallen leader went on to detail the ramifications of the growing Soviet domination of Eastern Europe.

Churchill, one of the great polemicists of the English language, thus invented a memorable and politically useful term: the Iron Curtain. The next year, American financier Bernard Baruch coined the term "cold war." Those two new additions to the international political vocabulary vividly captured the divided world that took shape in the wake of a cataclysmic world war. Nixon later wrote that Churchill's Iron Curtain speech "profoundly affected my attitude toward communism in general and the Soviet Union in particular."

There is no reason to doubt Nixon's account of his political evolution regarding communism and the Soviet Union. Such was quite common in his time and place. Still, many Americans were largely indifferent not only to communism and the Soviet Union but to the world at large. They wished to return to the isolationism of the past. Nixon was among those who understood that the world and America's role in it had changed. In this he was right in line with Truman and many Democrats. Republicans were by and large more isolationist and initially resisted Truman's determination to take America on the path of a superpower. But like Truman, Nixon believed that there was no guarantee of a lasting peace, as "freedom was now threatened by a new and even more dangerous enemy."

Even so, Nixon had not entered politics to crusade against world communism. He ran for Congress at the suggestion of a consortium of local Republican businessmen in his home district. He called them the Committee of One Hundred, and he seemed more interested in undoing the New Deal, as were his sponsors. President Truman wanted to update the old New Deal to postwar times and was trying to push programs of his Fair Deal through Congress. Nixon told the Committee of One Hundred that he would run against the incumbent Democratic congressman and suggest a program that he called "practical liberalism," which he would offer as an "antidote" to the incumbent's "particular brand of New Deal idealism." Whatever he meant by practical liberalism, the wording did not seem to trouble the conservative Republicans on the Committee of One Hundred, and Nixon won their backing for his congressional candidacy. The committeemen, and the majority of local voters, as it turned out, believed that the incumbent no longer represented the interests of their district. Actually, the committeemen *never* thought the incumbent represented their interests and were excited by the prospect of ousting him at long last.

Democratic congressman Jerry Voorhis, the inveterate New Dealer in question, presented a particularly obliging target for the young challenger. A solid, hardworking representative, he faced no serious challenge from the time he entered Congress in 1937 until Nixon came along. The changing times weakened his prospects for reelection, as Voorhis's district and much of the country took a postwar conservative turn. Voorhis's own political history now rendered him vulnerable to challenge in that volatile year. The liberal New Dealer had been a Socialist in his youth, then evolved into a liberal Democrat, and now stood ready for political extinction.

The business community in the Twelfth District never liked Voorhis, and he never liked them. Each side had a point. Voorhis was interested in agricultural reforms, cooperative farming, and related issues, and he had an eye for conservation and careful use of oil resources in California. His consistently liberal voting record in the House did not fit well in what was essentially a Republican district. Journalist Tom Wicker succinctly summed up Voorhis's situation in 1946: "He antagonized the banks with his 'funny money' views. He opposed a bill backed by insurance companies to exempt them from antitrust laws. He angered oil

companies by working for federal control of offshore oil . . .
He offended other corporations by trying to limit their tax
deductions . . . Farmers were upset with him for supporting
agricultural unions."

Surely, Voorhis was an odd duck in politics. Idealistic and religious, he had much of the evangelical crusader about him
despite his glaring lack of charisma as a campaigner. His liberal
views did not prevent him from authoring the Voorhis Act, which
required political organizations controlled by foreign nations to
register with the Department of Justice. The act required such
organizations to give the department information about their
membership, sources of contributions, officers, and a variety of
other matters. The Justice Department determined "foreign control" by examining a suspect organization's affiliation to or col-
laboration with any "international political organization" or if it
derived its policies and positions at such an organization's "suggestion." The bill's obvious targets were American Fascist and
Nazi organizations and the Communist party.

Voorhis served as one of the original members of the Dies
Committee. Voorhis never liked Dies and never fully approved of
the committee's methods, but he served at the request of the
House Speaker, Sam Rayburn, who wanted a liberal Roosevelt
man to keep an eye on things and help rein in Rayburn's rambunctious fellow Texan Martin Dies. Voorhis was one of two
members who served that purpose; the other was New Mexico
Democrat John Dempsey, and they both kept the White House
posted on the committee's plans and activities.

Voorhis later wrote that he considered some of the committee's work useful and honorable—in its first few years of
existence. He particularly approved of exposing Fascist agents
in the United States and believed that shady Communist activities deserved exposure, as was reflected in the Voorhis Act. What
Voorhis did not like was Dies's grandstanding and hostility to
Roosevelt and the New Deal. Voorhis also recognized that the
committee often crossed the line into witch-hunting, and soon

the California congressman turned into an outspoken opponent of renewing the committee's funding whenever the question came up for a vote on the House floor.

Although he bucked the Dies Committee and was outspoken in his support of New Deal reforms while representing a decidedly conservative area of California, Voorhis remained popular with the voters in his district. They elected him five times by sizable margins. But that was before 1946. Even then, many political observers considered Nixon, or any possible Republican candidate, a long shot against Voorhis. But many members of the Committee of One Hundred sensed that the congressman was vulnerable, and so did Nixon. Apparently, they correctly read the shift in the nation's mood—or at least the mood in the Twelfth District.

Nixon's first election campaign set the tone of his career for years to come, and in some ways for the rest of his life. The young navy veteran followed the same path as many other Republican candidates across the nation, accusing Democratic opponents of harboring Communist sympathies, or unwittingly serving Communist interests, or even of being Communists themselves. The Republicans who engaged in such tactics banked on popular weariness with the liberal policies of the Roosevelt-Truman years and some good old-fashioned fear of foreign subversion. Nixon, the future president of the United States, waged a campaign that can fairly be described as brutal and vicious.

He was careful and methodical. As he awaited his discharge from the navy in Baltimore, he familiarized himself with Voorhis's record and contemplated the congressman's weaknesses. By the time he returned to California as a civilian ready to campaign, Nixon had a pretty clear idea of how to defeat Voorhis. He attacked two critical areas. The first method of attack played on public weariness with the rationing and shortages of consumer goods that lingered from wartime, as well as inflation. Part of these difficulties had been caused by the war, but there had also been a series of strikes that helped restrict the availability of consumer goods. Consequently, one of Nixon's campaign slogans was, "Had enough?" Nixon and other Republicans thus portrayed themselves as agents of change, ready to set aside the "naive liberalism" of the New Deal and lead the country to progress and prosperity in the postwar era.

As the primary election approached, Nixon gave a hint of what was to come in the general campaign. Years later, Voorhis bitterly quoted one of Nixon's campaign statements: "If the people want bureaucratic control and domination, with every piece of human activity regulated from Washington, then they should not vote for me but for my opponent.... Next Tuesday the people will vote for me as a supporter of free enterprise, individual initiative, and a sound progressive program, or for my opponent who has supported . . . the foreign ideologies of the New Deal administration."

The foreign ideologies of the New Deal administration. There was the second tack: Red-baiting. He opened fire on this front in face-to-face debate with Voorhis in South Pasadena. Nixon wrote his own account of this confrontation. Voorhis, according to Nixon, opened with a "rambling, discursive" statement on the workings of government, involving the relation between the executive and legislative branches and "the need for progressive legislation." Voorhis defended President Truman and, according to other chroniclers, generally came across as lecturing the unfortunate audience.

When Nixon took the floor, the encounter turned into high drama. He had been an actor in high school and college and reputedly was excellent. One of his old drama teachers told a biographer that Nixon could have gone to Hollywood instead of law school and had a good career as a character actor, which is interesting in light of his frequent stiffness and discomfort in public. The fiery young candidate took thorough command of the proceedings and zeroed in on the federal bureaucracy, "meat and housing shortages," and the overall chaotic state of labor relations in the United States. Later in the debate, Nixon's real campaign theme emerged. He claimed in his memoirs that he had made no false charges, but an analysis of the exchange shows that he did. In South Pasadena, Nixon made his debut as a performing Red-baiter, and he treated the audience to one of the more impressive and devastating examples of the art.

Prior to the debate, Nixon and his supporters had charged that a Communist organization openly supported Voorhis's reelection. The group in question, a branch of the local Congress of Industrial Organizations (CIO) called the Political Action Committee (PAC), in fact did not support Voorhis. The CIO was angry at Representative Voorhis for what they considered his unsatisfactory stand on union issues. The CIO-PAC was subject to the bossism and ethical problems of Big Labor, and there also was a substantial leftist element within the group, some of it Communist. The Communists disliked Voorhis for authoring the Voorhis Act and for his anti-Soviet positions.

Nixon's advisers deliberately confused the CIO-PAC with another organization, called the National Citizens Political Action Committee—or NCPAC. The NCPAC was a liberal group and, like the CIO-PAC, had Communists in its membership. Its Southern California chapter numbered among its members such notable non-Communist liberals as actors Melvyn Douglas, the husband of Nixon's future opponent for the Senate, and Ronald Reagan, soon to take up the conservative cause. The chapter's many Communist sympathizers and Communists resented Voorhis, as did the Communists in the CIO-PAC, for condemning the Soviet Union's expansionist policies in Eastern Europe. Still, the non-Communist liberals endorsed Voorhis, an action the Communists bitterly fought. Voorhis, worried about the Communists in the group, did not welcome the NCPAC's endorsement. Nixon knew all this, but in the South Pasadena debate, he purposely confused the issue and declared that the heavily Communist CIO-PAC had endorsed Voorhis.

Voorhis unwittingly collaborated in his own destruction, as he gave Nixon the opening to capitalize on the PAC charge. Each candidate had plants in the audience to put hard questions to his opponent. A Voorhis plant asked Nixon why he was falsely accusing Voorhis of receiving the CIO-PAC endorsement and challenged Nixon to prove his charges. Nixon dramatically strode across the stage and thrust a piece of paper at Voorhis, proclaiming that here was the proof. It was just someone's position paper recommending that the NCPAC endorse Voorhis; it had nothing to do with the CIO-PAC. The flustered Voorhis did not respond effectively. Nixon had bluffed, and Voorhis blinked.

The rest of the evening was a triumph for the challenger and a disaster for the off-balance congressman. It was also a lesson in the politics of perception. Nixon's dramatic gesture thunderously upstaged the simple truth that the piece of paper he thrust at Voorhis did not substantiate a single one of his charges, but his performance electrified the audience and hobbled his opponent.

A quarter-century later, Jerry Voorhis offered his analysis of Nixon's campaign tactics in *The Strange Case of Richard Milhous Nixon*, a bitter attack on his former rival, published as President Nixon sought reelection. Voorhis pointed out, accurately, that much of Nixon's strategy and tactics originated with his campaign manager, a lawyer and Republican political operative from Los Angeles, named Murray Chotiner. Voorhis detailed what he called the "Chotiner formula for political success." First, discredit the opponent. Second, associate the opponent "with an unpopular idea, concept, or—better yet—organization." Third, "attack, attack, attack, never defend." When the opponent defends himself, then "learn to whimper." Whimper, and "accuse him, your opponent, of using unfair political tactics by calling you a liar!"

In the week after the South Pasadena debate, Nixon's Red-baiting intensified. Voorhis recalled an advertisement the Nixon campaign ran in local newspapers. It said, among other things: "Don't Be Fooled Again! Five times Jerry Voorhis has had the support of the radical groups because he was at one time a registered Socialist . . . While he has been carrying the Democratic colors in recent years . . . REMEMBER, Voorhis is a former registered Socialist and his voting record in Congress is more Socialistic and Communistic than Democratic."

In an earlier autobiography that he wrote shortly after leaving Congress, Voorhis recalled an editorial that ran in two newspapers in the Twelfth District. "Jerry is not a Communist, but not many members of the House have voted against more measures the Communists vigorously oppose than he. It takes a smart politician to get the support of the CIO Political Action Committee in Washington and appeal to the voters at home as a conservative."

In his memoirs Nixon gave his own spin to the 1946 campaign. "Despite later—and widespread—misconceptions," he wrote, "communism was not the central issue of the 1946 campaign." That is tricky wording, hinging on a technicality. He was right in that communism was neither a legitimate nor central campaign issue. But the thrust of Nixon's overall attack was Voorhis's alleged communistic and socialistic sympathies. While Nixon never directly said that Voorhis was a Communist, the implication was clear in his speeches, statements, and campaign literature.

Some Nixon supporters were more direct, and as Election Day approached, a telephone campaign commenced in the Twelfth District. Anonymous callers rang Twelfth District residences to deliver messages such as, "I think you should know that Jerry Voorhis is a Communist." There is no specific evidence other than hearsay that Nixon or his campaign staff authorized or administered the telephone calls, but such tactics characterized Nixon's campaigning and that he did not know of them strains credibility. The same thing happened in 1950, when Nixon ran for the Senate against Helen Gahagan Douglas.

Still, much of Nixon's later analysis of the 1946 campaign seems accurate enough. In his memoirs, Nixon cited Voorhis's autobiography. "The most important single factor in the campaign of 1946," Voorhis wrote, and Nixon quoted, "was the difference in general attitude between the 'outs' and 'ins.' Anyone seeking to unseat an incumbent needed only to point out all the things that had gone wrong and all the troubles of the war and its aftermath." Nixon added that he "took advantage of a nationwide phenomenon" that *Time* magazine described as voters' anger at "price muddles, shortages, black markets, strikes, government bungling and confusion, too much government in too many things." It is striking that Nixon left out of his analysis the fear of communism and the Soviet Union, since he utilized it so effectively.

Nixon and Voorhis met in several more debates around the district, and Nixon outperformed Voorhis every time. The local press, led by the prestigious *Los Angeles Times* gave the young Republican extensive and favorable coverage, in striking contrast to Nixon's press relations later in his career. Voorhis and his campaign people, as well as several historians in later years, charged that Southern California papers were refusing to carry his campaign advertisements but carried Nixon's, and that the editors willingly pushed Nixon's candidacy not only in their editorials but in their papers' reporting.

Nixon confused issues even further on the subject of party affiliation. California has never been a strongly partisan state, and in the 1940s and into the 1950s a practice called cross-filing was permitted and commonly used by candidates for elective office. Democrats and Republicans could run in each other's primaries and often did. Both Voorhis and Nixon had filed to run in both parties' primaries the previous June. Nixon won the Republican primary, and therefore the nomination, but in the Democratic primary Voorhis outpolled him by a wide margin. Many local observers considered this a test vote for the general election, and thus confirmed Nixon's underdog status, even though both he and the Committee of One Hundred felt reasonably sure they could beat Voorhis in November.

In those days California voters often were unsure of candidates' party affiliations, and candidates sometimes tried to keep it that way, because in confusion there can be strength. Nixon went that practice one better, and his campaign staff sent out mailers to registered Democratic voters that began, "As one Democrat to another . . ." In the general campaign, Nixon often impugned Voorhis's credentials as a Democrat, reminding voters of Voorhis's Socialist past and declaring that he had sold out the true principals of the Democratic party. It is not unusual for a Republican to appeal for Democratic votes, or vice versa, but one wonders how often a Republican does that by telling Democrats that their nominee does not really cut it as a Democrat.

Richard Nixon won election to the House of Representatives with 56 percent of the vote in the Twelfth District, 65,586 to 49,994. The voters sent Jerry Voorhis home, along with many other Democrats, as the Republicans took control of both houses of Congress for the first time since the Democrats won majorities in the House and Senate in 1932, the year Roosevelt won the presidency. Back in June, Nixon had promised his supporters that he would run a "rocking, socking campaign." As historian Stephen E. Ambrose pointed out, Nixon instead gave them a "dirty one."

Unsurprisingly, he never directly admitted that he had waged a dirty campaign, or that he had ever lied about Voorhis or Red-baited him. Writing in his retirement years, Nixon quoted a favorable *Time* magazine article that reported he had "politely avoided personal attacks" on Voorhis during the campaign. Both Nixon and *Time* were stretching the truth. While what Nixon called "the PAC controversy" supplied some fireworks and excitement at the debate, he argued, "it was not the central issue that motivated most voters." Nixon wrote that Voorhis in 1946 was not "in tune" with his constituents. Voorhis, Nixon went on, "believed in large-scale government intervention, and I did not. . . . He advocated policies that shackled and restricted American industry. His political views were 180 degrees away from most of mine. Most important, his votes in Congress . . . did not represent the wishes of the voters in his district."

Nixon was probably correct, since voters do tend to consider their immediate interests when voting. Former House Speaker Tip O'Neill said, "All politics is local," and Nixon likely would not dispute the point. But whatever influenced the Twelfth District voters, Nixon still waged a misleading campaign, and no amount of downplaying or disingenuous analysis can change history.

After pages of denying having Red-baited or personally attacking Voorhis, Nixon then admitted to doing so. He had a habit of denying something, then making a qualified or apologetic admission, and then denying the admission. It puts one in mind of the David Frost interviews three decades later, when Nixon said he would have "done the same thing" as his enemies did in the Watergate scandal.

In any case, Nixon wrote of the 1946 campaign, "If some of my rhetoric seems overstated now, it was nonetheless in keeping with the approach that seasoned Republicans were using that year." Nixon gave examples of other Republicans' Red-baiting, such as Representative Joe Martin's pledge to rid the federal government of Communists and Communist sympathizers. Martin became the Speaker of the House in the new Congress and asked Nixon to take a seat on the House Committee on Un-American Activities. That request had far-reaching results for Nixon and the United States.

NIXON, CHAMBERS, AND HISS

★ ★ ★

In January 1947, Richard Nixon took his place in the House of Representatives in the Eightieth Congress and, the following year, involved himself in the case that made him a national figure. The Alger Hiss case set Nixon on the path to the Senate, the vice presidency, and the presidency. For the rest of his life, Nixon was obsessed with the case and believed that it earned him the enmity of the press and liberal establishment. He saw much of what befell him in the succeeding decades as the consequences of antagonizing the liberals by exposing Alger Hiss as a traitor to his country. In so doing, Nixon wrote years later in *In the Arena,* "I earned the undying enmity of many powerful people who might otherwise have at worst taken a neutral view of me."

Nixon did not go to Washington expecting to sit on the House Committee on Un-American Activities—more commonly known as HUAC—but the new House Speaker asked him to serve. Nixon impressed Joe Martin, who figured that a young lawyer on the committee would "smarten it up." Assuming that HUAC had to exist in the first place, it surely needed smartening up, as it was a refuge for various eccentrics, racists, and anti-Semites in the House of Representatives.

Initially, Nixon actually fulfilled Martin's wish and served to moderate and contain some of HUAC's wilder excursions, particularly investigations of alleged Communist infiltration and influence of the Hollywood motion picture industry. The committee still did a lot of damage, but Nixon managed to curb a number of harsh and dim-witted interrogations of some witnesses who clearly wondered what they were doing in the dock before HUAC. While the freshman congressman was comparatively moderate, he was nonetheless the Red-baiter who had buried former committeeman Jerry Voorhis, and so not only found a home on HUAC but soon utilized it as a vehicle for bigger things.

The Hiss-Chambers case was a bigger thing. Rarely have so many elements of primal human urges, political and social upheaval, religious fervor and political faith, generational aspirations and idealism, disillusionment and betrayal come together so compellingly, thus forming one of the wrenching dramas of twentieth-century America. Every bit as compelling is the combination of personalities that came together to trigger the affair: Alger Hiss, Whittaker Chambers, and Richard Nixon.

The events and details of the Hiss-Chambers case were as familiar to Americans of a certain generation as Watergate and the O.J. Simpson case were in their times. Hiss-Chambers is the "other" major case in Nixon's history; as Watergate indelibly marks the end of Nixon's active political career, so the Hiss-Chambers case marks its beginning, or rather the beginning of his national prominence. But the case pertains to the entire state of the nation in the immediate postwar years and lends insight into crucial aspects of the effects on America of two world wars and one great depression during the course of three decades. The case also leads us down some of the dark alleys and cloudy byways of the times.

Our conductor on that journey is Whittaker Chambers, a haunted figure whom Alger Hiss described as "a possessed man and a psychopath." After a traumatic and tragic youth, Chambers became a Communist, eventually entering the Communist secret underground. In the late 1930s, he forsook communism, experienced a religious conversion, became a Quaker, and later denounced Hiss as a fellow member of the Communist underground. At least, he experienced a conversion in the sense that people who have such experiences define conversion. In his youth, he had been a believing Christian and a conservative Republican, as has been the case with many political radicals in succeeding generations, unto the present day. Many such radicals eventually revert to their backgrounds, but often with a zealous ferocity that matches their forsaken radicalism. Whether Hiss was innocent or guilty, Chambers, a creature of extremes, was definitely a disturbed, unstable man. He was entirely capable of extensive lying—after all, he spent six years as a Communist agent. But his testimony about Hiss may have been true, or at least largely true.

One man's psychopath is another man's icon. Chambers today is revered by the right, even as he is despised by the left. In 1984, President Reagan awarded Chambers a posthumous Medal of Freedom, America's highest civilian honor, and described Chambers as personifying "the mystery of human redemption in the face of evil and suffering." Hiss wrote the following year, "In the political mannequin that Chambers now is, it is impossible for me to see the unkempt, struggling freelance journalist I knew as George Crosley from the days of despair and hope that marked the New Deal of the mid-1930s." Hiss's harshness is understandable, since Chambers was instrumental in putting him in prison for nearly four years. So was Nixon.

Whittaker Chambers, at the time he came to Nixon's attention, was a senior editor at *Time* magazine and a former agent of the Soviet espionage underground working in the United States. Chambers told Nixon and HUAC that during his career as a Communist spy in the 1930s, he operated in cooperation with a number of other secret American Communists, one of whom was Alger Hiss, a bright young New Dealer. During the 1930s, Hiss served in several federal posts, eventually ending up in the Department of State. He accompanied President Roosevelt to the Yalta summit meeting with Churchill and Stalin in the Soviet Union, and presided over the first general assembly of the United

Nations as the secretary-general in San Francisco. Hiss personally carried the U.N. charter across the country to Washington to submit to President Truman. According to Chambers, Alger Hiss served as an espionage agent of the Soviet Union during his entire federal career.

Whittaker Chambers fell in with the Communists during the 1920s. In *Witness*, his morbid and tormented autobiography, he wrote that "a man does not, as a rule, become a Communist because he is attracted to communism, but because he is driven to despair by the crisis of history through which the world is passing." That sentiment tells far more about its author than about why anyone becomes a Communist. Chambers, given to self-dramatization and apocalyptic rumblings, came from an oppressively troubled family background and never lost the despairing outlook that gave such melodrama and pessimism to his writing. He comported himself gravely, almost humorlessly. One scholar wondered if a photograph of a smiling Chambers existed.

Sam Tanenhaus, Chambers's most recent and thorough biographer, however, wrote that in his pre-Communist days at Columbia University, Chambers was capable of collegiate humor and had some "hilarious" times with his friends there. But the Whittaker Chambers known to history is a mournfully serious figure, a crusader in the search for truth and salvation for himself and for an unwilling and unappreciative world. His memoirs' title itself carries a double meaning in that it describes his role as a witness to the international Communist conspiracy, and refers to the Quaker concept of witnessing before one's meeting, as Quakers call their congregations, and one's God.

Chambers spent his childhood and teenage years in Lynbrook, a suburban town on Long Island in New York. The characters of his youthful melodrama, which extended into his young adulthood, included a mad, almost homicidal grandmother; a cold, distant father who deserted the family for a homosexual lover and then returned; and an equally cold mother who had a penchant for telling the growing Chambers of the horrible childbirth pains he had caused her. His mother, a failed actress, imparted much of her self-dramatization to her elder son. Chambers's younger brother, Richard, unsuccessfully tried to convince Chambers to enter into a suicide pact with him. Richard Chambers tried to kill himself many times before he finally succeeded in 1926. Whittaker Chambers chronicled all of this in his memoirs.

He joined the Communist party in the mid-1920s. After some years as an open party member, he entered the secret Communist espionage underground and became an active Soviet agent. He wrote that he was drawn to communism after a trip to Europe in 1923. Chambers and a friend visited the German Weimar Republic and witnessed the country's "state of manic desperation, reeling from inflation, readying for revolution, while three Allied armies occupied the Rhineland . . ." Germany and the rest of Europe were caught in the convulsive aftermath of World War I. Chambers concluded that "the world had reached a crisis on a scale and of a depth such as had been known only once or twice in history."

To many people, particularly disillusioned young people like Whittaker Chambers, World War I represented the utter failure and bloody collapse of Western Civilization. The old verities of Christianity and nationalism appeared dangerously obsolete to such disaffected idealists, and the radical ideologies of socialism and communism offered more than just an answer to the monstrous problems that confronted a shattered world. These leftist belief systems appeared to be the last hopes for the world's reformation and the human race's salvation. The rebels, particularly the nascent Communists, embraced their new faith with a zealotry virtually identical to religious conversion. To many of the converts, the Soviet Union was the world's hope and inspiration, a sort of secular City of God. That is why, decades later, one critic would refer to communism as "the god that failed." For Chambers, in particular, the Communist creed offered an even more deeply personal solace, for his newfound Marxist outlook allowed him to view his family's disintegration as part of the overall failure of decadent bourgeois society.

To effectuate the victory of communism would be to destroy the conditions that destroyed his family.

Chambers in his memoirs described his conversion as "a choice against death and for life. I asked only the privilege of serving humbly and selflessly that force which from death could evoke life, that might save, as I then supposed, what was savable in a society that had lost the will to save itself. I was willing to accept communism in whatever terms it presented itself, to follow the logic of its course wherever it might lead me, and to suffer the penalties without which nothing in life can be achieved." Chambers found that communism offered him something that "nothing else in the dying world had power to offer at the same intensity—faith and a vision, something for which to live and something for which to die."

He joined the Communist party in 1925. At the time, the American party was, in historian Allen Weinstein's description, "small and elusive." Prior to the Great Depression, the American party was tiny, despite its potential appeal to lost youth like Chambers. But conditions in America had not reached the desperate level of those in postwar Europe, so the Communists made no real headway in the United States until after the economy crashed. Even then, the party never became a major force in American politics or society, but it did attract thousands of members. By then, Chambers no longer operated as a Communist in the open.

During the rest of the decade and into the early 1930s, Chambers served the party as a writer and journalist, working on the staff of the party's newspaper, the *Daily Worker*, and later for the magazine *New Masses*. In 1932, according to Chambers's account, the party ordered him to go underground. Thus began his career as a courier for Communist spies, both homegrown and from the Soviet Union. During the next six years he lived the secret life of the spy, carrying messages and other items between Communist contacts, while supporting a wife and family. He and Esther Schemitz Chambers, whom he had met in the party and married, had two children during the course of his clandestine career.

As an agent, Chambers said he received classified government documents from Alger Hiss. The relationship between Chambers and Hiss is one of the more controversial aspects of the entire case and, as one would expect, each man's account of the relationship drastically differs from the other's. When the case went to the courts, it was the dispute over the relationship— not the alleged espionage activities—that landed Hiss in prison.

According to Chambers, Hiss was one of his contacts in the government, a fellow Communist agent committed to carrying out the will of Moscow in subverting the United States and defeating the Western world. Chambers considered the evil efforts of the Communists to be headed for eventual success. Writing in his usual apocalyptic language in *Witness*, he included Hiss in a select group of Communist subversives. "If mankind is about to suffer one of its decisive transformations, if it is about to close its 2,000-year-old experience of Christian civilization, and enter upon another wholly new and diametrically different, then that group may claim a part in history such as it is seldom given any men to play, particularly so few and such obscure men." Chambers added, "One of them was Alger Hiss."

But in those days of alleged espionage, Chambers was fond of the man he would one day denounce. "Alger Hiss became our personal friend," Chambers wrote, referring to himself and his wife, "in a way that made my relationship with him unlike my relationship with any others in the underground." The "outstanding" thing that Chambers recalled about Hiss in *Witness* was "an unvarying mildness, a deep considerateness and gracious patience . . ." Chambers and his wife felt for Hiss and his wife "a tenderness, spontaneous and unquestioning that is felt for one another by members of an unusually happy family. Nothing in their manner led us to suppose the fact that they did not share the same feeling about us."

Something in Hiss obviously touched the morose Communist courier. On one occasion, Hiss, an avid bird-watcher, and Chambers heard a robin sing near a rural brook. "Do you know what he says?" Chambers wrote that Hiss asked him: "He says,

'Sweet bird, sing!'" Chambers explained that such moments caused him to tell HUAC, "Alger Hiss is a man of great simplicity and great gentleness and sweetness of character." On another occasion of testimony, Chambers described Hiss as "the closest friend I ever had in the Communist party." But he was, according to Chambers, a dangerous spy.

By contrast, Alger Hiss denied ever having been a Communist and until the day he died insisted that he was innocent of Chambers's charges. According to Hiss, he knew Chambers under the alias George Crosley and thought he was the sort of down-on-his-luck freelance journalist commonly found in New Deal Washington. Hiss later wrote that Chambers's or Crosley's financial troubles aroused his sympathy, and the young government lawyer tried to help him out. Hiss sublet a Washington apartment to the journalist and his wife, since he and his own wife had moved to a house in Georgetown. Hiss made Chambers a gift of an old Ford roadster after he bought a new car. "Little did I know," wrote Hiss in his second autobiography, *Recollections of a Life*, "that I was befriending a man without scruples or moral balance, who would make use of my kindness to destroy me." The sublet and the car would come back to haunt Hiss in 1948.

But in the meantime, Hiss felt a distinct affection for the endearingly precarious Crosley. Hiss thought him "a latter-day Jack London," an adventurous young proletarian writer who, Hiss claimed Chambers told him, had worked as a field hand, a streetcar tracklayer, and in any number of other odd jobs in his appealingly colorful journey across the American landscape. Hiss noted Chambers's broken teeth, "startling in so young a man," and considered them a badge of his friend's deprived past.

In the 1980s, Hiss wrote that he believed that he had "unconsciously identified Chambers with my brother Bosley," who died eight years before Hiss met Chambers. Bosley Hiss, older than Alger, was also a writer making a meager living as a journalist. Both Bosley Hiss and George Crosley were "bookish—indeed thought of themselves as men of letters." But there were differences. His late brother had a good sense of humor, but the man he knew as Crosley had "no humor and was utterly self-involved." Bosley was tall, handsome, and fastidious, whereas Crosley was short, heavyset, slovenly, and plain. But Hiss felt sure he had connected the two.

Hiss did not indicate in his memoirs if he also identified with the fact that Chambers, too, lost a brother, or that both men lost a close relative to suicide: Chambers's brother and Hiss's father. Hiss and Chambers had such losses in common with Richard Nixon, who lost two brothers to tuberculosis during his childhood and youth in Whittier.

One cannot help but wonder if Nixon and Chambers identified with one another to any conscious extent. Nixon always resented polished, upper-class types and was known to comment that he himself never was one of the "personality boys." Shy and awkward as a youth, Nixon retained a lifelong sense of being an outsider. Nixon and Chambers—also by no means a personality boy—shared a pessimistic view of Western society, which at times turned into a doomsday scenario. Both decried weak intellectuals and feared the strength of the Communist enemy. Both often struck others as oddly self-absorbed and almost humorless—although both displayed fairly heavy-handed senses of humor on occasion.

Eventually, Hiss stopped believing Crosley's colorful stories and came to consider him a bother and a sponger. Hiss wrote of Crosley's "constant importuning for money." That, finally, caused Hiss to terminate their relationship. When Crosley next asked for a loan, Hiss told him off, saying he doubted he would ever repay the standing loans, Hiss later claimed, and that he saw no reason to continue their association. After the break, according to Hiss, nothing brought Crosley back to his mind for the next twelve years. When Whittaker Chambers denounced Hiss to HUAC, Hiss did not connect Chambers with Crosley; the newspaper photographs of Chambers did not resemble Crosley. If Hiss were being truthful, then a simple memory lapse helped send him to prison. If Chambers is to be believed, Hiss lied about knowing Chambers as Crosley, actually knew him as "Carl," and knew him to be a member of the Communist underground, since he was one himself.

In his 1985 memoirs, Hiss wrote that years after Chambers's accusation, Hiss learned that, during the time he claimed to have known him as Crosley, Chambers was living a secret life as a homosexual. Hiss therefore believed that his rejection hurt Chambers "in a way that I did not realize at the time." Hiss thought that the rejection, "coupled with his political paranoia," motivated Chambers to destroy Hiss by denouncing him as a Communist.

Chambers admitted his homosexuality to the FBI agents after he first talked to HUAC. He secretly revealed his personal history in order to preempt any attempts to discredit him, although it is unclear how confessing homosexuality would protect him in the America of the 1940s. Chambers's father was a bisexual who for a time deserted his family to pursue his homosexuality. Chambers did not desert his wife and children, but he did live a nightlife of encounters in bars and city parks while traveling for the Communist underground during the 1930s. In *Witness*, while Chambers does not acknowledge his sexuality, his sections on Alger Hiss convey deep feelings of hurt and rejection. Some Hiss supporters have argued that Chambers's accusations were fantasies born of rejection, but the possibility that Chambers had mixed motives does not preclude the possibility that Hiss was guilty.

Hiss, unlike Chambers—and, incidentally and importantly, unlike Nixon—came from an old upper-class family in Baltimore and possessed all the old-fashioned social graces both Chambers and Nixon lacked, and that Nixon, at least, resented. Hiss was a graduate of Harvard, a law clerk for the distinguished Supreme Court associate justice Oliver Wendell Holmes, and a fast-rising government lawyer in the Roosevelt administration. However, during his childhood his father committed suicide and the Hiss family fell on hard times. As he grew up, the family bordered on genteel poverty. Hiss's father's suicide gives his life a striking parallel to Chambers's. Unlike Chambers, Hiss had surviving siblings, including younger brother Donald. As Hiss later theorized that he identified Chambers with his own lost brother, many chroniclers of the Hiss-Chambers case have wondered if Chambers may have in turn identified Hiss with his own suicidal brother.

Toward the end of the 1930s, Chambers started feeling disaffected from communism and the party. In 1938, he broke with it and considered himself an endangered fugitive from Communist vengeance. In 1939, he took his story to a journalist named Isaac Don Levine, who arranged for Chambers to talk to Adolf Berle, an assistant secretary of state who was close to President Roosevelt. Chambers described to Berle his life in the underground and said that Alger Hiss, then still in the Department of State, was a Communist.

Chambers's story went nowhere. According to Levine, Roosevelt scoffed at Berle's report. But that account has been disputed and no independent evidence confirms Roosevelt's reaction, if any. During the early 1940s, Chambers repeated his story to the FBI. That agency was interested, however, as apparently other sources cast doubt on Hiss, or, if Hiss is to be believed, FBI director J. Edgar Hoover was out to discredit him. Chambers, however, was reluctant to talk without securing immunity from prosecution for his espionage activities during the 1930s. After his contacts with the government did not lead to much, he moved on to a new career, becoming a staff writer for *Time*, where he rose to the rank of senior editor.

Representative Richard Nixon, too, had heard dubious reports about Alger Hiss. Even though he denied it in later years, Nixon knew of Hiss before Chambers appeared before HUAC in 1948. In his first book, *Six Crises*, written after he lost the 1960 presidential election to John F. Kennedy, Nixon claimed that when Chambers initially testified before HUAC, it was "the first time I had ever heard of either Alger or [his younger brother] Donald Hiss." Actually, Nixon had heard of both men from Father John Cronin. A curious figure in postwar history, Cronin was a Roman Catholic priest whose special interest was Communist subversion in the United States. In the coming years, Cronin would work with Nixon as a political adviser and sometime-speechwriter. Now, in 1948, Cronin informally advised and informed HUAC members concerning alleged subversives.

In 1944, Cronin wrote a report on communism in America that included Chambers's accounts to the FBI in which he named several alleged Communists in government service, including Hiss. In 1948, prior to Chambers's testimony, Cronin gave a copy of the report to Nixon. But it was another witness who led to Chambers's HUAC appearance—Elizabeth Bentley, also a former Communist underground agent. Bentley testified about her activities during the 1930s and named thirty-two government officials as Communist operatives. The committee then subpoenaed Chambers to corroborate Bentley's testimony, as well as to learn what else he might know.

Bentley had made headlines, but Chambers's testimony dropped a bombshell. He described his underground group in Washington, though he did not at that point mention any espionage activities. He told the committee that the group was part of the Communist infiltration of the U.S. government. Chambers named several people, including Alger Hiss. Under probing, Chambers added Donald Hiss to the list, as both brothers held government jobs during the 1930s.

In 1948, Alger Hiss no longer worked in the Department of State. In his 1985 memoirs, Hiss wrote that rumors of his alleged communism had circulated since at least 1942, and the FBI was involved in spreading them. The FBI's involvement did not surprise him, since he believed that FBI director Hoover harbored a personal animus against him. Hiss was "one of the early New Dealers who had complained of [Hoover's] disloyalty to Roosevelt's policies." The rumors motivated Hiss to remain in the State Department past the time he had originally planned to depart. "I did not wish to appear to be leaving under fire." So he stayed a year longer.

The mounting cold war led Hiss to figure that the U.N. would be fairly useless, as the League of Nations had been, so he decided "that my position as coordinator of [U.S.] policies toward the U.N. would no longer be rewarding." In 1947, he went to work as the president of the Carnegie Endowment for International Peace. John Foster Dulles, chairman of the Endowment's board of trustees, had recommended him to the board.

Hiss and Nixon actually had a mentor in common in Dulles, as he advised both of the younger men at various times in their respective careers. Dulles the Republican promoted Hiss the New Dealer for the Carnegie Endowment in 1947. In 1948, Congressman Nixon asked Dulles whether he should pursue the Hiss case on the basis of Chambers's accusation, and Dulles advised him to do so. It is worth noting that in 1948, Dulles was advising New York governor Thomas E. Dewey on foreign affairs. Dewey was the front-runner for the Republican presidential nomination and was widely expected to defeat Truman in November. Dulles expected Dewey to appoint him secretary of state. As things turned out, Dulles had to wait for that appointment until 1953, when Dwight Eisenhower took office as president.

When Chambers surfaced to accuse Hiss in 1948, Hiss detected the hand of Hoover yet again. The FBI director, according to Hiss's analysis, also expected a Republican to unseat President Truman in November, and so sought to curry favor with the Republicans and to pursue his animosity toward Hiss and other New Dealers. Hoover threw the full resources of the FBI into the Hiss investigation, and Hiss was sure that Hoover briefed Cronin and Nixon before Chambers's first HUAC appearance. Hiss later wrote that, besides currying favor with the Republican party, Hoover wanted to cultivate the party's "rising star Richard Nixon," and bolster HUAC "at a time when Congress seemed likely to terminate its existence . . ." Hiss came to believe that Hoover, Nixon, and Chambers in effect triple-teamed him, each for his own reasons: Chambers for neurotic vengeance, Hoover for political vengeance, and Nixon for ambition. Hiss referred to them as "an unholy trinity."

Many Americans had never heard of Hiss, even though he presided over the U.N.'s first general assembly in San Francisco.

But still it was big news that a witness before HUAC, an admitted former Communist agent, named as a fellow and possibly still active Communist agent a former Department of State official who accompanied President Roosevelt to the Yalta conference and now headed the Carnegie Endowment. Hiss took the unusual step of requesting to be heard by HUAC to answer Chambers's charges.

When Hiss testified on August 5, 1948, it was Nixon's first look at him. Nixon saw great contrasts between the smooth, aristocratic Hiss and the disheveled, mumbling Chambers. "Hiss's performance before the committee was as brilliant as Chambers's had been lackluster," Nixon wrote in *Six Crises*. In his later memoirs, Nixon described Hiss as "tall, elegant, handsome, and perfectly poised as he categorically denied Chambers's charge." The accused "immediately went on the offensive." He flatly denied ever having been a Communist or sympathizing with communism or the Communist party. Hiss denied ever having known anyone named Whittaker Chambers. The "elegant" witness displayed such aplomb that most of the committee was bowled over. When Hiss finished, several people, including committee member John Rankin of Mississippi, rushed to shake hands with the aggrieved witness.

Most of the committee was bowled over. Nixon was not. Hiss was the exact sort of "striped-pants type" that Nixon detested. Nixon saw Hiss as part of the Establishment—the elitist liberal Establishment. As early as his student days at Whittier College, Nixon had opposed the striped-pants set by founding a non-exclusive social club to offset their elite fraternity on campus. Nixon's club members eschewed neckties and wore their collars unbuttoned as a sign of their pride in being who they were. Biographers have made much of this episode of Nixon's college days. While it is probably excessive to assert that class resentment in and of itself motivated Nixon to pursue Hiss, it still is pertinent to observe that class resentment characterized much of his outlook on life and that he expressed many of his resentments in terms of class.

UPI CORBIS–BETTMANN

ALGER HISS, 1948.

As noted, Nixon believed he incurred the wrath of the Establishment by going after Hiss. The irony here is that Hiss, too, thought himself the victim of some sort of establishment. As is so often the case, the definition of "establishment" is up for grabs, twisted and shaped to the preference of whomever happens to be complaining.

"It has been said," Hiss wrote in the 1980s, "that Nixon was hostile to me from the outset because he thought I had scorned him." Hiss admitted to harboring a "low opinion" of HUAC and figured that his contempt probably showed. But Hiss claimed that when he first testified, "I had no reason for selective contempt for Nixon. He was simply a pale nonentity placed inconspicuously . . . among the well-known bullies of the committee who played major roles." Whatever the congressman's reasons, whether "hurt feelings" or ambition, he quickly became, Hiss noted, "my unofficial prosecutor."

Nixon certainly understood Hiss's attitude toward the committee and recounted that the accused displayed generous portions of arrogance and snobbery under questioning at that first session and in subsequent appearances before HUAC. Some displays are subject to interpretation. For instance, Nixon felt snubbed on one occasion when he mentioned that Hiss had graduated from Harvard. Hiss affirmed that he had and added, "Yours, I believe, was Whittier." Nixon earned his bachelor's degree from Whittier and his law degree from Duke. It is difficult to interpret that as it appears on paper, since one cannot hear the vocal inflections nor see the facial expressions behind it. But Nixon took Hiss's remark as a distinct slight. On still another occasion, Hiss appeared to correct one committee member's English, although, again, it is difficult to tell merely from the written record. The member, however, reacted angrily.

Therein lies one of the most vexing riddles of the case: Was Alger Hiss guilty or could he simply have been acting stupidly? Hiss aroused Nixon's suspicions at that committee session. By behaving in a manner that could arouse the suspicions of many observers, for, as Nixon put it, paraphrasing Shakespeare, Hiss protested too much. According to Nixon's accounts, Hiss asked if Chambers was present and theatrically scanned the room in search of his accuser. He played to the hilt the role of the wounded innocent, the indignant honorable man aghast at the outrageously false accusation. It was, Nixon recalled, simply too good a performance and it made him wonder.

According to Nixon's account, Hiss at first thoroughly cowed the committee, except, of course, for Nixon. As he told the story, after Hiss testified at the open hearing, most of the committee members thought they had made a mistake by putting Chambers on the stand without corroboration, never mind that Chambers had been subpoenaed to corroborate Elizabeth Bentley's testimony. Immediately after the hearing, a reporter approached Nixon to castigate him and the committee for Chambers's testimony and, later in the day, President Truman told a press conference that this latest HUAC investigation was a "red herring." As Nixon summed up the episode in *In the Arena*,

"The roof fell in on us. Most of the press were harsh critics of the committee anyway, because of its sloppy procedures and the unsubstantiated charges that were routinely made by its witnesses." Nixon added that reporters covering the hearings were "virtually unanimous" in considering Chambers yet another in the parade of bogus or crazy witnesses. They reported, correctly, that the committee's staff investigators had not verified Chambers's story.

The committee met for an afternoon executive session, in, according to Nixon, "a state of shock." There was talk of curtailing the HUAC investigation and turning the case materials over to the Justice Department. Nixon claimed that he objected strenuously. Not only would such a move be a tacit admission that the committee was incompetent and reckless, Nixon argued, but Alger Hiss might be guilty. Nixon saw problems in Hiss's testimony that his colleagues apparently missed and that might add credence to House Speaker Martin's desire that Nixon smarten things up at HUAC. Convincing the committee took some doing, and for a while that afternoon, Nixon had only chief investigator Robert Stripling on his side. Stripling's support may or may not have helped, since his investigators were the ones who had failed to check out Chambers's story.

Nixon was relentless. Hiss, he pointed out, had never actually stated that he did not know Whittaker Chambers, but had hedged by saying he knew no one by that name. Nixon conceded that, while it might be "virtually impossible" to prove that Hiss was a Communist, it still should be possible to determine whether Hiss and Chambers knew each other. If Hiss was lying about not knowing Chambers, Nixon added, "then he might also be lying about whether or not he was a Communist."

The freshman congressman won the day, and the committee agreed to pursue the question of whether or not Whittaker Chambers and Alger Hiss knew each other. That had to be determined before anything else and made it necessary for Nixon to form an odd alliance with Hiss's accuser. Whittaker Chambers was not a sociable sort and did not take to people easily. In the

Time offices his coldness and skittish aloofness were legendary. But he seemed to take to Nixon, especially after the congressman told him that he was a fellow Quaker.

Nixon visited Chambers and his family several times at their small Maryland farm. During one of those visits, Chambers purportedly remembered an intimate detail about the Hiss family: Priscilla Hiss, who had herself been raised a Quaker, sometimes used what Quakers call the plain speech, that is, addressing others as "thee" rather than "you." Nixon found that convincing evidence that Chambers indeed knew the Hiss family well, although someone who knew about Quaker customs could have fabricated this detail.

He may have been unsociable, but Chambers proved more than willing to continue talking to the committee. He displayed something very common among ex-Communists in that, after switching sides, he pursued his new beliefs with all the fervor and zeal he had brought to his conversion to communism. Some of the most strident anti-Communists were subversives and rebels who had seen the light and been reborn as patriots. Often, religious experiences accompanied these epiphanies, as they had for Chambers. Witnesses like Chambers frequently claimed that to testify was terribly hard for them and many of them showed a distinct martyr complex, claiming to sacrifice their civil existences for the sake of the anti-Communist cause. They often were highly melodramatic, and Chambers stood out even in this league.

Another thing many of the former Communists had in common was their stated conviction that in turning against their former comrades, they had left the winning side in the cold war for the losing side. The forces of evil, Chambers and many of his fellow "exes" believed, were heading for an inevitable victory over the forces of good. Interestingly, these individuals usually described their fears in language strikingly similar to the Communists' own—they took the language with them to the other side. Communists believed their eventual victory "inevitable"— that was the magic word, something of a mantra.

Communists and born-again anti-Communists believed in the coming Communist victory for many of the same reasons: The West was decadent, materially greedy, and spiritually demoralized. By contrast, the Soviet Union and the Communists whose loyalty it commanded were disciplined, dedicated, and guided by truth—though the ex-Communists parted company with their former comrades on that last point. The catastrophe of World War I and the economic collapse that brought on the Great Depression strengthened the convictions of those on both sides, who saw the inevitable Communist triumph slouching toward Bethlehem to be born.

Nixon and a HUAC subcommittee questioned Chambers further in an executive session on August 7 and heard his account of his alleged friendship with Alger Hiss and his wife, Priscilla. Chambers was so forthcoming in what seemed fairly intimate details, such as pet names that Alger and Priscilla had for each other ("Hilly" and "Dilly," which Hiss later denied), that Nixon and the rest of the committee were convinced of Chambers's veracity. An impartial reading of Chambers's testimony in that session shows that he could at least rattle off details, but there is nothing to corroborate what he said, and, as he was indeed a very creative writer, a novelist's imagination could well have been at work. But Nixon and HUAC apparently felt emboldened by their now-star witness's performance, albeit out of the public eye, and they called Alger Hiss for a subcommittee executive session on August 16.

In *Six Crises*, Nixon recounted that the subcommittee saw "a very different Alger Hiss" when he showed up to testify the second time. Instead of acting poised and confident, Hiss struck Nixon as nervous and evasive. Chambers's executive session testimony about the details of Hiss's life had been kept secret, but Hiss somehow got wind of it and now tried to make his own accounts answer the evidence that Chambers had given. Hiss looked at two recent photographs of Chambers but maintained that he could not identify the man in the picture. "May I recall to the committee the testimony I gave in the public session when

I was shown another photograph.... I testified then that I could not swear that I had never seen the man whose picture was shown me. Actually the face has a certain familiarity. I think I also testified to that."

Hiss did not consider the face in the photograph distinctive. He then set the stage for a confrontation. "I would like very much to see the individual face-to-face. I had hoped that would happen before. I still hope it will happen today." Hiss got his wish but not that day.

Nixon recounted in his memoirs that he told Hiss "there were substantial areas of difference" between what Chambers and Hiss had separately testified to, and the committee wanted to let Hiss give his explanations before it "arranged a public confrontation." That bomb hit its target. Hiss, perhaps unnerved by having his bluff called, reacted harshly and expressed anger and "hurt" that in a difference in testimonies between himself and Chambers, who was "a confessed former Communist," the committee would doubt his own credibility.

Hiss sounded his challenge: "I do not wish to make it easier for anyone who, for whatever motive I cannot understand, is apparently endeavoring to destroy me. I should not be asked to give details which somehow he may hear and then may be able to use as if he knew them before." Here was Hiss's initial defense: Chambers had somehow gotten hold of details of Hiss's life and then passed them off as eyewitness accounts. Stripling commented that Chambers either had carefully studied Hiss's life, "or he knows you."

Then, after some more fencing between Hiss and Nixon, came a sudden shift—one of great significance to the case, as it turned out. Hiss told the subcommittee, "I have written a name on this pad in front of me of a person whom I knew in 1933 and 1934, who not only spent some time in my house but sublet my apartment." Hiss did not think the photograph looked like the man he named. "If I hadn't seen the morning papers with an account of statements that he knew the inside of my house, I don't think I would even have thought of this name." But Hiss would not speak the name he had written. He did not want the name or any other details to leak to the outside world lest Chambers incorporate them into future testimony in his quest to destroy Hiss.

Hiss did not realize that he already had been had, for earlier in the session Nixon and another subcommittee member, John McDowell, sprang a trap. Chambers previously testified that Hiss once told him he had spotted a prothonotary warbler, a rare sight in the Washington area. McDowell, himself a bird-watcher, saw the possibility of trapping Hiss into corroborating at least that one bit of Chambers's testimony. Nixon assisted McDowell by asking Hiss if he had any hobbies. Hiss answered that he and his wife were amateur ornithologists. McDowell asked, "Did you ever see a prothonotary warbler?" Hiss answered enthusiastically that he had, "right here on the Potomac." He asked McDowell if he knew the place. Nixon interrupted and asked again if Hiss had ever seen one. Perhaps he had not heard Hiss's answer the first time. Hiss, speaking as one bird-watcher to another, asked McDowell if he had seen one "in the same place." McDowell answered that he saw his bird in Arlington, Virginia. Hiss bubbled on, "They come back and nest in those swamps. Beautiful yellow head, a gorgeous bird."

When the events of the session hit the newspapers, for a time the prothonotary warbler was the most famous bird in America. Readers in the 1990s might think of it as a bloody glove with feathers.

The confrontation between Hiss and Chambers came soon after, though not in public. It was a head-on clash between Hiss and that odd combination of Chambers and Nixon. The next day, August 17, the subcommittee, composed only of Nixon, McDowell, and J. Parnell Thomas of New Jersey (who arrived near the session's end), held its executive session in room 1400 of the Hotel Commodore in New York City. At 5:35 P.M., McDowell swore in Hiss as the session's first witness. Also present in the sitting room were Hiss's friend Charles Dollard, a Carnegie Corporation staff member, four HUAC staff members, and the official reporter to record the session. Whittaker Chambers sat out of sight in another room. Written accounts of the session differ; the author has pieced together several, but there is by necessity some uncertainty as to the participants' exact wording and the exact sequence of events.

Nixon described Hiss as "edgy, delaying, belligerent, fighting every inch of the way." Hiss was partly agitated by the sudden death by heart attack of Harry Dexter White, another former government official whom Chambers had named as a Communist. After a period of questioning and sparring about what Nixon called "some collateral issues," Chambers was summoned.

He entered and sat down on the couch reserved for him. Both Chambers and Nixon noted that Hiss did not look at his accuser. Then began what Chambers called the "sad play." Nixon asked Chambers and Hiss to stand. Nixon identified Chambers to Hiss and asked him if he recognized Chambers. Hiss said, "May I ask him to speak? Will you ask him to say something?" Nixon asked Chambers to state his name and occupation, which Chambers did. Hiss asked a few questions about Chambers's voice, to the bewilderment of Nixon. Essentially, he was asking if Chambers always sounded to the committee members the way he did at that moment, since Hiss did not recognize the voice as George Crosley's. Then Hiss spoke directly to Chambers. "Are you George Crosley?" Or he may have asked, "Have you ever gone by the name of George Crosley?" depending on whose account one reads.

Chambers answered, "Not to my knowledge. You are Alger Hiss, I believe." At that, according to Nixon, Hiss reacted as if slapped, and replied that he certainly was, and Chambers retorted, "That was my recollection." Chambers spoke further at Hiss's request, reading from a magazine. Hiss then said, "The voice sounds a little less resonant than the voice that I recall of the man I knew as George Crosley."

Hiss then did something that struck the others in the room as odd. He walked toward Chambers and asked, "Would you mind opening your mouth wider?" Hiss later wrote, "Chambers did not meet my eye. . . . He had given his name in a tight, rather high-pitched, constrained voice, barely opening his mouth." It did not seem to Hiss to be Chambers's normal voice, and he could not see his accuser's teeth. Hiss recalled that Crosley had rotten and missing teeth. Chambers merely repeated his name, according to Hiss, "in a strangled voice." Angry, Hiss demanded, "I said, would you open your mouth? You know what I am referring to, Mr. Nixon." Then, to Chambers again, "Will you go on talking?"

Hiss told the subcommittee that Chambers's teeth looked better than Crosley's, as if "there has been considerable dental work done since I knew George Crosley . . . " Hiss proceeded to question Chambers about his dental work. Nixon wrote that he "could hardly keep a straight face" as "the comedy" played out. Nixon lost any remaining doubt that Hiss knew Chambers as he watched the "incredible, and in some ways almost pitiful performance."

Nixon and his colleagues proceeded to question Hiss about the apartment sublet and the car he had given "Crosley" in the 1930s. Stripling questioned Hiss on several points, finally focusing on the issue of identification. The chief investigator expressed amazement that Hiss insisted on seeing Chambers's teeth and afterward claiming he could not recognize him but for the teeth. Stripling reminded Hiss that, by his own testimony, he knew Chambers as Crosley for a number of months at least, had sublet him an apartment, and given him a car. Yet he could not identify this person, except by his teeth.

Nixon thought that Hiss knew he was cornered. Hiss answered that, having seen some newspaper photographs of Chambers, he did after all detect "some similarity in features." Stripling noted that on August 4 Hiss had testified that he was unable to identify Chambers from newspaper photographs. Hiss replied, "He may have had his face lifted," which was something of a non sequitur. Nixon then allowed Hiss once again to question Chambers directly. Chambers denied subletting the apartment from Hiss but answered "yes" when Hiss asked him if he and his wife and child ever stayed at one of Hiss's Washington apartments while Hiss had resided at another one. Hiss then asked, "Would you tell me how you reconcile your negative answers with this affirmative answer?" Chambers replied, "Very easily, Alger. I was a Communist and you were a Communist." Chambers, in his account of the confrontation, wrote that he "answered very quietly, from the depth of my distress."

A few moments later Hiss, according to both Nixon and Chambers, was frustrated and angry and said, "I don't need to ask Mr. Whittaker Chambers any more questions. I am now perfectly prepared to identify this man as George Crosley." Later, McDowell asked Chambers to identify Hiss officially for the record. Chambers looked at Hiss and said, "Positive identification." That was when Hiss's composure broke.

Furious, Alger Hiss advanced across the room at Whittaker Chambers. His fists were clenched and he looked so angry that one of the investigators rushed in, grasped his arm, and asked him to sit down. Hiss recoiled and said, "I am not going to touch him. You are touching me." As various subcommittee members repeatedly asked Hiss to sit down, he responded angrily, "May I say for the record at this point that I would like to invite Mr. Whittaker Chambers to make those same statements out of the presence of this committee without their being privileged for suit for libel. I challenge you to do it, and I hope you will do it damned quickly."

Nixon wrote in his memoirs that Chambers "showed no fear" as Hiss advanced on him, "shaking his fist," but Hiss obviously was unnerved. Nixon regretted that the subcommittee had previously agreed to keep the session short so that Hiss could get to a dinner appointment at New York's Harvard Club, as Nixon sensed that Hiss was so agitated he might have broken down further if pressed. But the commotion soon subsided, and then it was time to let Hiss go. McDowell thanked Hiss, who replied, "I don't reciprocate." HUAC chairman J. Parnell Thomas, who arrived only a short while before, instructed the reporter to italicize Hiss's words in the record. "I wish you would," Hiss shot back as he prepared to depart.

Nixon believed the case was broken, and he wrote in *Six Crises* the chain of events that eventually sent Hiss to prison had been set in motion. Hiss biographer John Chabot Smith wrote, "Hiss was a gone goose when he left the Commodore that evening, but he was unaware of it." Hiss wrote, "...at the end of this hearing I wanted to make it quite plain that I resented the Committee's callous and ruthless procedures.... It was evident that the Committee and I were now at war." He should have caught on sooner.

Hiss put it aptly when he described Nixon as his unofficial prosecutor. As the committee member who convinced HUAC to go after Hiss, and as an ambitious young congressman, Nixon had much to gain by attracting press attention as Hiss's primary pursuer. There is no supportable reason to suspect that Nixon did not sincerely believe Hiss guilty, even though many of his enemies over the years have maintained that Nixon must have known he was helping to persecute an innocent man. Nixon never saw it that way. He believed Hiss was dangerous and reprehensible. On one occasion he told Chambers that if the American people realized the true character of Alger Hiss, they would want to "boil him in oil."

Nixon zeroed in on Hiss at the next full public hearing of HUAC on August 25, which featured the promised—or threatened—public confrontation of the accuser and the accused. Hiss endured approximately five hours on the stand, during which time the committee, in general, and Nixon, in particular, made it clear that they had arrived at the consensus of Chambers's veracity and Hiss's guilt. That session was, according to Nixon, "the first major congressional hearing ever to be televised." In 1948, there were far fewer television sets than just a few years later, which Nixon, in retrospect, thought unfortunate. "Had millions of Americans seen Hiss on the stand that day...," Nixon wrote in *Six Crises*, "...there would not have been the lingering doubts over the Hiss case, which have continued for so many years." Considering what television coverage did to President Nixon and his administration in the Watergate scandal nearly a quarter of a century later, that statement qualifies as yet another Nixonian irony.

Even with a limited television audience, the August 25 hearing definitely helped seal Hiss's fate even more than the executive session of August 17 had. The five-hour grilling allowed Nixon and his colleagues to build an intricate case against Hiss, pounding away on such details as the sublet and the car. Hiss also had to repeat his identification of Chambers as Crosley, which did not help his case with the public. Finally, after Hiss left the stand, Chambers was sworn in. When asked why their respective stories conflicted, Chambers said flatly that Hiss was lying.

Under questioning from Chairman Thomas, Chambers addressed the issue of communism's appeal to so many middle-class and even wealthy young people. "They seek a moral solution in a world of moral confusion. Marxism, Leninism offers an oversimplified explanation of the causes and a program for action. The very vigor of the project particularly appeals to the more or less sheltered middle-class intellectuals. . . . They feel a very natural concern, one might almost say a Christian concern, for underprivileged people." Such people are aghast at war, at economic depression, and at the evils of the world. When they seek ways to bring about social justices, "At that crossroads the evil thing, communism, lies in wait for them with a simple answer."

Chambers's declaration was meant to explain and further condemn Hiss; the fact that Hiss in his youth had not been privileged may have been lost on Chambers. It may have been lost on Nixon, too, as Chambers's words sound fairly close to much of what Nixon wrote and said in the coming years, which we shall see as the present study continues.

Meanwhile, the August 25 session had not yet ended. Nixon and Chambers had more for the press and the television audience. Nixon asked Chambers, "You were very fond of Mr. Hiss?" Chambers answered, "Indeed I was; perhaps my closest friend." Nixon asked, "Mr. Hiss was your closest friend?" Chambers answered, "Mr. Hiss was certainly the closest friend I ever had in the Communist party." Nixon went on, "Mr. Chambers, can you search your memory now to see what motive you can have for accusing Mr. Hiss of being a Communist at the present time?" Chambers seemed momentarily unsure of the question. "What motive I can have?" he asked. Nixon answered, "Yes. I mean, do you, is there any grudge that you have against Mr. Hiss over anything that he has done to you?"

Chambers launched into an aria. In *Witness*, he wrote that Nixon's question removed the restraint on the emotions that had been building in him all day. Chambers wrote that he struggled to control himself as he answered. He denied any grudge against Hiss and denied hating him. "We were close friends, but we are caught in a tragedy of history. Mr. Hiss represents the concealed enemy against which we are all fighting, and I am fighting. I have testified against him with remorse and pity, but in a moment of history in which this nation now stands, so help me God. I could not do otherwise."

The Nixon-Chambers side now pulled way ahead in the drama competition, far outdoing their enemy's theatrics at the Hotel Commodore. Alger Hiss, his own testimony for the day completed, sat listening in the gallery as the curtain fell.

The next act played out on the radio program *Meet the Press*. At the Commodore, Hiss challenged Chambers to air his charges in public. A witness cannot be sued for anything said under oath before a congressional committee, so Hiss was threatening legal action for slander or libel if Chambers accused him in an unprotected forum. Two days after the August 25 hearing, Chambers told the radio audience, "Alger Hiss was a Communist and may still be one." Hiss did not immediately respond with a lawsuit. Weeks passed. The press wondered loudly why Hiss was waiting. According to Nixon, press coverage had been largely favorable to Hiss and unfavorable to the committee, but Hiss's slowness to sue Chambers turned much of the press against him.

As Hiss seemed to delay in filing suit, Chambers felt certain that the leftist campaign against him had begun. During September, as the *Washington Post*, the *New York Daily News*, and Chambers himself wondered what may have become of Alger Hiss's threatened litigation, Chambers noticed "at least two strange cars prowling around the edge of the farm." Chambers was not sure what to do. If they stepped onto his property, cornering them "might be dangerous," but they usually stayed on the public roads. Chambers did not specify in *Witness* if the prowlers ever set foot on his property, but his wording suggested they might have. Chambers thought, "It made perfectly good sense to suppose that the Communist party might decide to remove me as the one dangerous witness against the conspiracy." He maintained that strangers began asking neighbors questions about his family. Finally, he told his wife that the strangers were Hiss's paid investigators. Chambers figured Hiss had hired them in preparation for the lawsuit that he in fact filed later that month.

At the end of September, about a month after his final HUAC testimony, Hiss sued Chambers in federal court in Baltimore for fifty thousand dollars. As part of that suit, Hiss hired private investigators who did, in fact, probe Chambers's background and may have been the men who questioned Chambers's neighbors. It also is possible they were the prowlers, assuming that Chambers actually saw any. The investigators wanted to find dirt on Chambers—specifically, according to several historians, they sought evidence of Chambers's past homosexual activities. One scholar observed that it is an interesting comment on those times that a confessed former Communist could have been discredited by being exposed as a homosexual.

Before Hiss filed his two suits, Nixon also believed that Hiss was delaying or bluffing. But Hiss related in his first book on the case, *In the Court of Public Opinion*, that his lawyer was out of the country. In the meantime he sought advice from several other attorneys, then filed suit shortly after his own counsel returned from overseas. Several weeks does not seem unduly long for putting together a fairly complex lawsuit, in the best of circumstances. Nixon's analysis of the slant of the press coverage is debatable, as well. Predictably, Chambers told the press that Hiss's suit was part of the Communist conspiracy. "I do not minimize the ferocity or the ingenuity of the forces that are working through him." Hiss shortly thereafter filed a second suit for twenty-five thousand dollars against Chambers for that statement.

Nixon likely agreed with Chambers's assessment of the lawsuit, for Nixon's siege mentality showed itself early in his career and was evident here. He believed that the Truman administration and the liberal establishment, that is to say, the left as Nixon defined it, had arrayed itself against his pursuit of Hiss. He believed that they had targeted Chambers as well, a belief Chambers ardently, and unsurprisingly, shared. Both men's fears were exacerbated by the results of the 1948 elections.

First and foremost, Harry Truman surprised the nation and probably the world—and maybe to some extent himself—by winning the presidential election. The Republican candidate, New York governor Thomas E. Dewey, had been expected by nearly everyone, including most of the nation's press, to defeat Truman. The major public opinion polls had predicted that Dewey would win by a wide margin. Truman, apparently personally unpopular, also faced a shattered Democratic party. Conservative Southern Democrats bolted when the Truman faction endorsed a civil rights plank for the party platform. They formed the States' Rights party, more commonly called the Dixiecrats, and ran North Carolina governor Strom Thurmond for president.

The Democratic far left wing also bolted and reconstituted itself as the Progressive party, reviving a venerable party name from the early part of the century. These latter-day Progressives were angry at Truman for what they considered lackadaisical pursuit of New Deal policies. Many of them resented Truman's anti-Soviet policies. Among the latter was their presidential candidate, Henry Wallace, who was Franklin Roosevelt's second vice president. Truman replaced Wallace in 1945 and became president.

The polls had never been so completely wrong before or since. To be fair, with the Democratic party so thoroughly scattered, it might have been hard even using today's polling techniques to untangle the mess in 1948. But Truman pulled off the impossible: He won with 49.5 percent of the vote to Dewey's 45.1. Thurmond and Wallace nearly tied, with approximately 2.4 percent of the vote each. Nixon and Chambers both dreaded the immediate future, knowing as they did of the victorious Truman's disdain for HUAC and the pursuit of Alger Hiss.

Adding to the bad news for the two were the results of the congressional elections. The Eighty-first Congress would have a Democratic majority. According to Nixon, the 1948 results "really jolted Whittaker Chambers." Hiss's accuser fell into a deep depression; he expected that Truman and the Democratic Congress would allow "the whole investigation of Communist infiltration in the United States and particularly in our government . . . to die." Both men feared that Truman would make good on a threat to seek the abolishment of HUAC itself. A federal grand jury in New York City had begun to look into the case and, Nixon wrote, Chambers even feared that the Truman administration might try to compel it to drop its investigation.

Nixon wrote of Chambers's fears in *Six Crises*, but it is difficult to determine to what extent, if any, he shared those fears. As for the Truman administration, if it wished to seek the end of HUAC and anti-Communist investigations, it soon lost its chance to act on its wish, since, in 1949, the Soviets detonated their own atomic bomb and the Communists won their civil war in China. Those terrifying developments significantly fueled cold war fears and domestic anticommunism, weakened the administration's position, and removed any inclination the congressional Democrats may have had to get rid of HUAC. Nor was the administration about to dismantle the executive branch loyalty board program it had initiated during 1947 at least partly in order to undermine HUAC's investigations by conducting its own. But Nixon and Chambers could not have foreseen all of this in November 1948, as they commiserated over the bleak election results.

The pending lawsuit presented its own problems for Chambers and Nixon. Chambers was called to a deposition in

Baltimore by Hiss's attorneys. Chambers hired his own attorneys, chief of whom was Richard F. Cleveland, a son of former president Grover Cleveland, to file a countersuit alleging Hiss had perjured himself. At the same time, the Justice Department considered the fact that either Chambers or Hiss had lied to HUAC, thereby committing perjury and so one of the men was liable to federal indictment. But Justice attorneys decided they had insufficient evidence to determine whom to indict. Eventually, when Justice made up its mind, Nixon found himself in a fight with a federal grand jury over the issue of who had jurisdiction over key evidence—the judicial branch or the legislative branch—which in this instance resided in the person of Richard Nixon.

But that lay in the near future, and for the time being, then, the battle shifted from HUAC to Baltimore, where Hiss had filed suit. Nixon believed the committee's work was done, but he remained active in the case and maintained contact with Chambers. As it turned out, Nixon and HUAC had a way to go before reaching the end of their part in the drama.

Until November 1948, Chambers had said nothing to indicate that he or Hiss was involved in espionage. Chambers had only told HUAC—and the several million Americans who listened to *Meet the Press*—that he and Hiss were Communists and that Hiss's job was to infiltrate the federal government. But Chambers had said nothing about the crime of espionage until he was specifically asked about it in front of the grand jury. On that occasion he denied that he or Hiss had committed any acts of espionage. When Chambers gave his deposition to Hiss's attorneys in Baltimore, he took the case into new territory.

Chambers had two bombshells waiting: He delivered the first at his deposition, and produced the second from a hollowed-out pumpkin on his Maryland farm. The melodrama's sinister and absurd new act consolidated Richard Nixon's starring role on the national scene, even as it threw him into conflict with the courts, the administration, and the die-hard liberals whom he hated so vehemently.

Since the committee's part seemed completed, Nixon felt it

might be safe to take a vacation with his wife, something they had rarely, if ever, done since moving to Washington. The Nixons were set to sail on a cruise ship on December 2. However, the day before, both Nixon and Stripling spotted a newspaper report that the Justice Department was contemplating dropping its own investigation of the Hiss-Chambers case. That seemed a realization of Chambers's fears. Stripling suggested to Nixon that they drive out to the Maryland farm to talk to Chambers. For one thing, Stripling had heard a rumor that Chambers had some evidence he had not shown to HUAC.

At this point, Stripling's account differs from Nixon's. Nixon wrote both in *Six Crises* and in his memoirs that he, and not Stripling, suggested visiting Chambers. Stripling, by contrast, recalled that Nixon did not want to bother, doubted that Chambers had any more evidence, and grew angry and even abusive when Stripling insisted that they go. Finally, according to Stripling, Nixon agreed, saying that he figured it was the only way to shut up the chief investigator. Stripling remembered that Nixon griped all the way to the farm.

When they arrived, they showed Chambers the article. He responded that he had been afraid this would happen, since he had submitted new evidence to the grand jury two weeks earlier, unknown to Nixon, Stripling, or HUAC. The rumors Stripling heard were correct. Chambers explained that the "documentary evidence" was so important that a Justice Department official had taken the material back to Washington and told all concerned that they must say nothing about the documents, under pain of a contempt of court citation. "So," Chambers concluded, "I can't tell you what was in the documents. I will only say that they were a real bombshell."

Nixon and Stripling tried to persuade Chambers to tell them something about the documentary evidence. Chambers refused, but he said his attorney had copies. Chambers's most startling news, though, was that he had more documentary evidence that he had not turned over to the Justice Department. "I have another bombshell in case they try to suppress this one."

We can only guess what raced through Nixon and Stripling's minds as they listened to Chambers. Nixon told him, "You keep that second bombshell. Don't give it to anybody except the committee." Chambers neither agreed nor refused, but Nixon had drawn a line between HUAC and the Justice Department. Nixon wanted HUAC, or more specifically himself, to have first call on that evidence. Nixon's instructions to Chambers were legally dubious, as he was advising him to withhold evidence from legal authorities. Apparently, there was not enough of Alger Hiss to go around.

On the drive back to Washington, according to *Six Crises*, Nixon and Stripling speculated on what Chambers's bombshell could be. Nixon wrote that Chambers's use of the word *bombshell* was striking in and of itself, since he so far had rarely used flamboyant language. One wonders what Nixon considered flamboyant, after listening to Chambers's testimony before HUAC and conversing with him over the past few months. In any case, Nixon wondered whether he should postpone his vacation. Not wanting to disappoint Pat, at least not at that moment, Nixon told Stripling that he would fly back to Washington if necessary. Stripling later claimed that Nixon, still angry at having been convinced to make the trip to Maryland, said on the drive back to Washington, "I don't think he's got a damn thing."

Before going home, Nixon went to the HUAC office and authorized a *subpoena duces tecum* to be served on Chambers "for any and all documents in his possession relating to the committee hearings on the charges he had made against Hiss." Stripling had it served on Chambers the next day. As the subpoena made its way to Maryland, Richard and Pat Nixon began their leisurely sail to the Panama Canal Zone. Both Nixons put to sea, but Richard did not make it to Panama.

Nixon received two wires from shore. The first, from Bert Andrews, a friendly reporter who had worked informally with Nixon on the Hiss case, told the congressman that the Justice Department "partially confirms" that Chambers's new evidence was "too hot for comment." The second message came from

Stripling. "Second bombshell obtained by subpoena. . . . Case clinched. . . . Immediate action appears necessary. Can you possibly get back?"

The next day a third cable arrived, from Andrews. "Documents incredibly hot. Stop. Link to Hiss seems certain. . . . Could you arrive Tuesday and get day's jump on Grand Jury. . . . My liberal friends don't love me no more. Stop. Nor you. . . . Hiss's writing identified on three documents. Stop. Not proof he gave them to Chambers but highly significant. . . . Love to Pat. Stop. (Signed) Vacation-Wrecker Andrews."

The media were treated to the spectacle of the congressman leaving a cruise ship in the Caribbean on a Coast Guard amphibious plane to make his way to a Coast Guard station in Florida and then north to the nation's capital. At a stopover in Miami, reporters asked Nixon what he had to say about the "pumpkin papers." He did not know what they were talking about. The reporters enlightened him. Chambers's second bombshell was a cache of five rolls of microfilm photographs of State Department documents that he claimed Hiss gave him during the 1930s. After Nixon and Stripling's visit to the farm, Chambers went out to his pumpkin patch, hollowed out a pumpkin, and stowed the microfilms in it. When the subpoena servers came, they were amazed to see Chambers retrieve the evidence from the pumpkin. Nixon could scarcely believe what he heard and for the first time wondered if Chambers might be crazy.

The pumpkin papers have occasioned considerable debate over the years. Advocates of both sides of the Hiss-Chambers case have argued over whether the State Department documents contained anything of any particular importance. Hiss supporters have pointed out, accurately, that there is no proof that Chambers got the documents from Hiss and that he could have obtained them in any number of ways. Others have held that Chambers should be believed, since so much else that he said in the Hiss case and in investigations of other accused Communist agents either proved true or at least were supported by considerable evidence.

To Richard Nixon and his HUAC colleagues, in 1948, the

pumpkin papers looked like pure gold, for both evidence and publicity. HUAC played them for all they were worth, and a famous news photograph of the time shows Nixon and Stripling examining the microfilms with a magnifying glass. But in the midst of the pursuers' jubilation, the good news temporarily turned sour and, for Chambers, nearly deadly.

The microfilm was manufactured by the Eastman Kodak company. Nixon had an associate contact the company's headquarters in Rochester, New York, to ask some technical questions. In the process, the Kodak representative told him that the type of film involved was manufactured in 1945, which meant that Hiss could not have given the microfilms to Chambers in the middle 1930s. Nixon and the group in the HUAC office were stunned. "This meant," Nixon wrote in *Six Crises*, "that Chambers was, after all, a liar. . . . We had been taken in by a diabolically clever maniac who had finally made a fatal mistake."

Accounts as to what happened next differ. According to some who were present, Nixon nearly went berserk, roared that his political career was over, and blamed the mess on the investigators. Since those investigators were there, according to this version, they took the full brunt of Nixon's fury. In Nixon's version, he was furious but remained calm and telephoned Chambers. He demanded an explanation. Chambers said, "I can't understand it. God must be against me."

According to Nixon's own account, he blew up at Chambers, taking out on him "all of the fury and frustration that had built up within me." He told the desolate informer, "You'd better have a better answer than that. The subcommittee's coming to New York tonight and we want to see you at the Commodore Hotel at nine o'clock and you'd better be there!" Nixon "slammed the receiver," without waiting for Chambers's answer. Then, again in his own version of the story, he instructed Stripling to have the staff call a press conference in thirty minutes. Nixon claimed he planned to eat crow since, he nobly wrote, "I reminded Stripling that it was the committee's responsibility not to prove Hiss guilty but to find out who was telling the truth." That might strike a reader as disingenuous, since only days earlier Nixon told Chambers not to give the pumpkin papers to anyone except HUAC.

Stripling made the arrangements, but then there occurred the sort of last-minute turnaround that one would think only happens in bad movies. Eastman Kodak called back. The spokesman had made a mistake. The company had indeed manufactured that kind of film in the 1930s and actually discontinued making it during the 1940s. The microfilms were real, and Chambers was back in the charmed circle. The happy crew in the HUAC office was back in business. Stripling waltzed Nixon around the room, which must have been something to see. It was several hours before the good news reached Chambers.

His initial reaction to Nixon's angry phone call had been despair. He knew that the films were genuine, but the world would believe Eastman Kodak's first report and thus favor the elegant Alger Hiss over the slovenly Whittaker Chambers. "The world's instinctive feeling was against the little fat man who had stood up to testify for it, unasked. The world's instinctive sympathy was for the engaging man who meant to destroy it." Hiss, not Chambers, "personified the real values of a world that could not save itself."

When word reached him of his vindication, he was not consoled. Chambers tried to kill himself. As he wrote in *Witness*, he was exhausted, experiencing what he said older Quakers referred to as "a dryness, a drought of the soul, a sense of estrangement and of being discarded." Also, by his account, he was having qualms over continuing to testify against Hiss, which he surely would have to do since HUAC was back on the case, the grand jury in New York wanted to hear him again, and he faced more depositions in Baltimore. By killing himself, he decided, he could ". . . spare the others [presumably Alger and Priscilla Hiss] by removing myself as the only living witness against them." He believed he had exposed the Communist conspiracy, and that was enough. He claimed to have no desire to send Hiss to prison.

He wrote suicide notes to his wife and children and to several friends, and one addressed "To All." The latter note asserted that he had told the truth about Alger Hiss but he considered the world was not ready to hear his testimony. By testifying, he wrote, he meant to expose the conspiracy but not to hurt any individual. He was removing himself in an act that was not "suicide in the usual sense," since he did not desire death for its own sake, but rather a "self-execution."

Having completed his valedictory to the world, Chambers poisoned himself with chemical fumes in his bedroom. He awoke in the morning, vomiting. Then his mother confronted him, saying, of all things, "The world hates a quitter." Even the almost humorless Whittaker Chambers found her words a little funny. He drank several cups of coffee and went to the federal courthouse in Baltimore, where he expected to testify. He felt terribly ill and weak but was not called to the stand that day.

While Chambers wrestled with his despair, plenty of political maneuvering was afoot. The Justice Department and HUAC fought for possession of the pumpkin papers. In what he called a "violent verbal battle" with Justice representatives at the Hotel Commodore, Nixon laid it on the line. He did not trust the department not to suppress the evidence and he suspected it would aid and abet what he saw as a cover-up by the Truman administration. As far as Nixon was concerned, the administration did not want Hiss proven guilty and would do any number of illegal things to avert that. He said then, and would say later, that the administration was obstructing justice. The warring parties reached a compromise: HUAC would provide Justice with copies of the microfilmed documents. In return, Justice would allow Nixon and HUAC to question Chambers again, even though Chambers was now under a Justice Department subpoena.

On the evening of the day of Chambers's suicide attempt, he testified that, yes, he and Hiss had belonged to an actual espionage ring. Hiss regularly gave documents to Chambers, who had them microfilmed in Baltimore. Priscilla Hiss sometimes typed copies of State Department documents for Chambers to have filmed. (The whereabouts and evidentiary value of her old Woodstock typewriter soon became hot questions.) Chambers would take what the Hisses gave him to his superior in the underground, a Soviet agent called Colonel Bykov, who regularly sent the materials to Moscow. After Chambers decided to break with the party, according to Nixon's summary of Chambers's testimony, he began hoarding documents so that after leaving the party, he would have something on the Communists; that is, if they threatened him, he had something to implicate them.

Chambers's admission of espionage raised new problems for him and for HUAC. The statute of limitations had run out on the alleged espionage, so neither Chambers nor Hiss could be charged with that crime. But whoever was lying about knowing or not knowing the other had done so under oath, and faced a possible indictment for perjury. Hiss might also have been lying when he denied being a Communist or belonging to the Communist underground. The Fifth Amendment privilege against self-incrimination did not pertain here, since being a Communist was not in and of itself illegal. As the case progressed, it appeared that Hiss was in greater danger of indictment than Chambers. That he ultimately identified Chambers as George Crosley did not help him, since he could not substantiate his assertion that Chambers ever used that alias, and he denied having known Chambers as Carl the Communist. The conflicting testimony over the sublet and the car looked like two more nails in Hiss's coffin.

But now Chambers, too, stood liable to criminal charges. He had earlier denied under oath before the grand jury that he and Hiss had participated in espionage, and now he was admitting it. Furthermore, Chambers currently possessed stolen government documents and had withheld evidence in a criminal investigation. When asked why he lied about committing espionage, he launched into one of his classical arias, telling the grand jury that since he believed in a merciful God, he wanted to be merciful himself and always tried to apply mercy in his worldly dealings. He said nothing about fearing consequences to himself for the series of criminal offenses for which he could now be prosecuted.

This was in early December and the grand jury's term would expire on December 14. On December 9, President Truman again called the investigation a "red herring," which Nixon took as a signal that Truman's Justice Department was set to let Hiss off the hook and hang Chambers. But Nixon had been playing his own game of hardball, which included using the press for his purposes. Years later, President Nixon told his national security adviser and later secretary of state, Henry Kissinger, how he did it. As reproduced in Stanley Kutler's wonderful collection of Nixon's White House tapes, *Abuse of Power*, Nixon told Kissinger that he initially refused to give up the pumpkin papers to the Justice Department "because they're out to clear Hiss. I played it in the press like a mask. I leaked out to the papers. I leaked everything, I mean, everything that I could. I leaked out the testimony. I had Hiss convicted before he ever got to the grand jury. And then when the grand jury got there, the Justice Department, trying desperately to clear him, couldn't do it. The grand jury indicted him and then a good Irish U.S. attorney, [Thomas] Murphy, prosecuted him."

There is no telling how much of this was mere boasting. It could all be accurate, but Nixon was in the habit of retelling the past in self-serving ways. Nonetheless, the grand jury only indicted Hiss for perjury. Chambers never faced any criminal charges. Hiss went to federal prison for forty-four months after two perjury trials in 1949 and 1950. The first ended in a hung jury, the second in conviction. The same year Hiss went to prison, Nixon went to the Senate. Those two events are by no means unrelated, and the Hiss case still had not concluded when Nixon's Senate campaign began.

Alger Hiss served his sentence and returned home to New York. Having been disbarred upon his perjury conviction, he could not practice law and, of course, he could not go back to the Carnegie Foundation. He worked a series of jobs, ultimately becoming a stationery-supply salesman. During the Watergate scandal in the 1970s, he returned to the public eye and went on lecture tours, mostly at college and university campuses, where he found receptive audiences composed of student radicals, various other Nixon-haters, and the merely curious. Although readmitted to the Massachusetts bar in 1975, he never had his perjury conviction overturned. After the 1970s, Hiss faded from the public scene.

In the late 1980s, he was back in the news when the media reported that a high official of the Soviet KGB announced that Hiss had never been a Communist agent and had been wrongly accused and convicted. His supporters claimed vindication, but critics maintained that the announcement meant nothing, as a perestroika-era KGB officer would not necessarily know who had or had not been a Soviet spy decades earlier. However, the KGB did not produce any documents that stated outright that Hiss was not a spy, and only days later the officer denied having said anything to clear Hiss.

Alger Hiss died in 1997, protesting his innocence to the end.

Whittaker Chambers died in 1961 of a heart attack. He had suffered from heart disease for some years. To the end of his life, he was gravely sorrowful and fatalistic about the fate of the Western world. Shortly before his death, he advised Richard Nixon, who the previous year had lost the presidential election to John F. Kennedy, to run for California governor in 1962, so as to keep his political career alive. Chambers wrote to Nixon that he still believed he would be president one day, although some biographers argue that Chambers thought rather less highly of Nixon than he had years before.

Chambers died apparently believing that Hiss had won and he had lost. He thought that most Americans believed Hiss was innocent. Chambers probably was mistaken. He was also mistaken in arguing that the American press had "buried" the Hiss-Chambers case; it was one of the most widely covered news stories of the century. In any event, in 1961, Hiss was a free man, while Chambers lived almost reclusively on his Maryland farm, still expecting the dark forces of the international Communist conspiracy to extinguish the light of Christian civilization. He took some comfort in his children's marriages, but he spoke of suicide and carried himself with so sepulchral a demeanor that inevitably his death gave rise to rumors of suicide.

For decades, the case has been a major point of conflict between the left and right in American political discourse, much like its near-contemporary story of the Julius and Ethel Rosenberg atomic spy case. For both cases, the arguments are nearly religious in that belief in Hiss's or the Rosenbergs' guilt or innocence are practically articles of faith on both sides. Although the term *politically correct* did not exist with its current colloquial meaning until recently, it was for many years politically correct on the left to believe that Hiss and the Rosenbergs were falsely accused, that those accusations were the products of postwar anti-Communist hysteria, and that all evidence of guilt in either case was easily explained away or was outright phony. But things are not so easy.

A fair examination of both cases produces uncomfortable results for the supporters of the accused. The Rosenbergs were clearly guilty, beyond a reasonable doubt. There are a number of excellent books on the Rosenberg case, if the reader wishes to pursue that inquiry. The Hiss-Chambers case is more ambiguous, although the author believes that the weight of evidence tilts against Hiss. As to whether or not that tilt goes beyond the requisite reasonable doubt, the author cannot in good conscience offer an opinion. There is evidence beyond what Chambers gave; some of it is problematic, but the case against Alger Hiss is, if not conclusive, then strongly suggestive of guilt.

For instance, the media recently reported that records found in the former Soviet Union indicate that there was indeed a Soviet agent among Franklin Roosevelt's retinue at the Yalta conference. The agent's code name was "Als." The newspapers and magazines put this forth as evidence against Hiss, but the author would be reluctant to assert that the name "Als" necessarily suggests the name "Alger Hiss." Would the Soviets assign a code name that might appear even slightly related to an agent's real name? For that matter, the designation "Als" could have been a decoy name. But the author is not prepared to argue strenuously that Als was not Alger Hiss. Suppositions, after all, are not evidence, and the history of international espionage is just as littered with the inexplicable and the stupid as any other field of human endeavor.

Several authors have asserted that Hiss had been identified as a spy in intercepted communications between Moscow and the Soviet embassy in Ottawa, Canada, during the late 1940s. It is troubling that Hiss himself never publicly answered this particular assertion. Hiss seemed quite selective about which evidence he refuted, both in courts of law and the court of public opinion.

Richard Nixon died in 1994, three years before Alger Hiss and thirty-three years after Whittaker Chambers. Nixon often quoted Chambers and publicly referred to him as a man of quality and an authority on world communism, as well as something of a sage on international affairs. Nixon liked to cite Chambers's judgment of the Korean War, for instance, that the war was not only about Korea but also Japan. By the same token, Nixon spent the rest of his life excoriating Hiss.

Indeed, Hiss and his case obsessed Nixon to the end. Nixon's writings, the writings of his associates, and the infamous White House tapes all attest to Nixon's obsession. He referred to Hiss constantly. During the Watergate crisis, many of his subordinate coconspirators grew weary of his continuous admonishments that they pick up their copies of *Six Crises* and reread the chapter on the Hiss case for whatever wisdom Nixon thought they might extract from it. More tellingly, Nixon complained again and again that the liberal forces were out to get him because he had gotten Hiss. He did not believe that the Hiss case was the only reason for his enemies' hatred, but he insisted that it was his first major victory over the liberal establishment. It was only the first of many, according to Nixon, but it was one of the two particular victories they could not forgive—the other being the Vietnam War.

The author cannot resist relating yet another irony. After Nixon left the vice presidency, he related in his introduction to *Six Crises* that Kenneth McCormick, an executive at Doubleday Books, convinced Nixon to write that book. Nixon never revealed whether he knew that McCormick was a friend of Alger Hiss's. McCormick kept Hiss supplied with Doubleday books in prison. McCormick also convinced Hiss to write his second book, *Recollections of a Life*, which was published in 1985. The author does not know if Hiss ever publicly revealed if he knew of McCormick's relationship with Nixon and his role in publishing *Six Crises*.

In *A Generation on Trial*, Alistair Cooke argued that the Hiss affair embodied the conservative backlash against the entire New Deal generation. Alger Hiss *was* his generation on trial, in Cooke's analysis. Nixon's own views on the matter largely bear out Cooke's analysis, as Hiss represented to Nixon the leftist evil of the New Deal era, the apotheosis of what Nixon saw as an irresponsible, ideological liberalism.

Despite Nixon's own moderate and even somewhat liberal social views, he saw the sort of liberalism that created the New Deal as sapping American vitality, a cultivation of a dangerous liberal naïveté, an abrupt and radical departure from American values of independence and self-reliance. Worse, in Nixon's view, the New Deal opened the floodgates to foreign ideologies and their agents, such as Alger Hiss.

According to Nixon's view, both the Roosevelt and Truman administrations harbored these subversives and actively interfered with attempts to expose them. Nixon's campaign rhetoric was loaded with this sort of thing—*The foreign ideologies of the New Deal administration*.

Nixon never successfully reconciled these accusations with the fact that Truman was the president who stood the line in the early cold war and committed the United States to the defense of Western Europe against possible Soviet expansion.

In one of his later books, *The Real War,* Nixon wrote that the Hiss case brought him "face-to-face with the ugly realities of

Soviet subversion in the United States." In his 1950 Senate campaign against Helen Gahagan Douglas, Nixon used that ugliness to generate plenty of his own. Chambers's "concealed enemies" testimony would echo in Nixon's campaigns, statements, writings, and thoughts for the rest of his life—sometimes predictably, sometimes surprisingly.

NIXON VERSUS DOUGLAS:
"PINK DOWN TO HER UNDERWEAR"

✯ ✯ ✯

Just as Jerry Voorhis looked formidable at the start of the 1946 campaign for the House of Representatives, so did Helen Gahagan Douglas when the 1950 senatorial campaign began. But Nixon knew that Red-baiting would work in 1950 as it had in 1946. He understood another crucial factor: Douglas's far left views would alienate many moderate and conservative sources of Democratic funding. That money probably would end up going to Republicans—hence, into Nixon's campaign coffers.

Nixon's heart was in the fight, as circumstances presented him with yet another adversary from the elite upper crust. He always denied his class resentments, even as he railed endlessly against upper-class, privileged liberals. He denied, for instance, that class played any part in the matter when he and some friends formed that open-collar social club at Whittier College. Yet, his writings and speeches are filled with attacks on the wealthy, liberal, educated elite; he was fond of saying that when societies become overly educated, they become soft. One way or another, Nixon expressed his anger and contempt for the liberal, rich elite all his adult life, and more than one of his associates and subordinates has recalled that he never let anyone forget his humble origins.

Fittingly enough, Nixon frequently found himself facing upper-class opponents. Jerry Voorhis came from a wealthy family. Alger Hiss was not a campaign opponent, but HUAC investigator Robert Stripling told journalist and Nixon biographer Tom Wicker that Nixon had it in for Hiss from the beginning, from the moment he sniffed Hiss's upper-class airs. Douglas was another elite enemy, and Nixon rose to the challenge like Robespierre with his guillotine.

Had Nixon been born in a different country under similar circumstances, he may have been a Socialist or Communist. It is a curious phenomenon that America usually produces a conservative working class that aspires to success under the existing system rather than follow a social or political doctrine that advocates changing the system to redistribute its wealth. The downtrodden in America—mostly the laboring classes and impoverished family farmers—have sought to move upward and claim a share of the wealth rather than overthrow the system by revolution.

Nixon the poor boy, the son of a farmer-turned-shopkeeper, saw himself as standing for basic American values that were threatened by those who had most benefited from American opportunity. The liberals and their extreme cousins the Communists were wealthy, intellectual, and spoiled. Nixon viewed Helen Gahagan Douglas as one of those privileged malcontents. Not long before his death, he told his biographer Monica Crowley, ". . . in 1950, I beat Helen Gahagan Douglas, who was closely associated with the Communist front organization— not so with Voorhis, who was a Socialist but not as far left as Helen Gahagan when I beat him in the Twelfth District. But with her, it was a clear titanic struggle. I am unique in that I'm neither left nor right, but I'm also not a mushy moderate. I always stood for something."

Following his usual manner, in later years Nixon's reminiscences were conflicting and probably disingenuous. In his memoirs he described Douglas as one of Congress's most left-wing members. Since she was a woman, Nixon wrote that he figured that he "must not appear ungallant" in his campaign attacks on her. His chivalrous sensibilities did not prevent him from describing Douglas as "pink down to her underwear" at the height of the campaign. Nor did he refrain from attacking her for opposing elements of Democratic President Truman's foreign policy, which is yet another in the unending series of ironies of Nixon's career.

Douglas herself waged a bitter and rough campaign. An argument can be made that Jerry Voorhis in a sense was Nixon's victim, although the author does not fully subscribe to it. But it is difficult to see how anyone can credibly argue that Douglas was any sort of victim. She waged a mean campaign, but Nixon was better at sounding the right chords for the voters. If she was a victim, then in many ways she was victimized by her own dense idealism. She was no Communist, but she could fairly be called a left-liberal ideologue, nearly indifferent to other points of view and blindly passionate in pursuing her causes. She showed a self-defeating stubbornness and an unwise disregard for some crucial political realities and imperatives. It was a rough time, politically, and the 1950 California Senate campaign was a rough affair all around.

Helen Gahagan was the daughter of an East Coast industrialist. Although her wealthy father insisted she attend college, she was determined to become an actress. She put in a couple of years at Barnard College to satisfy her father but then worked in the theater and achieved an almost overnight success on Broadway while still only in her early twenties. After several years as a dramatic star, Gahagan trained as an opera singer and achieved some success in European opera houses. During the 1930s she married film star Melvyn Douglas, moved to California, and starred in her one and only film, a dramatization of H. Rider Haggard's adventure-fantasy, *She*.

Both Helen Gahagan Douglas and her husband were politically active, liberal New Dealers. She later described herself as having been "converted" to political activism through her admiration of Franklin and Eleanor Roosevelt. In time, she and her husband became friendly with the president and first lady, and

Helen Gahagan Douglas began playing an active role in Democratic party politics in California. In 1944, she won election to the House of Representatives from California's Fourteenth District.

The Nixon-Douglas face-off came after a bloody Democratic primary campaign. Douglas challenged Senator Sheridan Downey for the 1950 nomination. She announced her candidacy in October 1949, and there was a good deal of antagonism between the two rivals. Douglas by then was associated with a wide range of liberal political affiliations. Downey, scion of a wealthy family, was an apostate liberal in the eyes of many New Dealers and Douglas supporters. In 1934, when he was young and liberal, he ran for lieutenant governor of California as the running mate of the Socialist gubernatorial candidate, muckraking novelist Upton Sinclair. Both Downey and Sinclair lost.

In 1938, Downey won election to the U.S. Senate as a Democrat. Despite his early support for Roosevelt and the New Deal, Downey evolved into a conservative and got on well with the state's major oil interests. During his liberal years, he and Douglas apparently got along well too, but as they grew further apart politically, they became enemies. When Douglas challenged him in 1950, things got ugly fast. Douglas later wrote that she was outraged when Downey supported the efforts of oil companies and agribusiness to secure state rather than federal control of California's oil resources. Downey also worked on exempting the Central Valley from the 1902 Reclamation Act which, as Douglas biographer Ingrid Winther Scobie explained, "required the limitation of water from federally funded projects to 160-acre farms"—in other words, large corporate farms.

Nixon watched these developments closely and found them immensely pleasing. Like Douglas, he announced his candidacy for the Republican senatorial nomination the year before the election, while still riding the wave of publicity from the Hiss case. He expected to run against Senator Downey, but when Douglas issued her challenge, Nixon shrewdly assessed that the primary campaign would cause crippling divisions among the Democrats. Whoever won the nomination would be seriously hobbled come November 1950. Early on, Nixon rooted for Douglas, since he pegged her as the easiest Democrat to defeat in the general election.

With his usual acumen, Nixon was entirely correct about the Democratic rupture. What he did not foresee, however, was an even greater boon to his own chances. Downey, aging and ill, did not last through the primary campaign, and dropped out of the race. Having done so, the Democratic senator made no secret of his desire to see his rival defeated by anyone who could do it. If no Democrat defeated her in the primary campaign, then Downey openly preferred that a Republican win in November. Before long, Downey and Nixon became unofficial allies in the cause of keeping Helen Gahagan Douglas out of the Senate. Meanwhile, Downey's battle with Douglas damaged her, and the next development damaged her further.

Another conservative Democrat arose to oppose her for the nomination. Manchester Boddy, owner and publisher of the Los Angeles *Daily News*, originally had promised Douglas his newspaper's support, so she felt a special sense of outrage and betrayal when Boddy stepped up to replace Downey as her main opponent in the Democratic primary. This was all fine with Nixon. In *In the Arena*, he called Downey's withdrawal and Boddy's entry a break for his own campaign. Nixon had assessed the damage that Downey had done to Douglas and now saw that Boddy hurt her further; he and other Democrats called Douglas "the pink lady," and attacked her for allegedly belonging to and supporting "a number of Communist front organizations."

On the advice of campaign strategist Murray Chotiner, Nixon stood back and let the Democrats savage each other. There were other reasons for his restraint: First, he wanted to run against Douglas, whom, as noted, he evaluated as the weakest nominee the Democrats could field. Second, he had to court Democratic voters in order to win the Senate seat, so it would play better to attack her personally in the general campaign rather than mount an attack on Democrats during the primary campaign.

Douglas won the primary and the nomination, but she'd lost

the support of the Democratic party organization. She threw that away by running in the first place. When she first made it known that she was considering a run in 1950, William Malone, the Democratic state chairman, advised her to wait until the 1952 election. Malone told her that to challenge Senator Downey would split the party. Douglas wrote in her autobiography, *A Full Life*, that she answered, "That's not the issue, going to the Senate." She argued that Downey neglected programs for veterans, but even more to the point, she cited the issue of the 160-acre limitation. The corporate practice of hogging land and water resources would destroy small growers and thwart reclamation programs aimed at helping migrants settle down and presumably become Democratic voters. "I really don't see how all of you can sit back and let our own Democratic senator destroy a program that is essential to the well-being of the West Coast."

Douglas should have listened to Malone. One can make a good argument that her ambition *was* the issue. Malone was telling her that a party split would hand the Senate seat to the Republicans. He clearly explained to her that her ambition could wait for two years, when she would not be challenging a Democratic incumbent and could thus run for the Senate without damaging her party and strengthening the opposition.

Douglas was in many ways a poor politician who did not always look before she leapt. She had an unfortunate tendency to lecture audiences, could be condescending, and often went her own way while disregarding some of the equally legitimate concerns of her colleagues. Even so, she encountered more criticism than did many of her contemporary male politicians who behaved as badly as she did. Then, as now, but even more so then, ambition in a woman was often considered unfeminine—even abrasive.

Chairman Malone had a point in arguing that 1950 was the wrong year for Douglas to run for the Senate, but in retrospect, the reactions of many of the Democratic committee's members seem particularly aggravated because Douglas was a woman. It was somehow unseemly and therefore aroused more anger when a woman challenged the state party discipline. The Democrats may well have been angry at a misguided male challenger under those circumstances, but Douglas's gender drove many conservative Democrats to unbridled fury. The smears to which they resorted were unjustified, and ultimately self-defeating.

Douglas had been coping with a certain institutional sexism since entering politics. For years, newspaper reports about her usually included descriptions of what she was wearing. When she first went to Congress, much of the Washington press corps tried to play her up as a Democratic counterpart to Republican congresswoman Clare Booth Luce. Since both women were young and beautiful, the press made much of a supposed rivalry, a pretty catfight on Capitol Hill. Even during the 1950 Senate campaign, Vice President Alben Barkley told an audience at a Douglas rally in California that the Senate would benefit from her "brains and beauty." But, she was widely disliked in Congress, and many of her male colleagues in both parties sometimes referred to her as "the bitch."

Douglas entered Congress in 1945, at the close of the Roosevelt era. The president had died in April, the war ended soon after, and Douglas and the rest of Congress faced the huge economic and social conversion to peacetime, the great debate over America's role in the postwar world, and the jarring imperatives of the cold war. She was an avid supporter of the United Nations but managed to antagonize President Truman by opposing some of his foreign policies because she believed they would undermine the U.N.'s authority. She supported the formation of NATO and considered it an important obstruction to Soviet expansion in Western Europe and a way of actualizing the principles of the U.N. She also supported the Marshall Plan but opposed other cold war measures, such as aiding Greece and Turkey, arguing that the latter actions would undermine the U.N.'s authority.

Douglas did not endear herself to Truman when she joined a group of Democrats who tried to convince General Dwight Eisenhower to displace Truman as the Democratic presidential candidate in 1948. She later wrote that she agreed to help sound out Eisenhower "in case Truman proved to be a disappointing president, as it seemed he would." The group visited the general to determine if he were a Democrat or a Republican, since no one actually knew. Upon discovering his Republicanism, they bid Eisenhower good day and reluctantly turned back to Truman. Douglas never quite understood why Truman seemed less than enthusiastic about her senatorial candidacy in 1950.

She may have been unpopular, but Helen Gahagan Douglas was not a Communist, nor a Communist sympathizer. She disliked the Soviet Union and disliked American Communists. She worried about Communists in California labor unions, and, she wrote in her posthumously published autobiography, *A Full Life*, her insistent public stand on that issue caused labor leader John L. Lewis to complain that Douglas "wants me to turn every union man upside down to see if a Communist card falls out of his pocket." Douglas worried about Soviet expansionist ambitions in Europe. In the 1948 congressional campaign, she refused the endorsement of former vice president and breakaway presidential candidate Henry Wallace, a hero to the American far left, because she detested his views on the Soviet Union. "After the Soviet aggression in Czechoslovakia, Wallace's policy of appeasement seemed to me dangerous nonsense. If I accepted his endorsement, I felt it would give the impression that I approved of his declaration that the Soviet Union was not a threat to world peace, which it unquestionably was."

Nixon was wrong in the 1990s when he called the 1950 campaign a "clear titanic struggle." At least, it could not be so characterized when it came to Communist infiltration and subversion, which seems to be what he meant. The campaign was a struggle between partisan candidates for the Senate, one of whom cast it in terms of a contest for the soul of America and the security of its political system. That had worked for him in 1946. He understood that such sentiments would move the voters in 1950. Douglas, on the other hand, spent a lot of time trying to direct voters' attention to the 160-acre limit and other issues she thought they should care about. She also spent a lot of time trying to outdo Nixon in throwing smears. In that arena, she was hopelessly overmatched.

Douglas and Nixon turned up on the opposite sides of many issues in the House, and Douglas particularly loathed the House Committee on Un-American Activities. In her autobiography, she wrote that, in 1948, when she and Nixon both won reelection to the House, she saw that Nixon intended to run for the Senate in 1950. HUAC "was creating the hottest news in the country with its daily accusations of espionage in high places." Nixon, of course, made headlines in pursuing "HUAC's biggest catch, Alger Hiss," whom Douglas described as "the brilliant adviser to the State Department who was accused by magazine editor Whittaker Chambers of carrying American secrets" to Soviet agents. In her view, HUAC "had been desperate to land someone important for the sake of its credibility." When Hiss was convicted of perjury and imprisoned, "the name of Richard Nixon was propelled into national prominence."

Douglas voted against making HUAC a permanent committee in 1945, and in 1949 and 1950 she opposed continuing its funding. "You cannot barter security for freedom, nor freedom for security," she said on the House floor. "They tried to do that in Germany; they tried to do that in Russia. I thought that was what we disliked about communism . . . Are we now to curtail our cherished freedoms by adopting Communistic and Fascistic patterns?" HUAC was popular in those days; Douglas was right in calling the Hiss case a "hot" news story. Opposing HUAC did not win her much support in political circles, regardless of how it may have pleased her supporters in the Fourteenth District.

The Fourteenth District was in Los Angeles and did not resemble the rest of California. Most of it was downtown and urban. Douglas's biographer Ingrid Winther Scobie described the district as including some of the wealthiest and poorest of Los Angeles residents, including a sizable African-American population. The district was largely Democratic and prone to support Roosevelt and the New Deal. Even in the postwar era, as

HELEN GAHAGAN DOUGLAS, 1950.

much of the nation slipped into a conservative mood, the Fourteenth and similar urban districts throughout the nation remained liberal Democratic country. Douglas's New Deal reputation kept her safely ensconced in the House, but running a statewide campaign for the Senate would be another matter.

In his postpresidential memoirs, Nixon described her as a "handsome woman with a dramatic presence," and noted she had many admirers in the press, the entertainment industry, and among the public. But, Nixon added, with undisguised glee, "she was not, to put it mildly, the most popular member of the House of Representatives." Nixon claimed that "even many of the House Democrats let me know that they hoped I could defeat Helen Douglas." One of those House Democrats was John F. Kennedy of Massachusetts, who one day dropped in at Nixon's office on the Hill and gave him a thousand-dollar campaign contribution from his father, Joseph P. Kennedy, Sr. "I obviously can't endorse you," JFK told Nixon, "but it isn't going to break my heart if you can turn the Senate's loss into Hollywood's gain."

Legend has it that even Vito Marcantonio wanted Douglas out of the House. An open Socialist and independent member from a district in New York, the convivial Marcantonio was personally popular on Capitol Hill, despite his status as a political near-pariah. According to some accounts, he got along with Nixon, amazingly enough. Marcantonio did not like Douglas and allegedly did not mind when his reputation was pressed into service against her during the California Democratic primary in 1950.

Both Senator Sheridan Downey and publisher Manchester Boddy hit on the bright idea of accusing Douglas of guilt by association by telling voters that in many House votes, Douglas voted the exact same way as had the Socialist congressman Marcantonio. The suggestion, of course, was that Douglas was herself a Socialist or even a Communist and so aligned with the leftist New Yorker. The only trouble with that device was that it was inherently dishonest: Many of those matching votes had been over routine bits of House business, or straight party votes, when Marcantonio aligned with most of the House Democrats. For that matter, quite a few Republicans, including Nixon, often voted with Marcantonio. In any case, again according to legend, when Marcantonio heard of how his name was being used by Democrats against Douglas, he got word to Nixon, suggesting that the Republican should try the same trick in the general campaign. "Tell Nicky to get on this thing," he supposedly told an acquaintance.

The author has never encountered a firsthand version of that story nor ever seen corroborating evidence, and is not trying to perpetuate a historical rumor. What is important here is that the story pops up in so many accounts and histories and that so many House members and Washington journalists believed it. The story survives even though it is never told firsthand but only as part of Capitol Hill's oral tradition. One always reads of it as something someone heard from someone else. That in and of itself indicates something of how many congressional Democrats and Republicans felt about Douglas. When the time came, Nixon followed in Boddy's footsteps and hurled Marcantonio's record at Douglas.

Douglas won the Democratic primary with less than 50 percent of the vote, defeating Boddy's 30 percent, that is, 730,000 votes to 400,000. The remaining votes were divided between other candidates, including Nixon. Cross-filing was still permitted in 1950, and both Douglas and Nixon filed in each other's primaries. Nixon won 300,000 Democratic votes. Counting his total from both primaries, he received one million votes. Douglas received 900,000 votes, so Nixon outpolled her in what many sharp observers saw as a test vote.

Nixon took the primaries seriously, despite having no serious opposition in the Republican party. He revived his old 1946 trick of trying to confuse some Democratic voters into believing he was a Democrat. Once again, the Nixon campaign mailed to Democratic voters pamphlets that purportedly came "from one Democrat to another." That tactic drew an attack from the Democratic committee, which ran an advertisement in California newspapers warning Democrats of the trick. The epithet "Tricky Dick" first appeared in that ad.

Despite his strategic decision to stand aside as the Democrats devoured each other in the Senate race, Nixon did not entirely refrain himself from attacking Douglas. He fired the occasional salvo that Douglas was not a true Democrat. Either Nixon simply could not resist attacking, or he may have judged that limited attacks would not seriously affect her chances to win the primary, as he preferred to run against her rather than Downey or Boddy. Nixon may have intended that his limited attacks would cause moderate or conservative Democrats to think about voting Republican in November. Meanwhile, he won the Republican nomination in a record turnout. He was entirely correct in assessing that he had a united party behind him, while Douglas had to contend with a major rift among the Democrats.

When the general campaign season arrived and Nixon began his attacks, he later wrote, "I did not question her loyalty, but, like her fellow Democrats, I criticized her judgment." He may not have *directly* questioned her loyalty, but, like her fellow Democrats, he criticized the color of her underwear. For Nixon to claim that he did not question her loyalty is absurd, as it was when he made the same claim about Jerry Voorhis. Nixon blamed "liberal historians" for the perception that he Red-baited Douglas.

Nixon later recalled that his campaign strategy involved keeping Douglas "pinned to her extremist record." That took some creative misrepresentation, or at least some omission of key facts. For instance, Nixon attacked her for voting against Truman's program to provide crucial aid to Greece, which was fighting a Communist insurgency, and to Turkey, on whose border the Soviets were mobilizing armed forces. Nixon accurately called the aid package "the key plank of the Truman doctrine," which was the first of the major cold war measures to turn back Communist expansion and contain communism in the areas where it already held sway, hence, the beginning of the containment policy, which largely defined American policy for the cold war's duration.

Douglas had indeed voted against the bill but claimed that Nixon only told part of the story. In her autobiography, Douglas gave her reasons for her vote. They may have been misguided, but Nixon's coloring them pink was misleading, although many voters bought it. It was clear, Douglas wrote, "that Russia was trying to expand in the Middle East and I agreed that something should be done about it. But what I believed then, and I believe today, was that Russia's military buildup on Turkey's border should have been brought to the Security Council of the United Nations, where it could be put in the context of a problem for the whole world rather than a U.S.S.R.–U.S. confrontation." Douglas believed that unilateral action in this situation undermined the United Nations.

As for the insurgency in Greece, Douglas was not convinced that the United States or any other nation should interfere in what she saw as the Greek people's attempt to overthrow an autocratic government. They had a right, she argued, to try to set up a better government, "even if some of them were Communists." Douglas wrote that she incurred the wrath of the Truman administration and argued with Secretary of State Dean Acheson, who pointed out that the Soviet Union, as a member of the Security Council, had the same veto power that all the permanent members had. If the United States put it to the United Nations to protect Greece and Turkey from Communist aggression, the Soviets could simply veto any such proposals. Douglas argued that, "If we tried to frighten the Soviet . . . it would only make the Soviet more frightened of *us*" (Douglas's italics). Douglas retained the antiquated habit of calling the Soviet government "the Soviet." She also displayed a quaint and glaringly naive outlook on world power politics.

Besides taking the odd view that the Soviet Union would be any less "frightened" by U.N. opposition than by unilateral American opposition, Douglas seemed oblivious to the effects of such a stand on her political future. Were she purposely eschewing Democratic support in a quixotic race for the Senate, that would be admirable in a quirky sort of way. That was not the case. Douglas expected the Democratic party, including the Truman administration, to line up behind her candidacy. She had little if any concept of political give-and-take; she in effect told her party and the administration that she was free to follow her conscience, but they owed her their unconditional partisan support.

Douglas had given Nixon some powerful ammunition. Then she made a key mistake in her campaign against him. As he tried to hang the pro-Communist onus on her, she tried to turn the attack back on him and accused Nixon of having the more pro-Communist voting record. Nixon's campaign manager, Murray Chotiner, noted that the Douglas campaign had erred badly; whereas Nixon had attacked Douglas's weaknesses, she was attacking his *strengths*. Douglas was an ultraliberal Democrat; even liberal Democrats did not oppose the Truman doctrine, nor did they proclaim such faith in the U.N., so Douglas was considerably to the left of her party. President Truman, after all, was a liberal Democrat. For someone with Douglas's record to get into a slugging match with a Republican over who was harder or softer on communism, especially Nixon, the world champion Red-catcher, was an exercise in futility, or worse.

Douglas was astute enough to know that the Red-baiting hurt her. During the primary campaign, she wrote, when *Daily News* publisher Boddy "talked about Helen Gahagan Douglas and the red-hots in the same breath, [the voters] paid attention." While some of her constituents stuck by her, including the local unions and, according to Douglas, most Democratic women, others besides Downey and Boddy Red-baited her. "The vice president of the California Democratic Women's League . . . ," Douglas wrote, "urged Democrats to vote against me because I showed my sympathies for the country's enemies when I voted against funds for HUAC." Senator Downey, attacking Douglas even after he dropped out of the race, told a California radio audience that she had given "comfort" to "Soviet tyranny" by voting against Truman's aid package for Greece and Turkey. In that same radio address, Downey compared Douglas to Marcantonio.

That spring, Douglas clearly was the underdog, and the Republican rising star, Richard Nixon, looked to be headed for the Senate. That was true enough before June 24, 1950, but on that day, the Communist North Koreans played a dirty trick on Helen Gahagan Douglas. They invaded South Korea and started the Korean War. U.N. forces, which is to say mostly American forces, landed in South Korea early in July. Amazingly, the Soviet delegate was not at the Security Council to veto the decision to intervene in Korea; the Soviets were boycotting the council to protest the U.N.'s failure to expel Taiwan's Chinese Nationalist delegation in favor of a Communist delegation from the Chinese mainland. For the Communists, that was terrible timing and the early phases of the war went well for the U.N., which is to say for the United States. But not immediately; in the first few days that the Americans engaged the enemy in Korea, the Communists seemed to have the upper hand, and that looked very bad for the Democratic White House and Congress back home.

Douglas wrote that many Californians panicked. Red-baiting became the order of the day, and Truman and the Democrats incurred massive voter mistrust. The cold war seemed to have swung against Americans in favor of the satanic Red forces overseas. There was widespread fear that the Soviets and the Chinese would intervene, thus turning Korea into the first battleground of World War III. Even when things began going well on the battlefield, many voters apparently figured it was no thanks to the Democrats, on whose watch, after all, the invasion took place.

North Korea had bestowed a golden springtime present on Republicans all over the United States—at the cost of thousands of lives. The Republicans had already been riding high for more than the past year. After their election victories of 1948, things quickly soured for Truman and the Democrats. The Communist takeover in China, the Soviet atomic bomb, and the perjury conviction of Alger Hiss strengthened the Republicans as the Democrats weakened drastically. Joseph McCarthy began his infamous Red-baiting rampage only a week and a half after Alger Hiss's conviction. Now, as the midterm elections approached, the Republicans knew that the Korean War was the icing on the cake. Douglas summed it up aptly enough when she wrote that ". . . what my campaign now needed was some luck. We got it— all bad."

Douglas believed that the war drove the voters even further into their conservative mood. "When people are nervous, they are ready to believe in muscle without asking too many questions," she wrote in her autobiography. ". . . All over the country, aspiring senators and congressmen rewrote campaign literature to show themselves as ardent anti-Communists." In Florida, Democratic senator Claude Pepper lost the Democratic primary after his opponent George Smathers taunted him as the "Red Pepper." Smathers, a Democratic congressman, was, incidentally, a friend of Nixon's. According to historian Greg Mitchell, Nixon asked Smathers for some collegial advice on Red-baiting Douglas.

Nixon's luck was all good, and he knew how to seize the moment. Douglas proved obliging, for in the wake of the North Korean invasion, she pulled one of the most boneheaded moves of the campaign: She attacked Nixon for opposing aid to South

Korea. In January, Nixon had voted against an aid package for South Korea that the White House sent to Congress. Douglas jumped on that as Nixon's failure to see that the Communists were a threat in Asia just as they were in Europe.

Nixon indeed voted against the Korean aid bill, but because it did not include aid to Chiang Kai-shek's government in Taiwan, not because Nixon was dreamily unaware of Communist designs in Asia. Worse, the Douglas camp pointed out that Vito Marcantonio joined Nixon in voting against aid to Korea. They went further, and circulated campaign literature claiming that Nixon and Marcantonio voted the same way many more times than Douglas and Marcantonio had. Douglas's bumbling attempts at turning the tables on Nixon only made her look ridiculous.

Historian Stephen E. Ambrose argued that in the mudslinging between the two, Douglas actually struck first. That is debatable, but the mere fact that who started the smears is difficult to discern goes a long way toward negating the classic image of Douglas as Nixon's victim. In his memoirs, Nixon described these tactics as "one of the most peculiar ineptitudes of the Douglas campaign." Even decades later, Nixon still marveled at the fact that Douglas tried to convince the voters that the HUAC member who "got" Alger Hiss was less an anti-Communist than she was.

Nixon considered Douglas's strategy "rooted more in desperation than logic," since there was no credible way she could brand Nixon as any sort of Communist sympathizer nor accuse him of indifference to the Communist threat, given his track record. It did not matter how many times Nixon's votes matched Marcantonio's; the public was not going to buy it. But Douglas, the left-leaning liberal, always stood vulnerable to Redbaiting, and, with the primaries over and the general campaign under way, Nixon lost little time in countering Douglas's lame charges and launching his own equally ridiculous but far more effective attacks.

In the late summer and early autumn, Nixon and his campaign

aides geared up to assail Douglas's record in Congress. According to historian Greg Mitchell, Nixon himself carefully thought out much of the strategy and tactics, and specifically instructed his assistants to dig up information on Douglas. Nixon had heard that she was "the only member of Congress" to defend Roosevelt's controversial Yalta agreement—a particular target of Republican Red-baiting during the postwar period. Nixon told aides to find material showing that Douglas was connected to subversive organizations. She had been mentioned in a book called *The Red Decade*; Nixon wanted to know what that was about. He wanted his staffers to find a 1944 article that reported a "left-wing PAC" had donated nearly a thousand dollars to her first congressional campaign. He wanted someone to "locate a newspaper quote by Mother [Ella Reeve] Bloor, the Communist heroine, praising Douglas." (The American Communists recognized two women as "mothers" of their movement: Bloor and Mother Jones. Bloor's son Harold Ware was an underground contact of Whittaker Chambers during the 1930s.) A 1945 article in the *New York Times* referred to Douglas as "one who uses and is used by Communists." Nixon wanted that found as well.

Nixon's official campaign began with a radio address in mid-September. "There will be no name-calling, no smears, no misrepresentations in this campaign," he insisted. It would not be "a campaign of personalities but of issues." Nixon would not permit Douglas to distort the record, hers or his, he promised. On the subject of her record, Nixon proclaimed that if Douglas would not reveal where she stood, then "I'll do it for her." Actually, the Nixon campaign had begun doing that even before the speech. On September 10, the day Eleanor Roosevelt arrived in Los Angeles to begin her tour of California to support both Douglas for senator and her son James Roosevelt's campaign for governor, according to Mitchell, Douglas supporters first encountered the notorious pink sheet.

The pink sheet was a leaflet that hammered away at Douglas for voting with Marcantonio, which was old news by then. But the leaflet could reach hundreds of thousands of voters who may have missed the smear in its previous rounds. As Mitchell described the pamphlet in his fine history of the 1950 campaign, *Tricky Dick and the Pink Lady*, it explained to voters that "While 'it should not be expected' that any member of Congress would always cast a vote contrary to Vito Marcantonio's ... it was significant that Helen Douglas had voted with him 'such a great number of times' and that the issues on which they always voted alike concerned 'Un-American Activities and Internal Security.'"

Fittingly enough, the pink sheet was printed on pink paper, though Nixon later claimed that the color of the paper was accidental. Campaign manager Chotiner had explained that he figured the leaflet would be printed on plain white paper, but the printer only had brown and pink; brown would have rendered the copy unreadable. Accidental or not, the paper's color made for one of the most effective double meanings in the history of American electioneering. It was just the sort of striking device that commands attention and sticks in the mind, even nearly fifty years later. For Nixon and the Republicans, his revival of the "pink lady" epithet combined with the pink sheet made for a powerful public relations offensive and surely turned pink into gold. Nixon's radio speech further set the tone of the coming fall campaign.

Douglas wrote in her memoirs, "Chotiner's strategy of keeping me on the defensive made me feel I was standing in the path of tanks. That effect was exactly what he intended. His instructions to Nixon workers were to refer to me as a 'supporter of the Socialist program running on the Democratic ticket.'" When Douglas attempted to counter the Nixon camp's Red-baiting by referring to her voting record both on the House floor and as a member of the House Foreign Affairs Committee, where, she wrote, she supported many anti-Communist bills, Chotiner wrote to the local Nixon campaign chairmen around California, "Helen Douglas is trying to portray a new role as a foe of communism. Do not let her get away with it! It is a phony act."

It is generally forgotten that the pink sheet actually came out *after* Douglas released a Red-baiting leaflet of her own, and at least one historian, Jonathan Aitken, argued that one of Nixon's motivations for issuing the pink sheet was that he had been "sufficiently stung" by Douglas's charges. Her leaflet was printed on yellow paper and in some histories, including Aitken's, is called the yellow sheet. The yellow sheet proclaimed that Nixon was using "THE BIG LIE! Hitler invented it. Stalin perfected it. Nixon uses it . . . LET'S LOOK AT THE RECORD . . . YOU pick the Congressman the Kremlin loves! Compare the voting records of Richard NIXON and Helen Gahagan DOUGLAS with the vital bills that concerned KOREA. Compare their votes with those of Vito MARCANTONIO, American Labor Party (Pro Communist) Congressman."

The rest of the pamphlet revived the inaccurate and incomplete analysis of Nixon's vote against the Korea aid package, and alleged that Nixon had voted with Marcantonio more often than Douglas had. Aitken noted that the yellow sheet was loaded with inaccuracies that the Republicans could easily rebut, and Murray Chotiner was ecstatic over its release. As noted earlier, the yellow sheet prompted Chotiner's explanation that Douglas made the fatal mistake of attacking Nixon's strengths instead of his weaknesses.

Douglas was vulnerable on her record in the House. She had voted against the McCarran Internal Security Act earlier in 1950, a tough antisubversion law that required all Communist organizations to register with the Justice Department. The law opened up new and vague vistas for prosecution on such grounds as "fomenting revolutions." The law regulated employment at defense plants and provided that Communists could be barred from these jobs. The law also provided that the federal government could refuse to issue passports to American citizens it determined to be Communists and could revoke passports on the same grounds. The bill passed over President Truman's veto.

The McCarran Act did not strike many voters as repressive. In fact, many citizens thought it perfectly legitimate and necessary in light of the Korean War and the cold war. Douglas had hit on something when she noted that nervous people did not question certain measures that appeared to enhance their security. Many Americans were not much concerned with the constitutional rights of citizens who professed Communist beliefs. When the bill came up for the House vote, several of Douglas's fellow Democrats, including Lyndon Johnson, a close friend who often defended Douglas in private against her congressional foes, advised her to vote for it. The law would be mostly unenforceable, some of them explained, and the only ones who would suffer would be Communists anyway. With one act of conscience, she would throw away her political future. "Douglas did not heed the advice."

Douglas also was told that she in effect was handing the Senate seat to Nixon and the Republicans, so her act of conscience had a dash of selfishness. By outdoing her fellows in virtue, she was furthering her enemy's career, especially ironic since Douglas was among the first in Washington to realize that Nixon had ambitions for higher office; she had commented to a political aide that, were Nixon ever to become president, "God help us all." One would be tempted to praise her for placing principle above politics in the face of certain defeat were it idealism winning out over pragmatism, but such was not the case. Douglas dearly wanted to go to the Senate and late in the campaign season, when she was far behind in the public-opinion polls, she was, in her own words, "desperate" to reverse the trend and salvage her campaign. She had not embarked on a moral crusade. She wanted to win.

Douglas later recalled that she "happened to catch Nixon's eye" on the House floor the day of the McCarran vote. "He was grinning broadly," she wrote. "I knew then that he would twist the issue so that my vote against the abuse of civil rights in the bill would be presented as a vote for communism, but I thought that few people would pay much attention to such an outrageous accusation." One may find that hard to believe, especially in light of her own Red-baiting of Nixon. Whatever the case, the events of the fall campaign bore out her friends' advice and justified Nixon's broad grin.

The Democrat from Los Angeles certainly continued doing her share to widen her opponent's grin. Shortly after Nixon and Chotiner issued the pink sheet, Douglas and her people committed more blunders in combating it. The Douglas campaign ran a newspaper advertisement that proclaimed, "THOU SHALT NOT BEAR FALSE WITNESS. Nixon's record of blind stupidity on foreign policy gave aid and comfort to the Communists. On every key vote Nixon stood with party-liner Marcantonio against America in its fight to defeat communism." As Nixon biographer Aitken tells the story, additional Douglas ads ran in the ensuing days and weeks; they slung even more mud: Douglas condemned "Communism, Naziism [sic], and Nixonism." She implied that Nixon was fascistic in his actions and ideas, and she kept referring to him in speeches and conversations as a "pip-squeak" and a "peewee."

When told of Douglas's language, Nixon exploded to a campaign aide, "I'll castrate her!" When the aide pointed out that castrating a woman was biologically problematic, Nixon insisted that he would do it anyway. Recalling the campaign more than twenty-five years later, Nixon still resented those insults. He particularly resented "Tricky Dick," the nickname that Douglas revived that fall.

But Nixon was doing all right. He led in the polls during the entire fall campaign, and he was no slouch in the mudslinging tournament. But it is odd that his mudslinging is remembered by the public while Douglas's has been largely forgotten. It was in the midst of this duel that Nixon began saying that Douglas was "pink down to her underwear." Aitken quotes one of Nixon's most typical attacks on Douglas: "If she had her way, the Communist conspiracy in the United States would never have been exposed and Alger Hiss . . . would still be influencing the foreign policy of the United States. . . . My opponent is a member of a small clique which joins the notorious Communist party-liner Vito Marcantonio of New York in voting time after time against measures that are for the security of this country." There was Marcantonio again. Both candidates must have loved him.

Aitken concluded that Nixon's attacks on Douglas are "hard to defend." But, he pointed out, Nixon "was constantly respond- ing in kind to outrageous charges that had been leveled against him by his opponent." There were times when his counter- attacks were too severe, wrote Aitken, but he was sorely pro- voked and Douglas's own behavior was pretty shabby. Aitken concluded, "If there had been a contest as to which candidate had the cleaner hands in this unsavory campaign, victory would have gone on points to Richard Nixon. But they were almost as bad as each other." Still, it seems beside the point to attribute Nixon's smears to Douglas's provocation when one remembers the campaign against Jerry Voorhis four years before.

In later years, Douglas was no more honest about her mud- slinging than Nixon was about his. In her autobiography she explained that she resorted to the Marcantonio smear in the later stages of the campaign, "when I grew desperate to counteract the effect of Nixon's" use of that particular smear. "I started to include in my speeches and literature the fact that Nixon and Marcantonio also voted together. My intention was not to paint Nixon as a fel- low traveler [a term meaning a Communist or Communist sym- pathizer], which would have been absurd, but to explain rather ineptly how Marcantonio switched his vote around. It wasn't help- ful to me and it didn't relieve the confusion."

Douglas was charitable to herself in that explanation, and a couple of generations of sympathetic listeners have taken her at her word, but it is difficult to determine if she meant it or if she was being disingenuous. Her explanation does not stand up to scrutiny, especially when one reviews the specific charges in her campaign literature. "As I look back over almost thirty years," Douglas wrote in the late 1970s, "I know we were affected by Nixon's tactics, but at the time I thought I was rising above them. Perhaps our approach should have been different. Perhaps I shouldn't have been so above it all, sticking to my record all the time with Gahagan stubbornness. I don't mean I should have played his game—winning isn't everything—but that I should have defended myself better." Indeed, memory is a funny thing.

But Douglas likely did shy away from confronting Nixon on a number of occasions. Probably hoping to repeat his debating triumphs over Jerry Voorhis, Nixon planned to debate Douglas. They were scheduled to meet for a formal debate in Los Angeles on September 20, but Douglas canceled. According to historian Greg Mitchell, she cited "urgent business in Washington," but Mitchell suggests she may have been reluctant to face Nixon because, in an informal joint appearance a while earlier, Nixon had jarred Douglas with a lead-weighted joke. He had produced a letter from Eleanor Roosevelt endorsing his candidacy and offering a contribution. The "joke" was that this Eleanor Roosevelt, a relative by marriage of Theodore Roosevelt's branch of the family, was not the former first lady. That did not sit well with Douglas, though Nixon thought it uproariously funny.

When Douglas canceled, the Democratic candidate for governor, James Roosevelt, decided to debate Nixon in Douglas's place. Nixon supporters had been publicly ridiculing Douglas for cowardice and, when Roosevelt decided to fill in for her, Nixon, according to Mitchell, said she "should speak for herself . . . so that everyone in California would know exactly why she had 'followed the Communist party line so many times.' " The debate took place, and Nixon danced rings around Roosevelt as he had Voorhis. Nixon concentrated entirely on the Communist threat, defended the pending McCarran bill, and altogether outperformed Roosevelt in front of a highly receptive audience. Media favorably reviewed Nixon's performance.

The mudslinging intensified as the campaign entered its later stages. Ingrid Winther Scobie wrote of a whispering campaign against Douglas unmatched by anything the Democrat had done to Nixon. Douglas was informed of the whispering campaign by none other than Eleanor Roosevelt—the Democratic one. The former first lady wrote Douglas to tell her that a California voter she knew was asked by a stranger on the street for whom she would vote. Roosevelt's acquaintance told her she would vote for Helen Gahagan Douglas. The stranger replied that Douglas and her husband were both Communists. Mrs. Roosevelt concluded, according to Scobie, "I thought you might like to know of this type of electioneering." There also were reports of a phone campaign similar to the one against Voorhis in 1946.

Other pamphlets called attention to the fact that Melvyn Douglas was Jewish, that his family name actually was Hesselberg. Neither Douglas had concealed these facts. As with the lowliest aspects of the campaign against Voorhis, Nixon claimed that he had nothing to do with such tactics, denied that various incidents ever occurred, and commented on occasion that a candidate cannot control all of his campaign workers.

In the same vein, the Nixon campaign put on one of the earliest television political spots. The twenty-second ad featured Richard Nixon looking into the camera, out at the television audience, and promising the voters of California that, as senator, he would represent them and their interests, "and not the half-baked theories of left-wing intellectuals at pinko cocktail parties."

In the last weeks of the campaign, Truman came through for Douglas. When all is said and done, no president wants an important Senate seat to go to the opposing party. Truman may have been less than thrilled with Douglas's candidacy, but when he realized that the tottering Douglas campaign was in serious trouble, he sent a series of important Democrats to the state to campaign both for Douglas and gubernatorial candidate Roosevelt. According to historian Stephen E. Ambrose, Truman, despite his lukewarm (at best) feelings for Douglas, wanted Nixon defeated. Nixon, with his harsh anti–Fair Deal rhetoric, had made himself a particular enemy of the Truman administration, and the president personally disliked the young congressman.

Vice President Alben Barkley showed up and hit the hustings in October. Truman's attorney general, agriculture secretary, and labor secretary, some famous out-of-state congressmen, and civil rights leader Mary McLeod Bethune, a friend of Eleanor Roosevelt, followed. Even W. Averill Harriman spoke in Los Angeles for Douglas. He was famous then as one of Truman's top foreign-policy advisers. In addition to these appearances, some out-of-state big guns sent recorded endorsements to California radio stations. Among them were Texas senator Lyndon Johnson, House Speaker Sam Rayburn, and Franklin Roosevelt, Jr., a Democratic celebrity by virtue of his name and parentage. President Truman did not travel to California or record a radio endorsement for Douglas, though at a Washington press conference he defended her record and commented favorably on her candidacy.

Nixon, however, found something to criticize in this cavalcade of Democratic stars who presented themselves or their voices on behalf of Douglas. He derided her and the California Democratic party for relying on out-of-staters, implying that outsiders had no business telling Californians how to vote. He labeled the troop of dignitaries the "foreign legion" and even revived the old Reconstruction label of "carpetbagger."

Nixon did not rely on many outsiders himself, and only grudgingly allowed Wisconsin senator Joseph McCarthy, the period's most famous and reckless Red-baiter, to make a single campaign speech for him in California. Despite his own Red-baiting, Nixon considered McCarthy prone to excess and potentially embarrassing. Historian Greg Mitchell accurately noted that "Nixon was no McCarthy; blacklisting and loyalty oaths made him uncomfortable . . . ," even though "his anti-Communist credentials were impeccable."

McCarthy's antics troubled Nixon, particularly since he needed Democratic votes to defeat Douglas. The senator's propensity for practically identifying the Democratic party as a large cell of the Communist party would make it more difficult to appeal to Democrats, no matter how leftist Douglas appeared to be. In any case, Nixon accepted McCarthy's offer to help in a limited way; the senator made a single campaign appearance for Nixon and spoke to a highly partisan Republican audience. McCarthy gave a crowd-pleasing, rousing speech that consisted of his usual diatribe about Truman and nearly every other Democrat working for the international Communist conspiracy. The senator made his speech and left California with no real harm done, and Nixon thereby managed to please Republicans without scaring off Democrats.

Meanwhile, Douglas answered the pink sheet with a monstrosity called the Blue Book—a lengthy defense and explanation of her positions guaranteed to put even the most avid Democratic reader to sleep in short order. It had little impact, and it certainly failed to counter the pink sheet. Mitchell identified the Blue Book's key problem: "The pink sheet could be reproduced in the hundreds and thousands, easily distributed and quickly read. The Blue Book was so cumbersome and so costly to produce it could be sent to only a few of Douglas's allies and members of the press (who took little notice of it)." That problem in turn highlighted a basic flaw in the Douglas campaign: the candidate's tendency to lecture the audience and to try to teach voters to see things correctly (that is, as she saw them), as opposed to Nixon's ability to sound the right notes and strike responsive chords.

Douglas herself understood this, though only in part, and recorded in her autobiography that a friend of hers went to a Nixon rally to hear him speak. She reported back to Douglas that Nixon was one of the most effective public speakers she had ever heard. His singular talent, she told Douglas, was to appear absolutely sincere, like a decent man fighting an evil that genuinely upset and perplexed him. His approach at that particular rally had been to ask a rhetorical question: But *why* does Helen Gahagan Douglas support the Communist line? It was as if he were asking God on behalf of the assembled listeners. *Why* would Helen Gahagan Douglas *do* such a thing? It was not his only approach, but Douglas believed he frequently used it, and it was effective in conveying the image of Nixon as a decent young family man, a navy veteran, who only tried to do good while his opponent, a highborn and wealthy star, had sold out to the Communists.

The wealthy star paid an awful price for the party split the state chairman had warned her about. Rather than contenting themselves to boycott the campaign and sit out the election, Manchester Boddy and Senator Sheridan Downey in late September let it be known that they supported Nixon. In the next couple of months, Democrats for Nixon played a formidable role as an organization in getting out the vote for him. Even more important, Downey and Boddy helped connect Nixon to major sources of corporate funding. All through the campaign, Nixon had an enormous advantage over Douglas in terms of money, especially after gaining access to benefactors who had previously funded Democrats.

Nixon's strategy of not alienating Democrats paid off, although toward the campaign season's end, things got a bit dicey. Only days before the election, the two candidates were again scheduled to appear together before a mixed audience of Republicans and Democrats in Beverly Hills in more or less formal debate. Accounts conflict on how the evening's events transpired, but apparently Nixon purposely arrived late and took a seat on the stage behind Douglas as she was speaking. Nixon is said to have fidgeted and looked at his watch, acting restless and bored and drawing scattered laughs from the audience.

Douglas grew progressively more nervous, according to some accounts, and left only moments after finishing her speech, after a quick handshake with her opponent. When Douglas was gone, Nixon went to the podium and addressed the audience. One eyewitness told Greg Mitchell that Nixon pointedly referred to Douglas as "Mrs. Hesselberg." Mitchell wrote that many Jewish Democrats present were "deeply offended," for "they knew an anti-Semitic appeal when they heard it." Mitchell wrote that some of the Democrats and Republicans nearly got into fistfights, as the tensions and resentments of the months of a rough campaign "had come to a full boil."

The temperature was about to rise even higher as a new twist came early in November, in the last few days before the election. Communist China entered the Korean War when General Douglas MacArthur's invasion of the north came too close to the Yalu River—the border between North Korea and China—for Chinese comfort. The day before the election there were confirmed reports that massive numbers of Chinese troops had crossed the Yalu into North Korea. This dealt a devastating blow to the American forces in Korea and to the Democratic candidates at home.

Nixon, as usual, was on top of things and blamed the Chinese intervention on the State Department's policies of "appeasement." The Democrats could not be trusted to stand up to our overseas Communist enemies, Nixon claimed, and so a Republican Congress was necessary to neutralize the Democratic appeasers in the White House. Further, Nixon charged that Congresswoman Douglas had not made it clear where she stood on the conflict in Korea, thus essentially accusing her of treason. He added that she deserved to lose the election because she would not say "whether she supports the government of Red China or whether she opposes it."

Nixon had purposely twisted something that Douglas said a day or two earlier, while reports from Korea were still confused. A reporter asked her if she thought Mainland China should be admitted to the U.N. According to Mitchell, she hedged since, like everyone else in the United States, Douglas was not sure what was going on in Korea. Her answer was politically clumsy under the circumstances, but she was hardly taking sides against the United States in Korea. Douglas had no time to answer these charges with the election literally only hours away.

"Toward the end of the campaign," Douglas wrote in her autobiography, "I knew I would lose." Everything had simply gone too wrong. A Douglas campaign worker told her of seeing Nixon tell a young mother that, if Douglas won the election, we would still be at war in Asia when her baby son was old enough to fight. Douglas was horrified. (It is worth noting, even though Nixon won in 1950, that we *were* still at war in Asia when that infant was old enough to fight.) Fatalistically, she decided that her "major concern was not whether I would lose, because I knew that I would, or by how much, because I was quite certain that Nixon's victory would be smashing." Rather, she decided that Nixon must not "have the final victory of destroying me along with my political career."

Nixon's victory *was* smashing. So were those of the other

Republicans in California. Nixon won election to the Senate with 2,183,454 votes; Douglas received 1,502,507. A Republican, Sam Yorty, won Douglas's House seat. Yorty later became mayor of Los Angeles. Governor Earl Warren easily defeated challenger James Roosevelt. In Congress, the Republicans made considerable gains on the Democrats, though they failed to win majorities. But times were good for the Grand Old Party, and they smelled blood with the 1952 presidential election looming on the horizon.

Nixon did not have to wait long to partake of the fruits of victory. Senator Sheridan Downey retired shortly after the election and Governor Warren appointed Senator-elect Nixon to fill Downey's unexpired term. So Nixon took up his duties as the junior senator from California even before the new Congress convened in January 1951. The rising star had risen farther and faster than any other contemporary newcomer, Republican or Democrat, and probably only a few observers actually thought that he would serve out the six-year term to which the voters of California had elected him.

Helen Gahagan Douglas was through with elective politics. She retired to private life, took a stab or two at reviving her performing career, but never made a go of it. She took active part in the antiwar movement, which drove a wedge between her and her old friend Lyndon Johnson. In the 1970s, she struggled against cancer but appeared in public and called for President Nixon's impeachment during the Watergate scandal. She worked on her autobiography and died in June 1980 before its publication. Melvyn Douglas wrote some concluding passages for the book, and Doubleday published it in 1982.

Richard Nixon, of course, went to the Senate, but his career there was predictably brief. In 1952, General Dwight Eisenhower won the Republican nomination for president and tapped Senator Nixon to join him on the ticket as the vice presidential candidate.

THE GENERAL'S SHOCK TROOPS:
GOOD SOLDIER DICK AND TAIL GUNNER JOE

✫ ✫ ✫

In May 1951, Senator Richard Nixon privately met General Dwight Eisenhower at NATO headquarters in Paris. Eisenhower told Nixon that he had read one of the first books on the Alger Hiss case, *Seeds of Treason,* by two of Nixon's journalist friends, Ralph de Toledano and Victor Lasky. "The thing that most impressed me," said Eisenhower, "was that you not only got Hiss, but you got him fairly."

The general was sizing up his young visitor. Eisenhower may or may not have realized that Nixon was sizing him up, too. There was talk back home of Eisenhower running for president as a Republican in the next election, approximately a year and a half away. The senator decided that the general was the best of the candidates for the Republican nomination, especially in terms of foreign affairs, Nixon's special area of interest. "I felt that I was in the presence of a genuine statesman, and I came away convinced that he should be the next president. I also decided that if he ran for the nomination, I would do everything I could to help him get it."

While at times Nixon could be shockingly honest in his writings, he also dissembled just like any other politician. His numerous accounts of this period never directly say that he wanted the 1952 vice presidential nomination, nor that he pegged

GENERAL DWIGHT D. EISENHOWER AND SENATOR RICHARD M. NIXON, 1952.

Eisenhower as his man, nor that the Paris visit had anything to do with his plans to obtain the nomination. But the message was received on both sides; Nixon indeed did all he could to help Eisenhower secure the presidential nomination, and Eisenhower chose Nixon as his running mate.

The stories behind the 1952 nominations are not among the concerns of this section; Nixon's role as Eisenhower's hatchet man against the Democrats is the pertinent topic. Nixon received considerable help in that task from Senator Joseph McCarthy, the newly prominent Republican Red-baiting firebrand who had emerged from relative obscurity in February 1950. The relationship between McCarthy and Eisenhower was uneasy and mistrustful on both sides, but many Republicans were afraid of the Wisconsin demagogue, and others at least considered him a necessary evil.

McCarthy was both valuable and dangerous, and he showed only guarded support for Eisenhower at the campaign's start.

When Eisenhower won the nomination, a reporter asked McCarthy what he thought of the ticket. The senator pointedly answered that he believed Dick Nixon would make a fine vice president. Nonetheless, McCarthy supported the ticket, soon jumped on the Eisenhower bandwagon, and turned into an enthusiastic campaigner. But during the campaign's early stages, the job of savaging the opposition fell to Nixon. Later, McCarthy joined Nixon in the dirty fighting that Eisenhower by necessity and inclination disdained.

Eisenhower had carefully cultivated a dignified, fatherly image, and in public the stern commander was nowhere in evidence. The American people saw only the kindly, thoughtful leader, the reassuring patriarch who pledged to go to Korea to personally assess the situation with his experienced military eye. He would finish the war that Truman could not, and he would not be caught napping, as Truman and the Democrats had been.

Ike conveyed to the voters that they could trust him to guide the country through the coming difficult years. His steady hand at the nation's helm would ensure strength in the face of the Soviet threat and a departure from the policies of the Roosevelt and Truman years. He would create prosperity for families at home, without resorting to Socialistic programs that would sap the American spirit and make it vulnerable to Communist subversion. At the same time, Eisenhower reassured nervous Democrats and annoyed stalwart Republicans by making it known he would not undo all the work of the New Deal. Social Security, for instance, was here to stay. Eisenhower told a political aide that any party that sought to repeal it would be committing political suicide.

Nixon's job was to take on the opposition directly: Nixon's British biographer Jonathan Aitken put it succinctly: "Flaying Democrats was Nixon's task for the election." Actually, Eisenhower said many inflammatory things about the Democrats and coined the memorable phrase "creeping socialism," but he successfully maintained the image of dignified restraint.

Nixon blasted the Democrats for appeasing the Communists

and called the New Deal and Fair Deal policies of the current and previous administrations un-American. He enthusiastically reminded the voting public of the various—and in historical perspective rather minor—scandals of the Truman administration. He spoke of the Hiss case, the "loss" of China, the Soviet atomic bomb. As he did in the Voorhis and Douglas campaigns, Nixon claimed that the opposition were not even true Democrats. Nixon attacked Democratic presidential nominee Adlai Stevenson, President Truman, and Secretary of State Dean Acheson as "traitors to the high principles in which many of the nation's Democrats believe." Clearly, this campaign was one for the books.

Eisenhower and his advisers recognized that Nixon's other assets were his California roots and appeal to Western voters. His nomination signaled that the Republican party understood the West's growing importance in postwar America. Nixon's candidacy, therefore, was tactically important for fighting Democrats and strategically important for addressing the changing national demographics.

As Nixon went to work, the campaign immediately turned into yet another ugly duel. He launched a series of characteristically Nixonian attacks on the Democratic presidential candidate, Adlai Stevenson. Eisenhower usually avoided mentioning his opponent and would not dirty his hands with such things, at least not often. Nixon fielded the standard Republican Red-baiting repertoire and went after Stevenson and the Democrats with a will, casting aspersions on Stevenson's loyalty and impugning his sexuality. The attacks were harsh even by today's rough standards.

Nixon and McCarthy served as the general's shock troops in the national campaign. The main theme of their campaign was that the Democrats had shown cowardice in the face of the Communist threat. Nixon ridiculed Truman's containment policy as "appeasement," which has been a dirty word since British prime minister Neville Chamberlain appeased Adolf Hitler's designs on Czechoslovakia at the Munich conference in 1938. Nixon went after Truman's secretary of state, telling voters of the

Dean Acheson Cowardly College of Communist Containment. Look what Truman and Acheson's policies have brought us to, Nixon and McCarthy proclaimed. We are losing in Korea, and if we lose Korea as we lost China, then Japan is threatened. If Japan is lost, then the Pacific is lost. It was terrifying stuff.

Nixon told an interviewer from the Kansas City *Star*, "There's one difference between the Reds and the Pinks. The Pinks want to socialize America. The Reds want to socialize the world and make Moscow the world capital." Stephen E. Ambrose explained that Nixon was not saying the Democratic party was pink, but he did implicate the "New Deal wing of the party." That was close to a direct accusation that Roosevelt and Truman had sold out the country to the Soviets.

Nixon told the nation that Acheson's policies had "lost" China and Eastern Europe, and "had invited the Communists to begin the Korean War." In Nixon's analysis, Acheson and Truman had announced to the world that their concern for Europe overshadowed any concern about Asia, giving the Communists the impression that the United States did not consider Asia an area of critical interest, and therefore would not fight to defend it. That, argued Nixon, virtually constituted a green light to North Korea.

Nixon went after Democratic presidential nominee Stevenson with a fervor born of personal disdain. "I felt instinctively negative toward Stevenson. I considered him to be far more veneer than substance, and I felt that beneath his glibness and mocking wit, he was shallow, flippant, and indecisive." Nixon's characterization of Stevenson contrasts with the more common and conventional view of the man. Historians and journalists generally describe him as contemplative and even professorial, an honest man, a politician with the makings of a statesman. In many of those accounts, Stevenson comes across as an intellectual, somehow out of place in the rough-and-tumble world of politics, a sophisticated man of wit and poise who would have made a good president—not the philosopher-king perhaps, but a more thoughtful and liberal leader than Eisenhower.

The one flaw that bothers his defenders is indecisiveness.

Stevenson's reputation for indecision dogged him during his career and persists to this day. But his admirers maintain that the voters missed a good bet by not electing Stevenson, and Democrats today recall him fondly. He was, after all, a protégé and close associate of the revered Eleanor Roosevelt, and in death, he retains the image of a man who was highly principled and only reluctantly became a politician.

In 1972, seven years after Stevenson's death, the author met a senior British politician, a Labour member of Parliament, who was a defense expert and an old friend of Stevenson's. The venerable MP told the author a story: Just after the war, he and Stevenson, then fairly young men in their forties, were delegates at the first U.N. General Assembly in San Francisco. The Britisher had just won his first election to the House of Commons and, one day at lunch, Stevenson asked him how it felt to "hawk yourself around, looking for votes." The MP replied that electioneering was a necessary evil and rather inconvenient. Stevenson was silent for some moments, then said, "I don't think I would like that." He was elected governor of Illinois not long after, in 1948.

Other analysts, less vulnerable to charming or seductive images and anecdotes, maintain that Stevenson was very much a politician and often got pretty scrappy himself. Nixon considered Stevenson opportunistic and dishonest and his tactics "crude," though he judged Stevenson's campaign behavior cruder in 1956 than in 1952. Still, Nixon's Stevenson is not the historian's Stevenson, and the difference in perception is striking.

Quick-witted and poised, Stevenson figured to be a dangerous opponent; his speaking style and crisp articulation contrasted sharply with Eisenhower's fairly slow vocal manner and tortured syntax. Historian Eric F. Goldman described Stevenson's use of the newest campaign medium, television, as "electrifying." The Democratic nominee did not shy away from using sarcasm and irony in his criticisms of the patriarchal Eisenhower.

Eisenhower was no fan of Stevenson; Eisenhower particularly resented his campaign rhetoric and took much of what he said as personally insulting. During Eisenhower's presidency, he never invited Stevenson to the White House, which is fairly unusual, though not unheard of, in the etiquette of American national politics. Eisenhower seems not to have considered that Nixon and McCarthy's Red-baiting, or his own, might have been just as personally offensive to Stevenson.

Candidate Nixon called Stevenson "Side-saddle Adlai," and cracked that he rode with both feet to the left. That hit on two fronts: Obviously, the "feet to the left" indicated Communist or communistic sympathies. The "side-saddle" was an oblique reference to rumors that the Democratic candidate, a divorced father, was homosexual. It was not unusual for Red-baiters to imply an association between leftist tendencies and homosexuality. Whittaker Chambers, for instance, in 1948 told HUAC that Alger Hiss walked with a slight "mince." The committee immediately grasped the implication.

Stevenson's sexuality remained a side issue and, for the most part, Nixon concentrated on the alleged Democratic failures in facing down the Communists. If Stevenson were elected president, Nixon told enthusiastic Republicans, "We can expect four more years of this same policy, because Mr. Stevenson received his education from Dean Acheson's wishy-washy State Department."

Nixon proclaimed that Eisenhower intended actually to defeat the Communists rather than contain them. Ike's goal would be to liberate the enslaved Eastern European nations. Containment was "cowardly," or, as Nixon put it on other occasions, the Democrats practiced "a negative policy of containment." Only years later did it become clear that every cold war president from Truman on practiced containment, no matter what name they gave it. Politics is a game of perceptions.

Nixon branded Secretary of State Acheson as the "architect of striped-pants confusion," and said that we need a "khaki-clad president" rather "than one clothed in State Department pinks." Many years later, in an odd twist of history, Nixon and Acheson actually became friendly. President Nixon valued Acheson as an important unofficial foreign-policy adviser. In his memoirs, Nixon expressed regret for the severity of his attacks on Acheson and praised him for his work in forming NATO and implementing some of President Truman's most important cold war policies.

Nixon even found kind words to say about Truman and the containment policy. In *In the Arena*, he wrote that "no one could question the anti-Communist credentials of the president who asked Congress to approve aid to Greece and Turkey to halt Communist aggression in Europe." In the nine books he wrote after leaving the presidency, Nixon joined historians in using the term "containment" to describe America's basic cold war policy, instead of politicizing the term as he had in 1952. But Nixon argued to the end that Acheson and Truman blundered badly in their Asian policy, which made the Korean War possible. Despite his later good feelings for Acheson, his admission that Truman did in fact oppose the Communists, and conceding that containment became standard American policy, Nixon never expressed regret for attacking Truman, nor for his attacks on Stevenson.

Stevenson taunted Eisenhower nearly as much as Nixon taunted Stevenson. The Democratic nominee derided the general's seeming vacillations on domestic policy, even though Eisenhower was clearly a moderate conservative. Still, Stevenson twitted Eisenhower for agreeing with certain New Deal innovations, such as Social Security, which other Republicans deplored and wanted repealed. Eisenhower correctly reasoned that the program was too popular to fool with, but such stands made him vulnerable to charges of being wishy-washy. Stevenson commented that he himself was proud of the Democratic party's record of the New Deal and Fair Deal years. "I was proud to stand on that record," he liked to say, but he wished that Eisenhower "would move over and make room for me."

More disturbing, Stevenson's criticisms of Eisenhower for tolerating McCarthy's attacks on George Marshall hit home and scored points. Marshall was justifiably widely respected among the voting public. Eisenhower's failure to defend Marshall against McCarthy's attacks was unconscionable.

Eisenhower, personally stung by Stevenson's sardonic witticisms, dropped his elevated stance and went after his Democratic rival. In the process, he engaged in some standard Republican Red-baiting. The general sought to convert Stevenson's main rhetorical weapon, his trenchant wit, into a liability. "The subjects of which we are speaking these days . . . are not those that seem to me to be amusing." How funny is it, asked Eisenhower, that "we have stumbled into a war in Korea . . . that we have already lost . . . 117,000 of our Americans killed and wounded. . . . Is it funny when evidence was discovered that there are Communists in government . . . ?"

That was getting into McCarthy's territory. Eisenhower and the Wisconsin senator did not get on personally, but the latter was important to the campaign. When Eisenhower won the nomination, there were questions as to how McCarthy might fit in, since despite McCarthy's formidable political power in 1952, his antics alienated many moderate Republicans, and it was no secret that Eisenhower did not like McCarthy's attacks on General Marshall.

McCarthy often referred to Marshall, Truman, and Acheson as some sort of incompetent triumvirate, and on other occasions he asserted that they were part of a subversive conspiracy. He stopped short of directly calling them conscious Communists, though he came close. The moderates did not object to McCarthy smearing the other two, but smearing Marshall was too much for many of them. The author of the Marshall Plan had been the army chief of staff during World War II and afterward served in President Truman's cabinet as secretary of state and then as secretary of defense. He was respected more than nearly any other living public figure, except for Eisenhower and General Douglas MacArthur.

Even so, Marshall was one of the right wing's special targets, and McCarthy had issued a long report the previous June charging that Marshall and Acheson were members of a vast "conspiracy of infamy so black that, when it is finally exposed, its principals shall be forever deserving of the maledictions of all honest men." Other career Red-baiters had also attacked Marshall and, several years before, twenty Republicans in the Senate voted against confirming him as secretary of defense. But none of that made Marshall a safe target, especially now that Eisenhower was the Republican presidential nominee. Ike served under Marshall's command during World War II, and most Republicans realized that to attack him might suggest that Eisenhower himself had been duped. However, McCarthy was getting away with it and doing quite well in the public-opinion polls.

McCarthy rolled about the deck as the proverbial loose cannon. He was excessive, embarrassing, and effective. Republican audiences loved him. Eisenhower privately asked him to soften his attacks on Marshall but otherwise did little or nothing to curb his rambunctious supporter. He acted cold and distant toward McCarthy in public, although he occasionally complimented the senator. At times, Eisenhower borrowed a spear or two from McCarthy's arsenal.

On one occasion, when McCarthy and Eisenhower shared a platform in Milwaukee, Wisconsin, Eisenhower engaged in some distinctly McCarthyistic Red-baiting. Referring to New Deal and Fair Deal policies, Eisenhower spoke darkly of a tolerance for communism having "poisoned two whole decades of our national life." He decried communistic trends in our schools, the news media, and government. He detected "contamination in some degree of virtually every department, every agency, every bureau, every section" of the government. As a result, China and Eastern Europe had fallen to communism. Domestic policy had been conducted by "men who sneered and scoffed at warnings of the enemy infiltrating our most secret councils." Eisenhower concluded that this all meant "treason itself." In that speech, he neither referred to McCarthy nor spoke of his Senate reelection campaign. He was angry at McCarthy for attacking Marshall, so he merely borrowed McCarthy's tools and ignored the man himself.

McCarthy, undaunted and unwavering, continued to speak of the Roosevelt and Truman administrations as "twenty years of treason." He sometimes pretended to mispronounce the name "Adlai" as "Alger"—as in, "Alger, I mean Adlai, Stevenson has said . . ." Eisenhower made no forceful move to quiet McCarthy, nor did he dissociate himself from such talk. Privately, the general was furious at McCarthy for more than just the attacks on Marshall. He winced at the liberties McCarthy took in private; Nixon wrote that McCarthy acted "crudely familiar" with Eisenhower. But rare was the Republican in 1952 who would dare to cross the Wisconsin senator in public. Eisenhower, the supreme commander of the European Theater and great hero of the nation, was not that rare Republican.

Nixon and McCarthy first met in 1947, when both were new to Washington. McCarthy Red-baited his way into the Senate in 1946, then promptly devoted himself to serving special interests. He quickly became known around Capitol Hill as the Pepsi-Cola Kid, since he allegedly spent most of his time looking after the soft-drink company's concerns. The Washington press corps regarded him as the least effective member of the Senate. Early in 1950, he realized that he stood a real chance of losing his bid for reelection when his number came up in 1952. He cast about for a good issue to play up for the next couple of years. He sought advice from friends and associates. He even asked a few reporters for suggestions.

On January 7, 1950, Senator McCarthy went to dinner with several acquaintances. One of them was columnist Drew Pearson's attorney, which was odd, considering the bad blood between McCarthy and Pearson. Another was Father Edmund Walsh, dean of the Georgetown University School of Foreign Service. Walsh, a Roman Catholic priest, took a special interest in communism, much like Nixon's personal political cleric, Father John Cronin. The boys spent some time kicking around various ideas for an issue for McCarthy, concentrating mainly on such things as housing for veterans and for pushing construction of the planned Saint Lawrence Seaway. None was, to use the 1990s term, sexy. Finally, Walsh asked, "How about communism as an issue?" It was something of a set-up, since Pearson's lawyer and another of the dinner companions, Georgetown University political science professor Charles A. Kraus, had been urging McCarthy to read Walsh's books and papers on anticommunism and suggested this dinner in the first place so that McCarthy could meet Walsh. Later, after McCarthy's orgy of accusations began, Walsh denied having given the notorious advice to the Pepsi-Cola Kid.

Assuming that Walsh gave McCarthy that advice, which Drew Pearson reported in his column (his lawyer was there, after all), the senator liked the idea and recalled to Walsh how he used the issue back in 1946 in his first Senate campaign. About a month after the dinner, McCarthy delivered his infamous and epochal Lincoln Day speech in Wheeling, West Virginia. His exact words are in dispute, since no cameras or sound recorders were there and none of the few bored reporters present took careful notes. McCarthy did not help clarify matters in the immediate aftermath of that small but historic political gathering in Wheeling.

Many Republican senators hit the road on Lincoln Day to make speeches on the rubber-chicken circuit. Lincoln Day actually was several days, ending on or about the February 12 birthday of the first Republican president. McCarthy headed for Wheeling on February 9. The big guns went to the big places, in Washington or New York or Los Angeles, but the Pepsi-Cola Kid went to Wheeling. McCarthy had four other stops scheduled for the Lincoln Day run, the last of which was in South Dakota. He began the journey with a bang, although it is not clear if he realized the attention his speech would draw. McCarthy had not, after all, intended to set the world on fire; he was trying to get reelected to the Senate.

In retrospect, it is pretty remarkable that McCarthy drew all the attention he did that day. His speech was standard Republican Red-baiting, some of it similar to a speech Congressman Richard Nixon gave only a couple of weeks before in California for his own Senate campaign. One particular section of McCarthy's Wheeling speech caused all the fuss. According to McCarthy biographer Thomas C. Reeves, the senator told his Wheeling audience that he had information "that would prove Secretary of State Dean Acheson guilty of treason." While he did not have time to "name all the men in the State Department who have been named as active members of the Communist party and members of a spy ring, I have here in my hand a list of 205—a list of names that were made known to the secretary of state as being members of the Communist party and who nevertheless are still working and shaping policy in the State Department." This was only about a week and a half after Hiss's perjury conviction, so the State Department made a particularly large and tempting target.

McCarthy waved a piece of paper at the assemblage but did not let anyone look closely at it. The paper disappeared soon after, and McCarthy never produced it for examination. Some reporter joked that for all anyone knew it could have been a list of laundry items, and so was born the document's unofficial name—McCarthy's laundry list. At any rate, word spread quickly that the senator from Wisconsin had named more than two hundred Communist spies in the State Department, and for the rest of his journey reporters met him at every stop. He relished the attention and gave a different, usually larger number of State Department Communists each time someone asked about it. By the time he reached South Dakota, the 205 grew to more than 600.

McCarthy's great days had come. The Pepsi-Cola Kid became Tail Gunner Joe, a nickname he or some Wisconsin staffer dreamed up at least as far back as 1946, but it had failed to catch on until the Wheeling speech made him a political celebrity. McCarthy claimed that he had served as a tail gunner in combat missions over the South Pacific. He was in the South Pacific, but he neither was a tail gunner nor had he flown in combat missions. Now, with his newfound fame, his preferred nickname edged out the old, derisive one and the Washington press corps' choice for worst senator instantly transmogrified into the nation's foremost Red-baiter. The hard-drinking, violent Joe McCarthy shambled into history, and for four long years America was transfixed and the national political scene electrified as this big, hulking brute carried Red-baiting to its absurd and grandiose zenith.

But there was a way to go still, and ahead lay days of sound and fury, signifying great publicity. Just after Wheeling, Nixon counseled McCarthy on the fine art of Red-baiting. Nixon told his first biographer, Earl Mazo, that he told McCarthy, "Now, the important thing . . . is one rule I would urge you to follow: Always understate, never overstate your case." McCarthy admitted to Nixon he was "sort of on a spot" over the Wheeling speech. Nixon told him that "you will be in an untenable position if you claim that there were umpteen, or however many, card-carrying Communists in the State Department, because you cannot prove that. On the other hand, if you were to say that there were so many people whose records disclosed Communist-front affiliations and associations, this you can prove. . . . But he did not listen and from then on that case was out the window."

The case was not out the window. What Nixon failed to grasp, assuming that he wrote truthfully about his thoughts, was that McCarthy did not care about proof.

The two men were friendly, although Nixon was wary of McCarthy. Early in their acquaintance Nixon recognized McCarthy's instability and unpredictability. When McCarthy took up Red-baiting, Nixon realized that potential disaster loomed, especially since McCarthy drank heavily and comported himself with uncertain restraint, sometimes acting thuggish and threatening. He was known on occasion to translate anger into physical action.

On one memorable night in December 1950, Nixon, McCarthy, and columnist Drew Pearson all attended the same dinner party in a Washington hotel. Pearson had been attacking McCarthy in his widely read "Washington Merry-Go-Round" column for some time by then, and he and McCarthy got into a series of nasty exchanges during the evening. When Nixon went to the cloakroom to retrieve his coat he found McCarthy strangling Pearson. McCarthy, twice Pearson's size and much younger, had his "big, thick hands" around Pearson's throat as the columnist gamely struggled for breath and tried to break free. According to Nixon, when McCarthy spotted him, he released the columnist and slapped Pearson's back "so hard that his head snapped back." McCarthy said, "That one was for you, Dick." Nixon stepped between them and suggested, "Let a good Quaker stop this fight."

It was hardly a fight. The burly McCarthy had simply assaulted a much older man. He was an alcoholic whose self-control was dubious at the best of times. After McCarthy released Pearson's throat, Nixon grabbed his arm before he could go for Pearson again and told him it was time to go home. McCarthy refused to leave before Pearson did. "I am not going to turn my back on the son of a bitch," he told Nixon. After the badly shaken Pearson left, McCarthy said, "You shouldn't have stopped me, Dick." Nixon then spent the next half hour helping McCarthy find his car.

The Wisconsin senator already was a national figure by the time of the cloakroom incident. As his national reputation grew, Nixon kept track of McCarthy's exploits mostly through the news media. What he heard and read he regarded with "great trepidation." McCarthy was new to "fighting Communists," as Nixon put it, and he worried that McCarthy might not understand "the need for absolute accuracy and fairness in going after them." Nixon probably differentiated between the wild accusations *he* employed to defeat election opponents, as opposed to an accusation that could send someone to prison.

Nixon grew increasingly dismayed as McCarthy "continued to strike out indiscriminately." He repeatedly told McCarthy that he had to be careful about facts. Referring to McCarthy's habit of talking about "card-carrying Communists" in his speeches, Nixon told him he "would be on firmer ground talking about the problems of national-security risks." Nixon, in fact, did not directly call his opponents Communists, particularly not card-carrying Communists. He contented himself to drop heavy hints, accuse them of Communist sympathies or weakness in the face of communism, and make snide remarks about pink underwear. He rarely accused anyone directly. Helen Gahagan Douglas commented that he did not have to, since his campaign workers did it for him. McCarthy, however, took the barnstorming approach, and Nixon did not like it. But McCarthy's antics seemed to work.

Eisenhower and Nixon both realized that while McCarthy was an asset during the campaign, albeit a troublesome one, once the election was over and the new administration in place,

McCarthy could easily and rapidly become a liability. The two running mates showed excellent political sense in that assessment, for events after January 1953 bore out their worries. Eisenhower may have been more acutely aware of this than Nixon was, since in private, the mutual dislike between Eisenhower and McCarthy grew increasingly evident as the campaign progressed. Out of public view, just before their joint appearance in Milwaukee, Eisenhower threatened to repudiate McCarthy for attacking General Marshall. McCarthy defiantly told Eisenhower that, were he to praise Marshall and criticize McCarthy that night in Wisconsin, he "would be booed." Eisenhower told McCarthy that he was not afraid of being booed, but when the moment came, Eisenhower did not praise or defend his old chief.

In the end, Eisenhower defeated Stevenson by more than 6.5 million votes. Considering Eisenhower's immense popularity, we never will know how great or small a role Nixon played in winning the 1952 election, nor the extent of McCarthy's campaign effectiveness. During the first term, Nixon continued to draw the partisan combat assignments. McCarthy predictably ran out of bounds and drew the administration's collective wrath. It fell to Nixon to handle the senator on the administration's behalf. Nixon wrote that the incoming administration "inherited" McCarthy as a liability from the Truman administration, an interesting way to state the matter.

Vice President Nixon was to serve not merely as the administration's attack dog but as the president's link to the party's right wing and to McCarthy. Nixon was a moderate on most social issues and verged on liberalism in many respects, including his support of racial integration. He was an internationalist in foreign affairs and while in Congress voted for many of President Truman's foreign policy initiatives, including the Marshall Plan and membership in NATO. But his Red-baiting endeared him to the party's most conservative wing, something it seems Nixon himself did not yet fully understand. Eisenhower did, though. At least the president's advisers did. Nixon never really gained Eisenhower's confidence nor even his full support, but he carried out important political tasks for the White House and soldiered on for eight years, attacking when unleashed and temporizing when constrained.

Therein lay the primary difference between Nixon and McCarthy as useful fighters for the administration. McCarthy was a loose cannon, while Nixon was a good soldier. The Wisconsin bully gave his allegiance to no one. Once he tasted blood, he was ready to destroy all in his path, although no one, perhaps including himself, could say where that path was supposed to lead. Perhaps his Red-baiting was in the end pathological. Whatever the case, McCarthy was just as willing to plague the Republican administration as he had the departed Democratic one. McCarthy's fall lay more than a year in the future when Eisenhower and Nixon took office in January 1953, so a lot of plaguing lay ahead.

McCarthy still commanded loyalty from many Republicans, and the president understood that to repudiate McCarthy outright would, as Nixon put it, split the Republican party down the middle, both in Congress and among Republican voters. Eisenhower assumed, perhaps correctly, that his own personal charisma and the overwhelming esteem in which Americans of both parties held him could not sufficiently withstand the possible split over McCarthy, and that such a split would severely compromise his ability to lead.

Problems arose almost immediately. When Eisenhower sent two high-level diplomatic nominations to the Senate for confirmation, McCarthy decided to denounce one of them, a Harvard professor, as a Communist on the grounds that all Harvard professors were Communists. Nixon heard about McCarthy's plan, personally intervened, and somehow managed to dissuade McCarthy from launching his attack. The following summer, when McCarthy learned that a fairly high-ranking official at the Central Intelligence Agency had contributed to Alger Hiss's defense fund, he prepared to investigate the CIA for Communist infiltration.

Allen Dulles, CIA director and brother of Secretary of State

John Foster Dulles, asked Nixon to intervene again. The official in question was no Communist, Dulles told Nixon, but his main object was to keep the CIA from getting any sort of publicity. Nixon went to see McCarthy, but the senator was hesitant to back off. Nixon enlisted the help of the other Republicans on McCarthy's Senate subcommittee, and Tail Gunner Joe backed off, but not happily.

Dean Acheson himself summed up the state of affairs for McCarthy and the Republicans in the early days of Eisenhower's presidency. McCarthy, Acheson wrote in his memoirs, *Present at the Creation*, "was essentially a lazy, small-town bully, without sustaining purpose, who on his own would soon have petered out. Flattered, built up by. . . the Republican right, and their accomplice, the press, printing what was not news and not fit to print, he served their various purposes." But things changed after the election of 1952, according to Acheson. Once Eisenhower was in office, ". . . they no longer had any use for him," but, knowing that people in high places feared him, "he was not shrewd enough to see that his day was over."

Clark Clifford, a longtime Democratic presidential adviser, had his own view of the matter. Clifford wrote in his memoirs, *Counsel to the President*, that "the harsh fact, which must never be forgotten, is that until he destroyed himself during the Army-McCarthy hearings, Joe McCarthy literally terrorized Washington and much of the nation. His popularity was growing steadily in the national polls, and the Eisenhower administration lay passive and supine before his depredations." Just before the Army-McCarthy hearings began, Clifford wished us all to keep in mind, McCarthy's ratings in the public-opinion polls were 50 percent favorable, against 29 percent unfavorable and 21 percent no opinion. Those were "very strong numbers for someone so controversial."

The key element in Clark's analysis is the Eisenhower administration's supine posture toward McCarthy. Even with the power of the presidency at his disposal, Eisenhower showed no eagerness to take on the senator. Perhaps Eisenhower feared a party rupture, or perhaps Ike listened to his vice president's

JOSEPH MCCARTHY AND ROY COHN, 1954.

advice, which was to let McCarthy sink himself, then turn on him. That is in fact what happened. McCarthy brought about his own downfall, and when the slide became obvious, the administration proved only too happy to give Tail Gunner Joe a downward shove.

McCarthy's fall came about in a strange and unexpected way. His right-hand man was a young lawyer named Roy Cohn, known in government and legal circles for his extreme viciousness and underhandedness. Clark Clifford later wrote that, "if McCarthy was ugly, crude, and self-destructive, Cohn was as close to a genuinely evil man as I have ever seen in American political life." Cohn was a homosexual who liked to smear others by charging that they were homosexuals. Utterly without ethics and without compassion for anyone he identified as an enemy, Cohn was made for McCarthy—up to a point. Cohn was the unwitting agent of McCarthy's undoing. The young lawyer's rise to power blinded him to certain important realities. The same could be said for McCarthy himself.

Acting as McCarthy's chief counsel, Cohn toured American embassies and consulates in Europe to inspect their libraries for works by supposedly subversive authors. He actually presided over book burnings. The Nazi book burnings of the 1930s were still a recent memory, but there Cohn was, stoking the flames and immolating the First Amendment to the Constitution of the United States. Standing beside him was a young man named G. David Schine.

Schine, wealthy heir to a large hotel chain, was the other unwitting agent who with Cohn worked McCarthy's ruin. In 1953, Schine was drafted into the army and Cohn immediately went about trying to secure special privileges for him. The army refused his requests, so Cohn approached McCarthy with the idea that the time had come to investigate the army for Communist infiltration. The case they selected to pursue concerned an army dental officer named Irving Peress.

Peress had been promoted to major as a matter of routine, though he had earlier refused to answer an army-loyalty questionnaire. That violated regulations, and the army had begun processing Peress for discharge before the whole matter came to Cohn and McCarthy's attention. Cohn found out that Peress once belonged to a leftist organization, and the dentist ended up in front of McCarthy's committee. The hapless Peress stood on his Fifth Amendment privilege not to answer potentially incriminating questions, and a few days after the hearing, requested and was granted an immediate honorable discharge. At that, according to Nixon, McCarthy "hit the roof."

The question "Who promoted Major Peress?" now resounded as McCarthy and Cohn's battle cry. How, they asked, could a known Communist rise through the ranks of the U.S. Army? McCarthy wanted the army's top brass hauled before his subcommittee. Brigadier General Ralph Zwicker, the commanding officer of Peress's station, Camp Kilmer, New Jersey, answered a subpoena to an executive session and explained that it was a simple case of bureaucratic confusion. The general took personal responsibility for the Peress promotion but declined to identify the specific personnel involved. McCarthy exploded. The senator upbraided the brigadier, accused him of protecting Communists in the army, and went on for a while about Zwicker's unfitness to command or even to wear an American uniform. Finally, McCarthy told Zwicker he would haul him before a public hearing if he would not name the Communists under his command.

After Zwicker's ordeal, Secretary of the Army Robert Stevens intervened and told McCarthy that he forbade his generals to testify in front of McCarthy's subcommittee. If anyone from the army was going to testify, Stevens insisted, it would be he. That idea appealed to McCarthy, since Stevens was a bigger fish than any active general could be.

The task of coordinating and presiding over the administration's war effort fell to Nixon by default, since the president was on a golfing trip and had made no communications concerning the looming crisis. Besides, dealing with McCarthy had been more or less designated as his department from the outset. Nixon considered himself well suited for the responsibility, since he had "enough credibility in both camps." Consequently, he held a private meeting in his Capitol Hill office with Stevens and the army's counsel, John Adams. Nixon found the two naively confident about their ability to handle McCarthy. As Nixon described it, Stevens and Adams figured they could "finesse the Peress case" by publicly conceding that the army had erred, but would then criticize McCarthy's treatment of General Zwicker. Nixon said he told them it was worth a try, but they should bear in mind that McCarthy would be the one in control of the hearing. They all agreed that Republican senator Everett Dirksen, a member of the subcommittee, should set up a luncheon meeting the next day. McCarthy would attend, with Dirksen, Stevens, and Adams, and two more members of McCarthy's subcommittee. Nixon did not attend.

Senator Karl Mundt, Nixon's old political friend who now sat on the subcommittee and attended the luncheon, told him that the meeting was stormy but, after a beginning that seemed hopeless, Stevens agreed to let army witnesses appear if McCarthy promised to behave himself and treat them respectfully. The secretary of the army called the vice president that same day and, Nixon wrote, seemed happy with the arrangement. Before the day was over, however, McCarthy boasted to a reporter that the army secretary had abjectly surrendered to him. That night, Stevens was back on the phone with Nixon, threatening to resign. Nixon tried to calm him and suggested they meet in the morning. That quieted Stevens for the moment.

Eisenhower returned to Washington the next morning. McCarthy proved unreceptive to the president's attempts to have everyone involved issue a single, conciliatory statement. Eisenhower told Nixon to meet with Stevens and presidential advisers Sherman Adams and Jerry Persons, and come up with a statement for Stevens to make directly from the White House.

The White House statement was a direct challenge to McCarthy. It declared that Stevens would tolerate no further "browbeating or humiliation of his officers" nor further abuse of army personnel "under any circumstances, including committee hearings." Some days later, Eisenhower told a meeting of the congressional leadership that he wanted to issue a statement to support Stevens. Nixon, who was present, recorded in his diary that the president said he wanted to make the point that "in fighting communism we could not destroy Americanism." Nixon noted that the president had grown emotional about the affair. He was, after all, an old army man, but he also saw a political threat in the situation, since the 1954 congressional elections were only months away. The clash with McCarthy was dividing Republicans and working to benefit the Democrats.

Nixon noted that Eisenhower was offended by McCarthy's personality and conduct, which by then was stating the obvious. The president told Nixon he wanted to make the point that the Red-baiters like McCarthy were every bit as dangerous as the Communists. He fumed that the investigators' methods were similar to Communist methods. Nixon counseled restraint; he still believed the time had not come to attack McCarthy, and he figured that the president's proposed statement would create more problems than it would solve—assuming it would solve any. In January 1954, Nixon reported, public-opinion polls still showed McCarthy with a 50 percent approval rating.

Eisenhower bowed to Nixon's logic and opted for a milder statement. On March 3, the president told a press conference, "In opposing communism, we are defeating ourselves if either by design or through carelessness we use methods that do not conform to the American sense of justice and fair play." There is no evidence that McCarthy felt at all wounded by that pallid rebuke.

The Democrats began their congressional campaign by hitting the Republicans for not controlling McCarthy. They had been quiet since the presidential election, as McCarthy turned out to be the viper in the administration's bosom. Now, in the wake of the Peress debacle and with the elections coming up, it served their interests to strike. The standard-bearer was Adlai Stevenson, who was still one of the most visible and respected Democrats. He blasted the White House for its failure to confront McCarthy. Stevenson said on television that the Republican party was now divided in two—"half McCarthy, half Eisenhower." As in the old days, Eisenhower assigned Nixon the task of answering Stevenson. Nixon unhappily did as ordered.

On March 13, he went on television to address the nation: "Men who have in the past done effective work exposing communism in this country have, by reckless talk and questionable methods, made themselves the issue, rather than the cause they believe in so deeply. When they have done this they not only have diverted attention from the danger of communism but have diverted that attention to themselves. Also, they have allowed those whose primary objective is to defeat the Eisenhower administration to divert attention from its great program to these individuals who followed those methods."

Nixon agreed that Communists were rats, but he cautioned that when you are shooting rats, you must not shoot wildly, because "it not only means that the rats may get away more easily—but you make it easier on the rats. Also, you might hit someone else who is trying to shoot rats, too."

Whether or not Nixon thought the time had come to do so, the administration now openly turned against McCarthy. Acting under orders, the vice president led the charge against Tail Gunner Joe.

During the following month, McCarthy commenced his public inquest into the Peress matter. Nixon called the proceedings "grotesque melodrama," and history calls them the Army-McCarthy hearings. They were the end of McCarthy and, though he largely self-destructed, he was given considerable assistance by his henchman Cohn. The administration did its part to help defeat him. But the star of the show turned out to be the lawyer serving as the army's counsel at the hearings, Joseph Welch, a natural actor with a phenomenal sense of timing. Before he was done, Tail Gunner Joe had been turned into the buffoon of the hour, and it all happened on national television.

Nixon's role in this last phase of the McCarthy saga was minimal, so we will take a quick look at how things transpired once the Army-McCarthy hearings were under way. Welch brought out the fact that the whole affair had started with Cohn trying to get special favors for G. David Schine. The television audience spent several weeks watching Cohn squirm and McCarthy bluster like the bully he was. Television, still new to America's national life, stripped bare the McCarthy mystique and mercilessly revealed the senator's coarse and belligerent ways. On camera, Roy Cohn looked like a nervous demon. Nixon watched the tragicomedy's first day of televised hearings and found it grotesque. When asked his opinion of the proceedings, he said he preferred watching professional actors to watching amateurs.

McCarthy behaved like a thug. His brutal treatment of Secretary Stevens, who suffered in the witness chair for fourteen days, soured many who either had supported McCarthy or at least had been neutral. Cohn made a poor impression by gratuitously insulting the army's lawyers and witnesses. But the most damaging aspect of the hearings was the sheer absurdity of McCarthy and Cohn's case. Welch skillfully shot it down, point by point, with surgical and gleeful precision.

The high point of the drama, the moment that many observers believed punctured McCarthy once and for all, actually had nothing to do with the case. On June 9, 1954, Joseph Welch crushed Joseph McCarthy in front of the national television audience. The irony is that McCarthy started the scuffle that gave Welch the opening of a lifetime. It came after an episode remarkable in its own right: Welch grilled Cohn, who foolishly allowed himself to get trapped in the witness chair. Welch twitted Cohn for his claim that he knew of Communists at Fort Monmouth, New Jersey. Welch wanted to know why Cohn had not informed Secretary Stevens or anyone else in the executive branch. Welch thought that if someone had that sort of information, then "before sundown" he should notify the proper authorities.

McCarthy thereupon launched his suicidal attack on Welch. Since Welch was so concerned with Communists in the army, McCarthy said, then he should know "that he has in his law firm a young man named Fisher . . . who has been a member for a number of years of an organization which was named . . . as the legal bulwark of the Communist party . . ." Cohn shook his head and gestured at McCarthy to stop. McCarthy went on: "Now I have hesitated bringing that up, but I have been rather bored with your phony request to Mr. Cohn here that he personally get every Communist out of government before sundown. . . . Whether you knew that he was a member of that Communist organization or not, but I don't know. I assume you did not, Mr. Welch, because I get the impression that you are quite an actor, you play for a laugh, I don't think you have any conception of the danger of the Communist party. I don't think you yourself would ever knowingly aid the Communist cause. I think you're unknowingly aiding it when you try to burlesque this hearing . . ."

Welch struck back. "Senator McCarthy, I did not know, Senator . . ." He broke off when he saw that McCarthy was whispering and laughing with an aide. "Senator, sometimes you say, 'May I have your attention.' May I have yours, Senator?" McCarthy answered that he was listening to his aide with one ear and to

Welch with the other. Welch demanded that McCarthy listen with both ears. But McCarthy continued to play at ignoring the man whom he clearly failed to recognize as his most deadly enemy.

"Until this moment, Senator, I think I never really gauged your cruelty or your recklessness. Fred Fisher is a young man who went to Harvard Law School and came into my firm and is starting what looks to be a brilliant career with us. When I decided to work for this committee I asked Jim St. Clair . . . to be my first assistant. I said to him, 'Jim, pick somebody in the firm to work under you that you would like.' He chose Fred Fisher and they came down on an afternoon plane. That night . . . Fred Fisher and Jim St. Clair and I went to dinner together.

"I then said to these young men: 'Boys, I don't know anything about you except that I've always liked you, but if there's anything funny in the life of either one of you that would hurt anybody in this case, you had better speak up quick. And Fred Fisher said, 'Mr. Welch, when I was in law school and for a period of months after I belonged to the Lawyers Guild . . .'" The Guild indeed was a left-wing organization. Welch continued, relating that Fisher next said, "I am the secretary of the Young Republicans' League . . ." Fisher made it clear that his youthful flirtation with the left was over.

But Welch saw the danger, ". . . I said, 'Fred, I just don't think I'm going to ask you to work on this case. If I do, one of these days, that will come out and go over national television and it will hurt like the dickens.' So, Senator, I asked him to go back to Boston. Little did I dream you could be so reckless and so cruel as to do an injury to that lad." Welch declared that Fisher would stay with his law firm. "It is, I regret to say, equally true that I fear he shall always bear a scar, needlessly inflicted by you. If it were in my power to forgive you for your reckless cruelty, I would do so. I like to think I'm a gentle man, but your forgiveness will have to come from someone other than me."

Welch had bounced McCarthy off the ropes and floored him with a combination left hook and right cross, and McCarthy knew it. He began blustering and nearly ranting. Welch interrupted, "Senator, may we not drop this? We know he belonged to the Lawyer's Guild." McCarthy did not stop and Welch delivered the knockout punch.

"Let us not assassinate this lad further, Senator. You've done enough. Have you no sense of decency, sir? At long last, have you no sense of decency?"

McCarthy still lacked the sense to shut up, but it was over.

Tail Gunner Joe's standing in the public-opinion polls dropped precipitously during and after the Army-McCarthy hearings. The McCarthy era itself came crashing to an end when the Senate voted to censure the senator from Wisconsin in December 1954. All sixty-seven Democratic senators voted for censure, but the Republicans split exactly in half, with twenty-two voting for and twenty-two against. The censure neither expelled McCarthy from the Senate nor deprived him of any senatorial privileges, but it marked the end of his power and influence. For the rest of his life, McCarthy had no particular impact on Washington and existed among his colleagues as a specter of the ugly recent past. He died of alcohol-related causes in 1957.

Nixon wrote that his feelings about McCarthy were "mixed." He did not look down upon McCarthy for his crude manners, as he believed Washington's fashionable circles did. Nixon thought him likable and felt sorry for the man whose hunger for publicity led "him and others to destruction." Nixon claimed to believe that McCarthy was sincere but that his excesses actually impeded real investigations of real Communists.

Joseph Welch caught Hollywood's eye and went on to a brief career as a movie actor. In his first and most famous role he played a judge in Otto Preminger's *Anatomy of a Murder*. He was good and the audience and the critics loved him. He died in 1960.

Roy Cohn continued to practice law. He died of AIDS in 1986. G. David Schine married and had a family and took over the family hotel chain. In 1996, he died in a private plane crash in Los Angeles.

With Senator McCarthy gone, Vice President Nixon soldiered on in service to President Eisenhower and his party for the midterm campaigns of 1954 and 1958, and the presidential election of 1956. In 1954, the year of the Army-McCarthy hearings, Nixon's Red-baiting was intense, and one might suspect that the vice president filled the void left by McCarthy's political demise. The Senate balance was precarious, since the Republicans ruled by only a single-seat majority, and the Democrats held the House. President Eisenhower was immensely popular, but Nixon and other Republicans felt they needed to conduct a hard-hitting campaign against the Democrats that year, since they could not count on Eisenhower's popularity to rub off on their candidates across the nation. Also staring them in the face was the political truism that the party that holds the White House almost always suffers congressional losses in midterm elections.

Nixon, of course, drew the shock-troop assignment. The president as usual wanted to stay "above the battle," and, Nixon recalled, Eisenhower said that at age sixty-three, he needed more rest. Nixon prepared to hit the hustings, but he had a divided party to lead into battle. The rifts of 1952 had not healed, and the damage McCarthy did in the interim was evident. Democratic leader Adlai Stevenson taunted the Republicans for having "more wings than a chicken."

In campaign appearances around the country, Nixon told audiences that since Eisenhower had become president "thousands of Communists, fellow travelers, and security risks" had been cleaned out of government service. Were the Democrats to win commanding majorities in Congress, Nixon proclaimed, the party's left-wingers would rule the roost. He told the voters that the Democratic candidates in all the "key states" were leftists, and the Communists openly supported them and opposed the Republican party. He charged the Democrats with blindness to the international Communist conspiracy and pounded home the theme that the Eisenhower administration needed a Republican Congress in order to crush the domestic Red menace. It was vintage Nixon.

He hit heavily on what historian Jonathan Aitken called the "K-1, C-3 formula"—Korea, communism, corruption, controls. It was, by now, the old Republican argument that Democratic foreign policy had caused or at least allowed the Communists to start the Korean War, that the Truman administration was hopelessly corrupt, and that the Democrats favored unreasonable federal controls and regulations on business. Nixon aimed his fire at the liberal wing of the Democratic party, which he called the "Truman-Stevenson-ADA left wing." The ADA (Americans for Democratic Action), an organization of Democratic liberals that had among its founders Minnesota senator Hubert Humphrey, was hardly a left-wing organization, but that hardly mattered, since Nixon and other Republicans attacked it as if it were a Communist cadre taking orders from Moscow. Adlai Stevenson fired back sharply. He called Nixon's taunts "McCarthyism in a white collar," and charged Eisenhower with "smiling" upon Nixon's smear campaign.

The vice president claimed that he was tired of campaigning in this manner and looked for ways to back out of the fray, at least to a degree, as Election Day approached. He disliked being called a demagogue by his opponents and the press—never mind that he acted like one. Years later, he told Aitken, "As the attacks [on him] became more personal, I sometimes wondered where party loyalty left off and masochism began." His daughters were "reaching an impressionable age," and he and his wife worried how they would feel if they started understanding that their father was often portrayed as "the bad guy of American politics."

The 1954 election results disappointed Nixon and the Republicans. The party lost sixteen seats in the House and two in the Senate, which cost the GOP its slight Senate majority. While the numbers were below the average losses for a presidential party at midterm, Eisenhower had to deal with a Democratic Congress for the rest of his presidency.

The 1956 election presented a new challenge for the president, the vice president, and their party. The year before, Eisenhower suffered a serious heart attack and Stevenson, again the Democratic presidential nominee, made the president's health an issue. That may have been fair enough, but Stevenson went further, asking the voters to consider the possibility that if they cast their ballot for the unhealthy, aged Eisenhower, they were, in effect, electing Nixon president. "Distasteful as this matter is," Stevenson said just before Election Day, "I must say bluntly that every piece of scientific evidence we have, every lesson of history . . . indicates that a Republican victory . . . would mean that Richard M. Nixon probably would be president . . . within the next four years."

Nixon considered the speech "crude and tasteless," and thought it actually lost votes for Stevenson. Not that it mattered, since Eisenhower again rolled to victory, this time with 57 percent of the popular vote.

The results of the 1958 midterm elections signaled the voters' weariness with Red-baiting. Even though the cold war was in high gear and the Soviets had launched their Sputnik satellite that year, the McCarthy era was over, and people were not as receptive to fear campaigns as they had been only a few years earlier. Nixon's Red-baiting now hurt his image and tarnished the hero's welcome he received when he came home after facing real danger in Peru and Venezuela in May 1958.

Nixon's own analyses of his and the Republican party's problems in 1958 appear in several of his books and take into account that the presidential party typically suffers midterm losses, but also note that there was a downturn in the economy early in the year, and the party was divided in crucial states, including California. Nixon recalled that for the first time Eisenhower's approval rating dipped below 50 percent that year. The vice president was reluctant to dive into the partisan battle since he now had more to lose. His own popularity rating was high after the South American trip, and, he wrote, "it would be risky to put myself again in the position of Eisenhower's political point man," since he planned to run for the presidency two years hence.

But after Eisenhower, Nixon was the country's most visible

Republican, and party officials nationwide beseeched him to help their campaigns. Nixon decided that sitting out the campaign would cost him a lot of Republican goodwill that he would need in 1960, so, weighing the risks, he decided to hit the campaign trail. It was a big mistake. The Republicans suffered a huge setback at the polls in November, and Nixon's association with such a disastrous defeat cost him his primacy as President Eisenhower's anointed successor.

Nixon had hit all the old themes and sounded all the old notes. He spoke of disloyal State Department officials, holdovers from Democratic administrations. He referred to the Truman administration's appeasement and compared Dean Acheson unfavorably to John Foster Dulles, in his usual inflammatory terms. He blamed Acheson for the Korean War. The voters did not like it, but Nixon failed to catch the change in the political climate.

The White House grasped the change. Someone realized that Nixon was turning voters off. Consequently, Eisenhower publicly rebuked Nixon at a news conference. The president told reporters that "foreign policy ought to be kept out of partisan debate." Nixon duly took some of his charges back. He told an audience in Baltimore that he never meant to question the sincerity or patriotism of the Democrats. All Americans want peace, Nixon conceded, and the Democrats are not the party of treason. That mantle belonged to the Communist party.

These sentiments were indeed a change in tone from his past campaigns, but they reflected no change in Nixon's thoughts and feelings. He resented Eisenhower's rebuke and disliked being made to rein in what he called his "normal partisan instincts." He found it especially frustrating that Stevenson operated under no such constraints and "bombarded us with malicious ridicule and wild charges."

The Republicans lost heavily in November. The Democrats picked up thirteen Senate seats and forty-seven in the House. Those gains gave them massive majorities and they also won control of thirty-four state governments. Nixon's position suffered

159

along with the party's, for now he no longer stood as the only logical Republican presidential nominee for 1960. The morning after the election, he heard a television commentator declare Nelson Rockefeller the big winner of 1958. Rockefeller had won election as governor of New York by a commanding margin. The commentator called Nixon the year's big loser; he had stuck his neck out and it got clipped. He now had a real rival for the 1960 Republican presidential nomination.

THE VICE PRESIDENT
MEETS THE COMMUNISTS

★   ★   ★

In August 1947, Richard Nixon joined a committee of nineteen congressmen and sailed to Europe on the *Queen Mary*. The special committee, appointed by House Speaker Joe Martin and chaired by Massachusetts Republican Christian Herter, intended to observe and evaluate conditions in Europe and report back to the House, which was considering the Truman administration's proposed Marshall Plan for massive financial aid to fund European recovery. Secretary of State George Marshall had announced the proposal in his June commencement address at Harvard University.

In Nixon's conservative Twelfth District, the Truman administration and its Marshall Plan were unpopular. In 1947, many Republicans still clung to isolationism and wanted to withdraw from the international scene as much as possible. The Democratic administration realized it would have to drag them kicking and screaming into the new world order. Conservatives, much of Nixon's constituency among them, had a hard time understanding the responsibilities of world power and the new realities of the cold war. Six of whom Nixon called his "strongest supporters" sent him a letter shortly after his appointment became public.

"It is our hope and belief that . . . you will be able to maintain the levelheaded course you have followed in Congress . . ."

These supporters believed that the "hangover policies of the New Deal" had to be swept out of Washington, but for that to happen, "the Republican members of Congress" must be "wise enough to refuse to be drawn into support of a dangerously unworkable and profoundly inflationary foreign policy . . ." The letter concluded that the Democrats must not be permitted to succeed in dividing the Republicans by means of "bipartisan internationalism." If that happens, the letter writers feared, then it would be impossible to tell Republicans apart from Democrats.

Nixon was determined to win his constituents over to the new internationalism that so many of them feared. Younger and in many ways more worldly than the men on the Committee of One Hundred, Nixon grasped the inescapable fact of America's status as a world power, and the equally inescapable fact that the world was more dangerous for the United States in the twentieth century than in the past. During the nineteenth century, the European powers mostly left America in peace. That happy state of affairs had much to do with America's size, the Atlantic Ocean, and European policymakers' recognition of America's potential strength. Another and possibly more crucial guarantee of America's safety was the British Navy. Britannia ruled the waves prior to World War I and contributed heavily to American security. Britain was the only power that could credibly threaten us, and as long as we were at peace with the British, we were safe. Britain valued its access to American markets, and until this century, no other sea power had a navy that could challenge the British on the high seas, which meant that no other navy could reach American shores.

The two world wars of the twentieth century ended America's "free security" forever. The United States not only had to defend itself, but when World War II ended with the fall of the Axis powers, the exhaustion of the Western allies and the social and economic disarray in Europe meant that only the United States could counterbalance the looming menace of the Soviet Union. In 1947, the United States was the world's only atomic power, but Nixon and other internationalists understood that the bomb alone could not guarantee world peace and American security.

Now, with World War II ended and East and West squaring off at the start of the cold war, Nixon and other internationalists knew Western Europe had to get back on its feet. That could not happen without massive U.S. aid. Germany had to be rebuilt, otherwise there could be no viable European economic recovery. A stable, prosperous Germany would also help counterbalance the growing Soviet sphere of influence in Eastern Europe. Western European leaders, particularly the British, looked to a continued American presence in European affairs to ensure stability and protection. The Marshall Plan offered substantial and nearly unlimited aid to all of Europe, including the Soviet Union and the embryonic Eastern bloc. The Soviets refused the aid on behalf of themselves and their puppet states, which came as no surprise and thus permitted the plan to proceed as a bulwark against direct Soviet expansion and the spread of extensive Communist influence in Western Europe.

The threat of Soviet expansion was by no means imaginary, nor some clever propaganda device invented by American leaders bent on demonizing the Communists. Soviet expansionism had ample historical precedent; expansionism figured prominently in Russian foreign relations long before the Communist era. Much of the Soviet Union itself was the old Russian Empire conquered during the three centuries before the Bolshevik revolution of 1917. In the middle-nineteenth century, Russia and Britain played the "great game" in Central Asia, where they competed for territory and influence as Russian agents tried to undermine British rule in India and Afghanistan. Historian David Fromkin, in his brilliant and valuable contribution to the study of American foreign policy, *In the Time of the Americans*, explained that Russian expansionism grew largely out of fear. "Russians never could feel secure; they were driven to protect themselves by seizing whatever lay on the other side of their frontiers."

They felt particular anxiety about the postwar status of Poland; Stalin insisted that Poland had traditionally served as a corridor for European powers to attack Russia. The Soviets had plans for a puppet state in Poland, which made for severe contention with the United States and Britain. So, during the war's final phases and the beginning of the postwar period, the Soviets ran true to their old Russian form and expanded their power into Poland and as much of Eastern Europe as they could manage. It was more feasible, for reasons both military and political, to dominate and dictate through neighborhood hegemony using the enormous Red Army as Moscow's big stick than to seize and conquer through outright imperialism. Hence, the proliferation of puppet governments in the Eastern bloc rather than overt annexation by the Soviets.

In his internationalist outlook, Nixon was more aligned with the Democratic administration than with much of his own party. He was in close agreement with Dean Acheson, who in 1947 was still an undersecretary of state. Both men, for an instant a pair of politics' proverbial strange bedfellows, wondered how to educate the population about America's inescapable role. President Truman also wondered how to garner support from Congress and the people for aid to Greece and Turkey, and then later for the Marshall Plan. On the first imperative, Republican senator Arthur Vandenberg, a recovering isolationist, told Truman, "Mr. President, if that's what you want, there's only one way to get it. That is to make a personal appearance before Congress and scare the hell out of the American people."

Vandenberg said that right after, Dean Acheson scared the hell out of Vandenberg and a number of other senators and congressmen. The occasion was a meeting of the congressional leadership with President Truman, Secretary Marshall, and Undersecretary Acheson on February 27, 1947. Marshall outlined the Communist threats to Greece and Turkey, but the air did not catch fire. Acheson wrote in his memoirs that he realized that Marshall had "flubbed" his presentation and asked for permission to speak. Marshall, only too glad for some help, gave him leave, and Acheson proceeded to tell the august assemblage that the world now faced a crisis unlike anything since ancient times.

Historians Walter Isaacson and Evan Thomas, in *The Wise Men: Six Friends and the World They Made*, summarized Acheson's speech, as follows. "Not since Athens and Sparta, not since Rome and Carthage, had the world been so polarized between two great powers. The U.S. and the U.S.S.R. were divided by 'an unbridgeable ideological chasm.' The choice was between 'democracy and individual liberty' and 'dictatorship and absolute conformity. . . . This was not an issue of pulling British chestnuts out of the fire but of preserving the security of the United States, of democracy itself.' " So spoke the cold warrior whom Red-baiters later taunted as the "Red Dean."

Acheson's own summary in *Present at the Creation* omitted the rather extravagant classical allusions but still conveyed the impression that Armageddon had for all intent and purposes arrived. "These congressmen had no conception of what challenged them." The undersecretary figured he needed to "bring it home" to them. Getting down to the nuts and bolts of the situation, he told them that, during the past year and a half, "Soviet pressure on . . . Iran and on northern Greece had brought the Balkans to the point where a highly possible Soviet breakthrough might open three continents to Soviet penetration." The "infection" might spread "to Africa through Asia Minor and Egypt and to Europe through Italy and France, already threatened by the strongest domestic Communist parties in Western Europe. The Soviet Union was playing one of the greatest gambles in history at minimal cost. It did not need to win all the possibilities. Even one or two offered immense gains." Only the United States could "break up the play." Those words convinced Vandenberg and the other legislators.

President Truman took Vandenberg's advice and proceeded to scare the hell out of everybody, with Acheson's—and Nixon's—hearty approval. The president proclaimed the Truman Doctrine, which pledged that the United States would aid any nation facing an insurgency from outside elements, meaning, of course, Communists. The Truman administration depicted the conflict between the West and the Soviet Union as a battle between good and evil, as the recent world war had been. Truman and his spokesmen scrupulously avoided explaining the international situation in such terms as critical interests, international economics, or strategic goals. Instead, the administration couched the conflict in terms saving the free world from the blight of communism. To strengthen the argument for voter consumption, the Soviets had to be painted as supermen, despite their lack of atomic weaponry and the grievous losses they sustained in World War II, though the massive Red Army in Eastern Europe was no chimera.

In Europe with the Herter Committee, Nixon had his own ideas for some additional fact-finding. He wanted to meet Western European Communists. Nixon later recalled that he insisted the committee should meet local Communist leaders in each country visited. The American embassy personnel charged with shepherding the committee were reluctant and wary about seeking out Communists, but Nixon thought it important, and other committee members agreed. Nixon wanted to see these Western adversaries at firsthand, get an idea how their minds worked, and see if he could determine the nature and extent of their relationship with the Soviet Union.

During the Herter Committee's tour, Nixon formed basic impressions and concepts of world communism from which he never deviated. First, he concluded that all Communists, no matter their country of origin, were free of nationalism and gave their loyalty only to the Soviet Union. Second, he believed that the Communists he met in Italy, France, and other countries with shaky governments, were more vigorous, mentally sharper, and considerably more ruthless than their local non-Communist counterparts. The Communists' intelligence and vigor, Nixon reckoned, signified that Western Europe stood in precarious balance and imminent danger of Communist overthrow. In Greece and Turkey, the process already had started. For the rest of his life, Nixon held to the belief that the Communists were resourceful, sly enemies, and he harbored serious doubts that the United States could match the enemy in willpower and resolution.

In Italy, Nixon had one of his first talks with a real, live Communist, as opposed to an election opponent with allegedly pink underwear. He met the secretary-general of the Italian Labor Confederation, Giuseppe Di Vittorio, in his office; Nixon noted the red curtains and red walls, and the tiny red flag Di Vittorio wore on his lapel. Speaking through an interpreter, Nixon asked Di Vittorio what governmental labor policy he favored for Italy. He responded with a call for free labor unions and the right to strike. Nixon told him that the United States had that kind of policy and that labor unions were on strike in America at that very moment. Nixon contrasted this fact with policy in the Soviet Union, where there had been no labor strikes in at least two decades. Di Vittorio glared at Nixon and retorted that strikes were not necessary in the Soviet Union, since there were no capitalists to exploit workers and deprive them of their rights.

Nixon asked him to comment on American foreign policy, and Di Vittorio poured out what Nixon described as a series of severe criticisms in a manner that would "make Henry Wallace look like a piker." Then Nixon asked Di Vittorio if he had criticisms of Soviet foreign policy. Di Vittorio obviously did not like the question and explained that American foreign policy was imperialistic, as it was "dominated by capitalists, reactionaries, and employers." Since such people did not exist in the Soviet Union, Soviet foreign policy by definition could not be imperialistic and so there were no grounds for criticizing it.

Nixon noted that Di Vittorio framed his answers in almost precisely the same phraseology as had Communists he met in Britain and France. That strengthened his suspicion that Communists the world over were loyal to the Soviet Union, not their own countries, and followed whatever party line Moscow dictated.

From Italy, the Herter Committee flew to Greece to take a firsthand look at the real Communist insurgency rather than confine themselves to talking to the tamer Communists who functioned as politicians in the more or less conventional way in Britain, France, Italy, and elsewhere in Western Europe. In a Greek mountain town, the mayor introduced them to a girl who had refused to turn her anti-Communist brother over to the local Communist rebels. The rebels cut off her left breast.

Before the Herter Committee's tour was over, Nixon and other committee members witnessed a bloody riot in Trieste, a port city on the Italian-Yugoslav border, between Communist and non-Communist elements. The congressmen had left the safety of their hotel to watch what began as a Communist parade. It quickly turned into a riot and at one point Nixon heard a gunshot. A young man's head had been blown off. Nixon saw the fresh, headless corpse; he and other onlookers froze in horror as they watched blood gush from the neck. A few minutes later, the police arrived to disperse the crowd. One Communist rioter fled and crashed into an old woman; she flew several feet, then lay motionless in the street. The committee returned home and prepared a series of reports.

Nixon wrote later that all the reports basically argued that the Marshall Plan was necessary. His own view was that the violence he witnessed in Trieste and the crises in Greece and Turkey would recur all over Europe unless substantial American aid were forthcoming. Nixon assessed the Communists as "strong and vigorous," resourceful, ruthless, and crafty. Most important, in Nixon's view, they were all part of a cohesive, coordinated international effort orchestrated in Moscow.

Nixon also noted that the Western European Communist leaders were smart enough to cloak their strategy and tactics in nationalistic terms, often omitting the classic Communist hammer and sickle insignia from their campaign posters and literature in national and municipal elections. In Rome, for instance, Communist election posters showed pictures of Garibaldi, the great hero of Italy's national unification in the nineteenth century.

Further, Nixon considered democratic Europe effectively leaderless and unfocused. He recorded in his memoirs that on the European trip, he understood for the first time the importance of strong national leadership and "the sad consequences when such leadership is lacking or fails." Nixon concluded that the Communists would respect only opposition that could show and deploy power. One had to confront the Communists with strength at least equal to their own, as well as convince them that such strength would, if necessary, be used. Nixon held this view for the rest of his life, and wrote himself a note in Trieste that one should never bluff the Russians, because they will always test their adversary.

As Nixon and other internationalists saw it, the Marshall Plan would serve several purposes at once: a display of America's sheer economic power, a humanitarian distribution of aid to a devastated Western Europe, and a convincing demonstration to Moscow that the United States would not retreat into isolation but would face down the Communists in Europe.

Once home, Nixon found that his dilemma in the Twelfth District persisted in rearing its provincial head. His staff took a poll, which showed that three-quarters of the district's voters opposed the Marshall Plan and any other form of foreign aid. Nixon wrote a series of articles and columns for Southern California newspapers and made a number of speeches to sell his voters on the Marshall Plan. The plan itself passed the House in December by a wide margin, 313 to 82. Apparently, Nixon successfully appealed to his district as well, since in 1948 he faced no serious opposition for reelection.

It is difficult to assess how successful or unsuccessful Nixon's efforts were to educate the Twelfth District's voters to the world's realities, since the events of 1949 did much of the internationalists' work for them. The Communist takeover in Mainland China and the Soviet A-bomb effectively eliminated serious opposition to cold war policies in mainstream American politics. The events of the year had the paradoxical effect of damaging the Truman administration, while demonstrating that Truman, Marshall, and Acheson's theories were true. The Republicans' "soft on communism" campaign against the Democrats by necessity ignored the fact that for the most part, the Democrats—not the Republicans—had to sell Congress and the voters on facing the facts of cold war life and America's unarguable superpower status.

In early 1958, President Eisenhower's relations with Vice President Nixon had been bumpy, despite Nixon's protean service during the past five and a half years. Nixon performed numerous services for his chief, in addition to the partisan combat assignments he carried out with such flair. The most notable and impressive moment came when Eisenhower suffered a major heart attack toward the end of his first term, and the vice president stepped in to guide the administration and assure the nation that the government was not in crisis. That was not easy, since the Twenty-fifth Amendment did not yet exist, so the vice president actually had no distinct constitutional role when the president was disabled rather than dead. Nonetheless, Nixon won good reviews from pundits and goodwill from voters for his responsible and reassuring performance as Ike lay fallen.

In 1956, Eisenhower was still waffling as to whether he wanted Nixon back for another term as vice president. The president even came up with the astonishing suggestion that Nixon step down and take a cabinet post to gain administrative experience before running for president. Eisenhower never seemed to understand that that would appear to be a demotion for the vice president and thus signal the president's lack of confidence in him. One evening, one of Eisenhower's closest and most trusted friends defended Nixon to the president and asked, "Ike, what in hell does a man have to do to get your support?"

The president's answer is lost to history, but Eisenhower never fully endorsed Nixon for the second term until Nixon himself made it clear he would not voluntarily step aside. When Nixon told Eisenhower he wanted to stay on, the president told him he could tell the press that he was "delighted" with Nixon's decision. However, the press had the impression that the president did not fully support his boy for the 1960 Republican nomination.

Despite Eisenhower's lukewarm posture toward Nixon, by 1958, the smart money was on the vice president for the 1960 nomination. When Eisenhower sent Nixon on an official tour of several South American countries in 1958, that distinctly enhanced Nixon's status as the heir apparent. When Nixon and his wife were physically threatened by hostile crowds in Lima and Caracas, the trip turned into a baptism by fire, not the sort of thing high-ranking American officials generally experienced. His grace under pressure impressed much of the world, and the ubiquitous pundits judged Nixon to be Eisenhower's inevitable successor. Such was the conventional wisdom when Nixon returned home after nearly getting killed in South America.

While Nixon faced dangerously hostile crowds in Lima and Caracas, in May 1958, he also met friendly crowds there, but leftists turned out in impressive numbers to protest his presence and condemn the United States. Several times Nixon stepped out of his car to talk to protesters, showing for the first time a life-long tendency to meet his adversaries and establish contact with rank-and-file leftists rather than confine himself to dealing with their leaders. The South American contacts prefigured his 1970 trip to the Lincoln Memorial in the dead of night to talk to anti-war protesters.

Leftist students at San Marcos University in Lima abused Nixon first, when he got out of his car to talk to individual demonstrators. Some threw rocks at him. A couple of the men with him were hit, one in the face. Nixon kept his companions calm, instructed them to back away from the crowd slowly, and told them not to turn their backs on the angry students. It worked; the students continued screaming taunts and curses and lobbing a few rocks, but the mob did not rush the vice president and his party and beat them to death. Nixon and his guards were essentially unprotected, literally at the crowd's mercy, and only their calm and pluckiness saw them through. As Nixon's convertible drove away from the roaring students, he stood up and shouted back at them that they were cowards who feared the truth. One of his guards grabbed his legs so the vice president would not pitch out of the speeding car. Nixon's next stop was Catholic University, across town, where a decidedly more pro-American crowd gave him a standing ovation upon his arrival.

The San Marcos incident worried the Secret Service about

the planned trip to Caracas. At a stop in Bogota the Secret Service received a CIA report of a plot to kill Nixon in the Venezuelan capital, but the vice president, accompanied by his wife, decided to continue. The Venezuelan government assured the Nixons that everything was under control, which turned out to be wishful thinking.

Both the vice president and his wife showed considerable physical courage in Venezuela. Things went wrong immediately; the Nixons were surrounded by hostile demonstrators inside Maiquetia airport. As the Nixons stood at attention and the band played the American and Venezuelan national anthems, a group of demonstrators on an observation deck above them spit on them repeatedly, creating an almost rainlike effect. Nixon watched as his wife was literally soaked by spittle, but both maintained their poise. When the ceremony ended and the party headed for the cars, a young woman jumped in front of Pat Nixon and spat in her face. Mrs. Nixon put her hand on the young woman's shoulder and looked into her eyes. According to the vice president's account, "something seemed to snap inside the young girl," and she turned away and sobbed.

Nixon and his wife entered separate cars; the vice president rode with the Venezuelan foreign minister. When the cars reached the city, a mob attacked them. Rioters showered both cars with rocks, then surrounded Nixon's car and rocked it. That was the first moment it occurred to Nixon that he and the others might be killed. He looked back at his wife's car and was glad to see that the crowd was pretty much ignoring her in its bloodlust for him.

The rioters rocking Nixon's car chanted "Muera Nixon, Muera Nixon" (Kill Nixon, Kill Nixon) and some of them pounded on the windows with rocks. The windows did not shatter, but slivers of glass flew; one lodged in the foreign minister's eye and two or three caught Nixon in the face. One rioter pounded a window with a lead pipe. When a Secret Service agent in Nixon's car pulled his gun, Nixon told him not to shoot. The agent said he wanted to "get some of those sons of bitches," and another agent added that if they were about to die, then he wanted to take about six of the rioters along. But Nixon feared that a gunshot might drive the crowd completely berserk. After some minutes, which Nixon said felt like an eternity, the press truck in front of the cars managed to break out and clear a path for the others.

Over the foreign minister's objections, Nixon decided to head for the American embassy. The hostile crowds were everywhere and Nixon reasoned that the Communists probably had more stunts planned, so it would be unsafe to go anyplace on the announced schedule. At the embassy, the Nixons discarded their spit-soaked clothes, showered, and contemplated their next move. Members of Venezuela's ruling junta accepted the vice president's suggestion that they meet with him there rather than having him venture out to see them. Crowds still roamed the streets as night fell, and one group organized a march on the embassy.

Nixon's limousine had sustained dents and broken windows. Someone suggested that it would be tactful to move the car from in front of the embassy before the junta members arrived, so as not to embarrass them. Nixon told the embassy personnel to leave the car where it was. He was angry, made a few choice comments about the authorities' failure to control the crowds, and said that the junta should see the limousine so that they might come to understand what they were facing from Communist agitators. When they arrived, Nixon plainly told them that they were foolish to have formed a coalition government that included Communists.

Before he was through, Nixon lectured both the Venezuelan leadership—except for the Communists—and a group of American businessmen that operated in Venezuela, telling them that many of the rioters in Lima and Caracas were not themselves Communists, although Communists had organized, led, and agitated the demonstrations and turned them into riots. He did not believe that the Communists were the problem; the terrible poverty of Latin America led to riots and uprisings, and gave the Communists the material to build leftist revolutions. "It is essential," he told the American businessmen and the others, for

Americans operating businesses overseas "to adopt practices which are above suspicion of any charges of exploitation of the workers."

At a press conference that evening, Nixon said that the demonstrators in Caracas and Lima "used the same slogans, the same words, the same tactics" that Communist-led demonstrations had employed in all the South American countries he had visited. They were, Nixon said, "directed and controlled by a central Communist conspiracy." He never abandoned that view of Communist strategies and tactics, and during his presidency was obsessed with the idea that foreign Communists were behind the antiwar movement. Government investigators never turned up a shred of evidence to support the idea, but Nixon never gave up his contention that the Soviets organized and funded the protests.

Nixon could not let go of the idea that the Soviets had something to do with antiwar protests in the United States because he never abandoned his early conclusion that Moscow ran the entire international Communist conspiracy. Nixon biographer Tom Wicker wondered if Nixon ever really distinguished between Soviet and non-Soviet Communists, and the author of this book wonders, too. Although Nixon clearly understood that the Chinese acted independently of Moscow, at least after the rift between the Soviets and the Chinese in the late 1950s and early 1960s, he never took certain critical factors into account in his overview of world communism. The Soviet-Chinese antipathy itself predated the open rift and it is not at all clear that Beijing *ever* took orders from Moscow. The author finds it difficult to agree with Nixon's argument that Communists are *never* nationalists and they *always* put their communism above any nationalistic feelings. By the time Nixon was living in retirement, enough time had passed for analysts to see that communism had lost its battle with nationalism.

In the Soviet Union itself, when the Germans invaded in 1941, Stalin thought it wise to appeal to the Russian people's nationalism rather than their shaky loyalty to communism. The Soviet government rallied its people with propaganda about defending Mother Russia rather than preserving the Soviet system in the land of Lenin.

When the Vietnam War ended, Communist Vietnam and Communist Cambodia went to war against each other. Rather than the dominoes falling in Southeast Asia, as earlier cold warriors predicted, the Communist nations fought among themselves. China itself invaded Vietnam, prompting a short and bitter war between the two Communist countries. (Garry Trudeau had one of his *Doonesbury* characters crack that Vietnam was China's Vietnam.)

While many non-Soviet Communists proclaimed loyalty to the Soviet Union, the functional reality has been different, and many other analyses hold that in the end, nationalism has always proven stronger than communism. Nixon, in all of his statements and writings on the subject—before, during, and after his presidency—never really tackled these problems in his analysis.

The Latin American trip was for the most part a personal triumph for Richard Nixon, albeit with mixed results. After the riots in Lima and Caracas, the White House fell into a state approaching panic when communications with South America grew difficult. President Eisenhower dispatched a naval force to the Venezuelan coast, which angered the government in Caracas, distressed much of Latin America, and caused Nixon some embarrassment. Nixon thought the president's action understandable but unfortunate; the danger was past and nothing merited an American military response. Nixon further thought Eisenhower's move was a diplomatic faux pas.

Nixon returned home to a thunderous hero's welcome from the government, the people, and the press. His political stock soared. In his book, *Hail to the Chief*, Robert Dallek related a story that, when Nixon met the cheering crowds at Andrews Air Force Base, Senate Majority Leader Lyndon Johnson embraced the vice president. The next day a reporter asked Johnson why he had done that when, only a few weeks ago, Johnson told him that Nixon was "nothing but chicken shit." Johnson told the reporter, "Son, you have to understand that in politics, overnight chicken shit can turn to chicken salad."

To some extent, Eisenhower may have shared Johnson's sentiments. Amid the hoopla, the president decided to send Nixon to the Soviet Union to meet the biggest Communist of all, Nikita Khrushchev. The visit to Russia proved to be one of the defining episodes of Nixon's career and the so-called kitchen debate still holds a niche in American political lore.

It was not so much the president's idea as a recommendation by the United States Information Agency, which figured it would be good to have the vice president represent the country at the American National Exhibition scheduled for Moscow in July 1959, since Khrushchev had accepted the president's invitation to visit the United States later in the year. Nixon set about intensively preparing for the trip; knowing what he knew about Khrushchev, he anticipated some sort of showdown. The vice president tried to learn everything he could about the Soviet Union and its leader.

Nixon went to Moscow loaded for bear. He knew that Khrushchev, the bear in question, would challenge him. It was the man's style to be loud, physically imposing, argumentative, and boisterous. To this day, many Americans of a certain age remember the amazing spectacle Khrushchev made of himself when he attended the general assembly at the United Nations in New York. An amused and bewildered American television audience watched Khrushchev heckle speakers by shouting and pounding on his desk with his hands. When his hands grew tired, he pounded the desk with his shoe. It was quite a performance for the leader of the world's second superpower. He held impromptu press conferences from his hotel-room balcony, and bellowed down to reporters in the street that he was under house arrest, then prodded his bemused interpreter to translate his words exactly. He complained that the American government refused to let him visit Disneyland. All this was later in 1959, after Nixon's visit to the Soviet Union.

Khrushchev and Nixon did not exactly hit it off. At their first meeting, shortly after Nixon arrived in Moscow, Khrushchev harangued the vice president over the Captive Nations Resolution. Congress had passed the resolution once a year, every year since 1950. It was pure cold war symbolism, calling on the American people to "study the plight" of the Soviet bloc nations and "recommit themselves to the support of the just aspirations of those captive nations." Nixon should have expected the Soviet premier to object and confront him about the resolution, but the vice president somehow thought Khrushchev would understand and accept the resolution's symbolic nature and think nothing of it. Khrushchev told Nixon the resolution was McCarthyistic. McCarthy was dead, Khrushchev said, but his spirit lived on in Washington.

Nixon wanted to discuss other topics, but Khrushchev kept on. He could not understand why Congress would pass the Captive Nations Resolution just as the vice president was about to make this important official visit to the Soviet Union. "It reminds me of a saying among our Russian peasants," he said, "that people should not go to the toilet where they eat." Khrushchev had more bathroom metaphors up his sleeve. "This resolution stinks. It stinks like fresh horseshit, and nothing smells worse than that."

Nixon knew that Khrushchev once worked herding pigs, so the vice president fired back what he considered a clever rejoinder. "I am afraid the chairman is mistaken. There is something that smells worse than horseshit, and that is pigshit." Nixon recalled years later that Khrushchev looked like he was hovering on the edge of rage, but after a moment broke into a grin. He agreed to move on to another subject but told Nixon that he would hear more about the resolution during his visit.

The manure debate has not resonated in history as has the kitchen debate, which took place that same day at the American exhibition. Surrounded by American technology and consumer products, Nixon and Khrushchev went at each other with almost unseemly fervor. During the initial stages of the debate, after they exchanged a few shots about their nations' respective states of technological progress and labor conditions, Nixon said, "You must not be afraid of ideas. After all, you don't know everything." Khrushchev, visibly angry, snapped, "If *I* don't know everything, *you* don't know anything about communism, except fear of it" (Nixon's italics). Khrushchev was by then shouting.

The kitchen debate properly got under way at the model kitchen exhibit. Nixon told Khrushchev that it was the sort an average American steelworker might have in his house. Khrushchev insisted that Soviet houses soon would have all the modern conveniences that the Americans claimed theirs had. They argued about whether it was necessary to have more than one type of washing machine available for consumers. Nixon then changed the subject slightly; was it not better, he asked, for them to argue about washing machines than about rockets?

Khrushchev took that as a cue for some blustering and declared that while American generals say they have the power to destroy the Soviet Union, the Soviet Union can also destroy the United States. "We are strong. We can beat you." Nixon commented that if the two countries went to war, both would lose.

Not long after that exchange, they decided to calm themselves, and, bowing to diplomatic nicety, they agreed that each nation ultimately wanted friendship with the other.

The rest of Nixon's visit seesawed between confrontation and socializing. Even Pat Nixon fired a shot. One night at dinner, after Khrushchev and Nixon had spent several hours arguing about a variety of subjects, Nixon began asking questions about Soviet submarines and rocket fuel. Khrushchev said that these were technical matters that he was not qualified to discuss. Mrs. Nixon interjected that she found that surprising, since Khrushchev, with his one-man government, surely must have a grasp of every important subject. Another Soviet official present cut in and told Mrs. Nixon that even Comrade Khrushchev could not do everything, which was why he had people to help him.

Nixon wrote in his memoirs and in *Six Crises* that he saw that Khrushchev actually could be a charming host and had a sense of humor, but that did not alter his opinion that the Soviet leader was a ruthless and dangerous adversary. Sergei Khrushchev, in his book, *Khrushchev on Khrushchev* (edited by William Taubman), recorded some of what his father told him about that day.

Khrushchev had a poor opinion of Nixon and felt that the vice president asked "inappropriate questions" while they toured the exhibition. When Nixon asked him what type of fuel the Soviets used in their rockets, Khrushchev told his son he did not know what to answer. Nixon "didn't act like a statesman in that kitchen but like a second-rate spy. He, the vice president of the USA, asks . . . what kind of fuel we use in our ICBMs! It wasn't his business to find out whether we used solid or liquid fuel or something else. Everybody's got special services for that sort of thing. One should think about the questions one asks."

In Khrushchev's own memoirs, translated and edited by diplomat Strobe Talbott, Khrushchev referred to "that son of a bitch Nixon." Writing during Nixon's presidency, Khrushchev judged Nixon "unpredictable . . . I'd say even unbalanced. I don't know what motivates him, other than his obvious ideological hatred for communism and everything progressive."

Nixon and Khrushchev disliked each other for the rest of their lives, but their relationship ended on a note of decency on Nixon's part and appreciation on Khrushchev's. During the mid-1960s, when they were both out of office, Nixon visited the Soviet Union as a private citizen. Khrushchev was also a private citizen by then, having been ousted by the coup that Brezhnev and others had engineered. He lived as an outcast, with no real active life outside his family. Nixon and Pat went to Khrushchev's Moscow apartment, hoping to visit their fallen adversary, but the old man was not there. Khrushchev wrote in his memoirs, "To be honest, I very much regretted missing him. I was touched that he would take the trouble. I was especially touched in view of the fact that our relations had always been so tense. On the occasions that we met, we rarely exchanged kind words. More often than not, we bickered. But he showed genuine human courtesy when he tried to see me after my retirement. I'm very sorry I didn't have an opportunity to thank him for his consideration, to shake hands with him and his wife."

That final salute to his old enemy was published posthumously. Khrushchev died in 1971.

PART II
NIXON AND THE PRESS

★　★　★　★　★　★　★　★

THE FUND CRISIS AND BEFORE

★   ★   ★

"The press is the enemy."

That effectively sums up Richard Nixon's entire attitude toward the press in the most basic terms. H.R. Haldeman, John Ehrlichman, William Safire, and a number of others who worked for him have written extensively on his hatred for the press. President Nixon even warned Senator Edward Kennedy, by way of comradely advice from one adversary to another, that the press was his enemy, too.

Nixon firmly believed that the press would quickly turn on anyone, even one of their favorites, if there was a juicy scandal to report, such as Chappaquiddick. That advice was even more extraordinary in light of Nixon's chronic suspicion that much of the press were the Kennedys' unpaid shills—although he likely saw no similarity to the early days of his own political career, when Southern California newspapers like the *Los Angeles Times* endorsed and publicized his campaigns for the House and Senate while burying his opponents in the back pages, or not covering them at all.

Nixon, like most other politicians, had mixed relations with the press. He exploited it when he could, snubbed it when he could, and complained about it endlessly. He was by no means the only president, nor the only politician, to consider journalists enemies even as he understood the public relations value they could provide. But, as with so much in Nixon's life, the story of his particular relationship with the press has its own special quality. One might call it a modern epic of enmity, and it began long before his presidency.

By and large, presidential press relations have always been bumpy, and only a few presidents typically got along with reporters. Apart from exceptions like Franklin Roosevelt, whom the Washington press corps treated with a deference bordering on worship, presidents from George Washington onward have, with varying degrees of justification, felt unfairly treated and victimized by the American press. Journalist Kenneth T. Walsh, author of *Feeding the Beast: The White House Versus the Press*, quotes one newspaper's editorial on George Washington at the end of his presidency: "If ever a nation was debauched by a man, the American nation has been debauched by Washington. If ever a nation has suffered from the influence of a man, the American nation has suffered from the influence of Washington. If ever a nation was deceived by a man, the American nation has been deceived by Washington. Let his conduct then be an example to future ages. Let it serve to be a warning that no man may be an idol." That editorial is as harsh as anything any mainstream journalist ever wrote about Richard Nixon.

Since the end of World War II, bad feelings between presidents and the press have been aggravated and obvious. All the chief executives since Franklin Roosevelt have had difficulties with the press and some have been adept at causing journalists their share of headaches in return. Lyndon Johnson alternately tried to cultivate and bully reporters, which was how he handled people in general. Jimmy Carter's press relations were decidedly chilly: Before starting one press conference, he told reporters to put away their coloring books. Ronald Reagan and George Bush managed the news to the extent that their photo opportunities and sound bites amounted to staged pageants that resembled campaign commercials. Reporters and editors howled in protest but did little, fearing expulsion from the charmed circle.

So both sides have felt misused and abused, and both sides like to let everyone know it. When the Oval Office's current tenant, Bill Clinton, grouses about the press, if you close your eyes, you might think you are hearing Richard Nixon.

What, then, is so unusual about the spats and outright clashes between the press and Nixon? For one thing, there really was a fierce animus between Nixon and the Washington press corps. Nixon took his press problems, as he took so much else, very personally. He felt the press, as the strongest arm of the liberal establishment, spearheaded all the powerful forces that opposed him. Nixon was more vindictive and vengeful than most other presidents, and his administration fought and harassed reporters like no other, outstripping even Johnson in that regard. In turn, much of the press hated Nixon.

Such was not always the case. When Nixon began his political career in 1946, he only had to contend with the local Southern California press, and those newspapers were overwhelmingly favorable to him. For the most part, reporters applauded and on occasion assisted him when he Red-baited Jerry Voorhis and Helen Gahagan Douglas. The largest paper in the region, the *Los Angeles Times*, led the pack in endorsing, praising, and helping young Dick Nixon as he slew liberal dragons and promised solid conservative representation for the Twelfth Congressional District and then the state of California. The press lords in Southern California were conservative, angry over the New Deal, and Red-baiting was fine with them.

In Nixon's view, his press relations deteriorated during the course of the Hiss-Chambers case. He thought that most Washington reporters were liberals and Alger Hiss was some sort of liberal hero-cum-martyr. Consequently, the liberal establishment turned on him when they figured he had turned on them via his pursuit of Hiss. Nixon ever after recalled press coverage of the Hiss case as highly favorable to the accused man and blisteringly hostile to Hiss's accuser, Whittaker Chambers, and to himself.

That is a characteristically Nixonian interpretation, but it is not entirely accurate. Much of the press coverage conveyed the message that Hiss was guilty, and, also contrary to Nixon's interpretation, there was widespread assumption of Hiss's guilt among liberal Democrats. But that both President Truman and Secretary Acheson at first spoke out in defense of Hiss only strengthened Nixon's suspicions.

Next, in Nixon's own analysis, the lines were drawn and cast in stone when the fund crisis erupted during the 1952 campaign. The crisis left Nixon permanently hostile to the press and, according to all his later recollections, took all the fun and excitement out of politics for him, although one may have trouble fully believing that. John Ehrlichman wrote that the Checkers speech left Nixon feeling violated rather than vindicated. As Nixon saw it, the press universally assumed him guilty of collecting and using funds illegally and unethically, and then never forgave him when he prevailed, stayed on as Eisenhower's running mate, and, consequently, was elected vice president. Having both nailed Hiss and survived the fund crisis, Nixon felt that he would forever be sighted in liberal reporters' crosshairs.

In his memoirs, Nixon dated his resentment of the press to his mother's funeral, when he claimed reporters harassed him and showed no respect for his and his family's grief. But he and others have given contradictory accounts of the origins of Nixon's animus toward reporters—and of theirs for him. There seems no reliable way of ascertaining when exactly Nixon started actually hating the press. He apparently resented it even when newspapers largely supported him or gave him favorable coverage. At the risk of indulging in amateur psychoanalysis, the author suspects more than a tinge of paranoia in Nixon's point of view.

Nixon believed that the press singled him out in particular, subjecting him to a double standard. He believed that it jumped on him for doing things that they ignored when other politicians did them, especially liberal politicians like Stevenson and the Kennedys. Nixon filled his diaries, published writings, and conversations with bitter complaints about press mistreatment and abuse. He griped about reporters' love for the Kennedys. He called the press the tool of the liberal establishment and wrote endlessly about how it targeted him, bore him special animosity, and sought to bring him down.

The feeling was mutual. Walter Cronkite, the living icon of CBS News, accused the Nixon administration of conducting a conspiracy to discredit the American press. When Nixon was president, his public clashes with correspondents such as Dan Rather, Roger Mudd, and others were almost legendary. President Nixon's heated confrontations and pitched battles with reporters were like nothing seen before or since. In his excellent and entertaining book, *Before the Fall*, William Safire, a Nixon speechwriter who managed to get out of the White House before Watergate brought everything crashing to earth, asked, "Was there a conspiracy . . . to discredit and malign the press? Was this so-called 'anti-media campaign' encouraged, directed, and urged on by the president himself? Did this alleged campaign to defame and intimidate Nixon-hating newsmen succeed, isolating and weakening them politically? And did it contribute to the us-against-them mentality that then cracked back at Nixon after his election victory?"

Safire wrote that those questions were "slanted" to elicit an answer of "Nonsense!" But, he sadly revealed, the answer to each was "yes." Safire described the press as the "quintessential them" in Nixon's world of "us against them." The press was "the fount and succor of other thems," the organ of all the *thems* that hated and fought Richard Nixon. It was the *them* that had the power. Academics had no power, and many of the other opposition *thems* were destroying themselves through their own silly fads and political follies, but the journalistic *thems* had real power and could empower all the other *thems*, giving the *thems* an instrument to have *their* way and work Nixon's ruin.

It is unsettling to see this pronounced us-versus-them attitude in a man who, when all is said and done, was so politically successful in his career—until he destroyed himself with Watergate. Nixon won election to the House, the Senate, and the vice presidency all before he turned forty. He nearly won the presidency in 1960. Only forty-seven years old, he was young enough to live to run another day. Even after his disastrous run for governor of California in 1962, he came back from the political graveyard and won the presidency in 1968. In 1972, he won a second term by a landslide. He was widely respected by the voters and well regarded by world leaders, who respected him and took seriously his ideas and opinions on world affairs, even when he was vice president.

Here was a politician of considerable stature and achievement, one who earned much of his standing while quite young, and who throughout his career, throughout his presidency, felt besieged, misunderstood, and abused. He identified the liberal establishment as Goliath to his David. He considered the press the primary instrument of his enemies, and no slingshot would bring it down. But a steady, sustained campaign of harassment and intimidation might.

Nixon's fund crisis was a potential disaster that turned into a public relations triumph. Probably a major reason for his everlasting bitterness was his innocence of any wrongdoing in that instance. There was nothing illegal or dishonest about the fund; Nixon was correct in considering the scandal a red herring with which the opposition slapped him about the head. The fund crisis was a scandal without substance, but it nearly wrecked his career.

From Nixon's viewpoint, the press jumped on him unjustifiably, played the story sensationalistically, and ignored similar funds that benefited other politicians, including Adlai Stevenson. His complaints are not without merit, but, as usual, Nixon felt himself victimized and failed to understand that the press was no more merciful or generous to his opponents (although years later Washington reporters certainly were besotted with President John F. Kennedy). Nixon's customary siege mentality contributed mightily to his anger, which he maintained for the rest of his life.

The issue arose on September 18, 1952, when the *New York Post*, which historian Eric F. Goldman called a pro-Stevenson newspaper, ran the headline SECRET NIXON FUND. According to the *Post*, a group of California millionaires had built a "slush fund" for Senator Nixon to live on above and beyond his Senate salary. The implication was obvious: These rich contributors controlled the corrupt vice presidential nominee. By the next day, the story had sparked a media feeding frenzy. Goldman quotes Nixon's immediate response: "This is another typical smear by the same left-wing elements which have fought me ever since I took part in the investigation, which led to the conviction of Alger Hiss." Vintage Nixon.

Murray Chotiner had the original idea for the fund; he figured that Nixon needed a standing campaign war chest to cover political costs and to keep him ready and flexible for whatever political requirements might arise. The fund was set up shortly after Nixon took office as senator, and it did indeed help finance many of his political activities before the 1952 presidential campaign. The fund enabled him to operate a more or less permanent campaign, and he did a lot of campaigning for other Republicans across the country. The fund also took care of any number of purely political expenses for which many other officeholders would not hesitate to use public money. The fund gave Nixon the flexibility and wherewithal to stay in the public eye in California and have a head start on his reelection campaign of 1956—which never occurred, of course, since he was elected vice president in 1952. The fund was maintained by several contributing supporters and was administered by a trustee. Nixon never used the money for personal reasons. Records were scrupulously kept because Nixon, Chotiner, the trustee, and the major contributors realized that in the future the fund might come under political or journalistic scrutiny. Not every politician kept such a fund, but enough did so that the arrangement was not unusual and should not have been shocking.

The careful records and aboveboard nature of the war chest provided scant protection when the *Post* broke the story. The press immediately played the revelation as a national scandal, and by the next day, several major newspapers, including the

New York Times and the venerable Republican *New York Herald Tribune*, published editorials calling on Nixon to resign from the ticket and let Eisenhower pick an untainted running mate. The *Times* editorially doubted Nixon's judgment in accepting such "gifts" from wealthy supporters.

Press and public perceptions ran far ahead of reality. Within hours of the original *Post* story, Nixon's vice-presidential candidacy and his entire political career were in jeopardy. Other than his family, his close aides and advisers, and some supporters, almost no one was in his corner, not even Eisenhower.

The *Herald Tribune*'s call for Nixon's resignation jolted him, because he interpreted it as a signal from Eisenhower. The general's own initial public statement on the scandal did nothing to comfort or reassure Nixon, since Eisenhower told reporters that he personally believed Nixon to be an honest man, that he was sure he would place the facts before the American people, and that he would talk to his running mate as soon as they could hook up on the telephone.

That was not exactly a ringing endorsement; Eisenhower was clearly hedging. He made no effort to contact Nixon directly; his only communication was that unsupportive message sent through the press. Eisenhower's waffling caused Chotiner to fume that if the "political amateurs" who advised Eisenhower would use "the brains they were born with," they would see that the scandal was nothing more than a purely political attack.

Chotiner was correct, and there was no proof or even any evidence suggesting any wrongdoing, but the scandal gathered momentum. Nixon's own interpretation was fairly predictable; he believed the Democrats were keeping the story in the newspapers. By his reasoning, the newspapers were doing the liberal establishment's bidding both to damage the Eisenhower campaign so as to elect their own anointed champion, Stevenson, and to torpedo Nixon's career, since he was the man who got Hiss.

In his memoirs, Nixon referred to the *New York Post*'s "extreme liberal-left politics," showing that even two and a half decades later, he still believed what he said at the time that the entire mess was a way for those "same" leftist elements to smear him. He who once proclaimed, "If the record smears, then let it smear," was now being smeared six ways to Sunday, and he was mortally offended. Nixon never saw any of this as politics as usual, which is how he tended to view his own misdeeds and misadventures, especially during his presidency. When he did the smearing, it was "normal partisan instincts," but when he was the target, it was unfair reporting, double standards, or the liberal establishment out to crush him.

Nixon made no attempt to conceal the fund nor duck any questions once the *Post* story appeared. Just before it ran, Nixon appeared on the television program *Meet the Press*, on September 14. After the show, a reporter, Peter Edson of the Newspaper Enterprise Association, asked him about the fund. Nixon explained it and gave him the trustee's telephone number for any specific questions about how the fund was administered. Edson was one of the few who published a sober, factual article on the fund and its origins.

On September 19, Nixon issued a press release titled "The Basic Facts About This Fund." The statement consisted of seven points: "(1) It was set up to pay for strictly political activities in which all public servants must take part, in which those who are not independently wealthy and financially unable to participate without assistance. (2) It enabled me to keep my speaking and mailing schedule without recourse to padding my federal office payroll, free government transportation, misuse of the Senatorial franking privilege [free postage], or any subterfuge. (3) I had never received one penny of this fund for my personal use. (4) This fund has been a matter of public knowledge from its inception; no attempt has ever been made to conceal its existence or purpose. All its disbursements were made by [the trustee] by check. . . . (5) Contributors . . . are longtime supporters of mine who sincerely wish to enable me to continue my active battle against communism and corruption. (6) None of them ever asked for or received any special consideration from me. (7) This fund represents a normal, legitimate, open matter of permitting constituents actively to support the political activity of a candidate of their choice. Any other interpretation is a grave injustice to a fine group of public-spirited community leaders." The release was reprinted in full in *Six Crises*, where Nixon noted that it had been buried amid the avalanche of other news stories about the scandal.

As the weekend wore on, the men around Eisenhower contemplated ways to defuse the scandal, all of which involved sacrificing Nixon in one way or another and enabling Eisenhower to wash his hands of the matter. Both running mates had been harping on Democratic corruption, and now here was a Republican scandal over an alleged slush fund. The important thing to the general's men was preserving his candidacy. They viewed Nixon as a secondary consideration, at best.

Nixon was correct in his estimation that, except for Thomas E. Dewey, the former New York governor and 1948 Republican presidential candidate, Eisenhower's circle constituted a "hanging jury" for his own continued candidacy, and Dewey seemed unsteady. Some of them already had a successor in mind, California senator William Knowland. Their reasoning was obvious: Knowland would preserve the ticket's demographic appeal while dissociating Eisenhower from Nixon's scandal. Nixon, kept apprised of developments in the Eisenhower camp by Dewey, was furious.

Eisenhower's further public statements did nothing to soothe Nixon's anger. The general simply would not express real confidence in his young running mate. He offered superficial confidence, saying that he himself believed Nixon honest, but he continued to say that Nixon should give the American people a full description of his finances, explain the fund, and then privately come east for a meeting with Eisenhower himself—to explain all the same things to the general in private.

On September 20, the reporters riding on Eisenhower's campaign train took a vote among themselves, and it came out forty to two that Nixon should go. Eisenhower sat down with them to talk informally and said that he had made no decision on Nixon, regardless of their vote. Then, in one of the campaign's more memorable quotes, he rhetorically asked them, "Of what avail is it for us to carry on this crusade against this business of what has been going on in Washington if we, ourselves, aren't clean as a hound's tooth?"

Nixon and Eisenhower were campaigning on opposite sides of the country; Nixon was tooling around the West on his train, the Nixon Special, and Eisenhower was touring the Southeast. Eisenhower got word to Nixon that he wanted him to show up for a private meeting in West Virginia. Nixon chafed at the imperious summons and pointedly ignored it. Meanwhile, Eisenhower and Nixon's aides communicated with each other, but the only one in the Eisenhower camp to have any significant direct contact with Nixon was Dewey, who claimed to be on Nixon's side, but he, too, appeared to lean toward the idea that Nixon should leave the ticket.

From what Dewey was telling him, Nixon understood that opinion in the Eisenhower camp had started to swing away from public disclosure to resignation. It infuriated him that no clear signals came from Eisenhower; the general neither said anything definite to the press nor directly contacted Nixon to tell him what he wanted him to do. Eisenhower's waffling meant that Nixon had to decide what to do on his own, without knowing how Eisenhower would respond. Dewey had already suggested that Nixon address the American people on national television and ask them to wire or phone the Republican National Committee to make their feelings known. Dewey recommended that Nixon leave the ticket if the public response fell short of a 90 percent vote for him to stay on. That sounded impossible, and perhaps it was, although Dewey was talking only about Republican voters. In any case, Nixon had the distinct feeling that Eisenhower wanted to throw him to the wolves to avoid making a decision himself.

By September 21, many newspapers not only recommended Nixon's resignation from the ticket but were predicting it. That was the very day that Dewey told Nixon that Eisenhower's advisers wanted him to address the nation on television and earn that magic vote of confidence. Eisenhower finally called later that night and told Nixon what he wanted to hear on the broadcast. "Tell them everything there is to tell, everything you can remember since the day you entered public life. Tell them about any money you have ever received." Clearly, Eisenhower wanted to wash his hands of this problem. Nixon could make his case to the American public, then resign, and Eisenhower could stand above the fray, regret the loss of his running mate, but then choose a new one.

Nixon fought back. He tried to pin Eisenhower to make a decision or at least to tell him what he was thinking. In *Six Crises*, Nixon wrote that he told Eisenhower that the time had come "to fish or cut bait." Years later, in his memoirs, perhaps in the interest of full disclosure, Nixon revealed that he really said to Eisenhower that there comes a time to "shit or get off the pot." Nixon imagined Eisenhower was not used to that sort of language, which was unlikely. Despite the choices Nixon offered, Eisenhower did neither, and Nixon still had to lay his finances bare to the American people before the general would make any decision about Nixon's continued candidacy, assuming that Eisenhower intended to decide at all.

Nixon went to Los Angeles to prepare for the broadcast, although he was not sure what he would say. Dewey stayed in touch, apparently trying to get a line on Nixon's intentions. Then, only two hours before broadcast time, Dewey called to tell Nixon that a majority of Eisenhower's advisers had decided he should resign. Dewey said that he did not agree, but since he and Nixon went back some years, they asked him to call with their decision. Dewey recommended that Nixon tell the nation he had done nothing wrong, but he was resigning for the good of the ticket, since his continued candidacy would only hurt Eisenhower's chances to win in November. Dewey wanted to know what he should tell the others. What, he asked, was Nixon going to do?

Nixon blew up. He told Dewey he "didn't have the slightest idea, and they should listen to the broadcast." Before hanging up, Nixon raged, "And tell them I know something about politics, too!"

The Republican National Committee paid for the television time. Nixon broadcast from the El Capitan Theater in Hollywood. The speech was remarkable for many reasons, not its least soaring banality. His language florid, the tone unabashedly sentimental and self-pitying, Nixon told the nation exactly what Eisenhower said he should. He revealed his entire financial history, his current state of debt, and the exact nature of the fund, and gave a dramatic and sentimental account of his life and travails.

Television was still new in 1952, and audiences had never before seen anything like that speech. Today, we have had several decades of political television, and we have grown used to such things as President Nixon telling us that he was not a crook, Senator Edward Kennedy telling the voters of Massachusetts that he was not drunk that night in Chappaquiddick, President Clinton saying that he did not have sexual relations with that woman. In 1952, Senator Nixon's was the very first of these political confessionals and pleas for mercy and understanding.

Nixon recounted his war service. He described his financial achievements as modest and reasonable. He helped his parents, he was raising a family. His wife, he said as the camera cut to her sad but bravely smiling face, had no furs and wore a "respectable Republican cloth coat." That memorable phrase resonates even today. It also reminded the viewers of the Truman administration's scandals, one of which concerned gifts of fur coats to female staffers. Smiling shyly and affectionately, Nixon confided in his millions of viewers that he told Pat she would look good in anything.

Then came the passage that gave the speech its name. After denying taking improper gifts from supporters, he told of one a supporter had sent after hearing that Nixon's two daughters had no pets: a cocker spaniel puppy. "And our little girl, Tricia, the six-year-old, named it Checkers. And you know the kids love that dog and I just want to say this right now, that regardless of what they say about it, we're going to keep it." So did Nixon's dog enter history. When Checkers died during the 1960s, it was front-page news.

Press reaction to the speech was fast and furious. One paper called it "incredible corn," and it was, but the pundits failed to understand something that pundits often fail to understand: People love corn. Not for the first or last time, the pundits misread the public mood, for there arose from the land a great cry that Nixon stay on the ticket. Eisenhower heard, and answered, "You're my boy." But not that evening. Nixon had more twisting in the wind ahead of him.

The speech was a roaring success as public relations, though Nixon left the studio thinking he had blown it. He mistimed the speech and never got to tell the viewers to send their letters to the Republican National Committee. The broadcast ended before he finished what he had to say, and he thought that would do him horrible damage. But the audience loved it and found out for themselves where to send their telegrams. That same night and during the following day the RNC and other Republican addresses were inundated with messages of support for Richard Nixon. The public loved Checkers even if the press did not.

One viewer who did not love Checkers was Eisenhower. According to those who watched the broadcast with him, he was displeased, especially when Nixon called for *all* the other candidates to reveal their financial records. But a good general knows when an opponent has outmaneuvered him, even when the opponent is his own subordinate.

The margin of support for Nixon was closer to 60 percent than to Dewey's magic 90, but Eisenhower did not dare dismiss Nixon in light of what was, Dewey be damned, a large vote of confidence. Nixon had done it. He had sold himself to the American people by means of the new medium whose power hardly anyone understood.

In later years, Nixon compared the Checkers speech to Franklin Roosevelt's equally famous speech about his pet Scotch terrier, Fala. The press made fun of how Nixon invoked Checkers, but the way Roosevelt used Fala went down in history as a campaign master stroke. There, Nixon insisted, was a prime example of the double standard. "The reporters thought the Fala story was cute," Nixon wrote in 1990. "They thought the Checkers story was corny." He thought that the Checkers story "particularly irritated" reporters. When Roosevelt, the liberal demigod, spoke of his dog, it was genius; when Nixon, the pursuer of Alger Hiss, spoke of Checkers, it was incredible corn. Nixon griped about that at some length in his memoirs and other places. He felt quite passionate about it, but he was dead wrong.

Nixon ignored the fact that he invoked Checkers in an overtly maudlin play to the voters' sympathy and sentimentality. Roosevelt used Fala in one of history's great presidential comic turns. That is a crucial distinction—FDR played his dog for *laughs*, to devastating effect. Nixon pressed Checkers into service to costar in a sob story.

Eisenhower knew that the speech had a powerful effect on the public and kept Nixon on the ticket. He approached him face-to-face and said, "You're my boy." Shortly thereafter Nixon, overcome by the events of the past few days, publicly lost his composure. This supposedly inhibited man burst into tears and buried his face in the shoulder of his rival, the man who nearly displaced him, Senator Knowland.

The Checkers speech did not end Nixon's troubles with the press in the 1952 campaign. In late October, Drew Pearson, whom Nixon rescued from Joseph McCarthy's strangler's grip in 1950, ran a column charging that Nixon and his wife improperly claimed a fifty dollar veteran's exemption on their California state taxes. According to Pearson, the Nixons lied about the total worth of their real estate properties. However, Pearson retracted the column several weeks after the election, since the charge was false; a married couple with the same names, Richard and Pat Nixon, had legitimately claimed the exemption.

Senator Nixon was furious. In common journalistic practice, Pearson should have asked Nixon for his comments before going to print. But Pearson never contacted Nixon and printed the calumny only five days before the election. It would not surprise the author if Nixon wondered why he troubled to peel McCarthy off Pearson that night in the cloakroom.

Nixon's bumpy relations with the press probably had as much if not more to do with Nixon's attitude toward reporters than with reporters' attitudes toward him. He at times admitted that reporters often gave him favorable coverage, but to his dying day maintained that the press had it in for him in particular. The record really does not bear him out. For instance, many news agencies praised Nixon's responsible conduct when Eisenhower fell ill in 1955, and much of the press reacted favorably to his 1958 South American trip. Some of the reporters who were with him when the angry mobs attacked him in Lima and Caracas later told him that his courage made them proud as American citizens.

Even so, Nixon usually saw the glass as half empty. During Eisenhower's major illnesses, for instance, some newspapers ran editorials suggesting that the president either resign or delegate interim powers to the vice president (although no constitutional means then existed to delegate presidential powers). Nixon noted the press's approval in his memoirs but could not resist adding, ". . . much as they recoiled at the idea of my succeeding him in office."

Another of Nixon's favorite complaints was that the press blatantly favored John F. Kennedy over Nixon in the 1960 presidential campaign. That is by no means undebatable; Nixon always believed the press was enamored with Kennedy and let him get away with all sorts of political misdeeds for which they would have nailed anyone else (by "anyone else," Nixon meant himself). It can indeed be argued that the press later fell in love with President Kennedy, but the 1960 campaign coverage was another matter, and this author, at least, never has had the impression that the press was as besotted with JFK the senator as they were with JFK the president. But Nixon and others would argue otherwise.

The next major clash between Nixon and the press came when he ran for governor of California. At the end of his campaign, the day after Nixon lost the election, he told the press and the world that he was through with politics, and in parting he decided to tell off the press on national television.

CALIFORNIA 1962:

NOT WITH A BANG, BUT A SNARL

★   ★   ★

Nixon did not really want to run for governor of California. State politics and issues largely failed to interest him, and he had not given up on winning the presidency someday. The governorship did not strike him as a logical stepping-stone to the White House—not for a man who had been vice president of the United States and the 1960 Republican presidential nominee.

But the California Republicans wanted to field a strong candidate against the fairly popular Democratic incumbent, Edmund G. "Pat" Brown, and Nixon was the only viable contender. Early polls showed him ahead of Brown. Whittaker Chambers, in his final letter to Nixon before his death in 1961, urged him to run. Eisenhower and Dewey thought he should run, and more than one of his mentors and associates made the point that if he failed to answer the party's call when it needed him, then the party may not answer his call later.

Yet, former president Herbert Hoover and General Douglas MacArthur advised against running. They thought that if Nixon ran for anything that year, it should be Congress. MacArthur told him that California was too parochial; Nixon was a man of Washington and belonged there, not in Sacramento. After weighing matters, Nixon overcame his reluctance to run, but his heart was never in the campaign.

As Nixon tells it, the *press's* heart was in the campaign. Nixon was rising from the dead; they did not like it and sought to drive a stake through his heart. As usual, Nixon, in his accounts, portrayed himself as almost an innocent party unfairly treated and unreasonably put-upon, and ignored his own conduct. For instance, in the 1962 campaign, Nixon revived his old practice of Red-baiting, though in a rather lower key than in earlier years. That Red-baiting was particularly inappropriate and even silly in a gubernatorial campaign never figured into his analysis of why he lost. He preferred to concentrate his ire on the press and the liberal establishment he always believed the press served and promoted.

Nixon Red-baited for a number of reasons in the 1962 campaign. It may have been misguided, but from his standpoint it was not merely a cheap device for smearing Governor Brown. A 1961 statewide poll showed a high percentage of California voters agreed with a statement that Communists threatened the United States from within. During the campaign, audiences responded when Nixon spoke of domestic subversion. He seemed to have hit on something, but his political instincts had steered him wrong.

In the final analysis, anticommunism did not prove an effective weapon against the Democratic incumbent. Brown had governed effectively, and his administration expanded California's freeway systems, markedly improved the state's school systems and the University of California, found efficient ways to supply the state's urban centers with water (always a major issue in California), and in general provided solid governance that California voters appreciated. For more than one reason, Nixon had entered the wrong race at the wrong time, against the wrong opponent.

In a way, Nixon may have felt he was stuck having to do a certain amount of Red-baiting. His Republican primary opponent was a right-winger and Nixon had to patch things up with the Republican right wing. Right-wing voters would not support Brown, but Nixon knew that some of them would sit out the election, or refuse to contribute anything to his campaign in the autumn, or would do nothing to help rally support for his candidacy. Democrats so outnumbered Republicans in California that a Republican nominee for statewide office badly needed his party solidly behind him. Attacking Brown for being soft on communism seemed a good way to woo these recalcitrants, especially since Nixon had angered them when he publicly repudiated the support of the extreme right-wing John Birch Society.

The Society's founder, Robert Welch, the fruit-juice magnate, some years earlier had called President Eisenhower a Communist and said that Eisenhower's foreign policies amounted to treason. But Nixon could not dismiss the group's endorsement as mere noise from the political nether-regions, since the John Birch Society was strong enough in California that Birchers held local elective offices in Republican areas around the state; a number of Birchers were the Republican candidates for local offices in the coming election. That put Nixon in a bind, since repudiating the Society meant automatically repudiating Republican candidates. But Welch's attacks on Eisenhower meant that Nixon absolutely had to speak out, which made reassuring right-wing voters all the more urgent. Consequently, Nixon attacked Brown and the Democrats for trying to abolish the state loyalty oath, a holdover from the McCarthy era, and called for requiring the state's schools to teach California's children about communism so that they might know the enemy. He hoped that this fairly pallid exercise in Red-baiting might assuage some of the Birchers' feelings and keep the right wing behind him.

In a radio address during the fall campaign, Nixon included among his "Twelve Goals for Californians" fighting communism in the state. At a time when Communists were pressing their cause in Cuba, Berlin, and Southeast Asia, he said, "our goal in California must be to intensify our opposition to communism at home." Nixon objected to giving Communists "a forum on the campuses of our tax-supported colleges and universities. Communists lie to gain ground. . . . A free educational system dedicated to the truth should have no place for speakers who vow to overthrow our Constitution by any means to serve their ends." Nixon wanted to bar from California's state campuses anyone who refused "to testify before a legislative committee investigating communism or who [refused] to comply with the Subversive Activities Control Act of 1951 . . . which I helped to write."

At the time of that speech, October 1962, the Cuban missile crisis had claimed the public's attention and made his chances for victory look bleaker than ever. Worse for Nixon, President Kennedy summoned Brown to Washington to chair a governors' conference on civil defense and then publicly praised him for putting national security ahead of his own reelection campaign. That may have had some bearing on Nixon's choice of subject in the broadcast, but it also made the soft-on-communism argument ring hollow.

Clearly, circumstances did not favor Nixon, and his own conduct played its role in his defeat. Nonetheless, his memories of the ill-fated campaign tended to dwell on the press. As Nixon remembered it, reporters gave him trouble from the beginning, long before the general campaign began in 1962. When he announced on September 27, 1961, in Los Angeles, that he would run in the Republican primary the following June, Nixon told reporters that he would not run for president in 1964. He had decided beforehand that he had no desire to face Kennedy, "or his tactics," a second time, and he figured that the president would be unbeatable in the next election, though he did not share those thoughts at the press conference. Many of the reporters obviously doubted that he was serious and fired a barrage of questions about whether he intended to serve a full term as governor if elected.

Nixon insisted that he had only the governorship on his mind. What, one reporter asked, would he do if the national party insisted on his 1964 candidacy? Would he answer a draft? Nixon insisted again that he would not run for president in the next election. The reporter, Nixon recalled, referred to General William Sherman's famous response when queried about running for president: "If nominated I will not run, if elected I will not serve." He asked Nixon to comment. For the third or tenth time during that one news conference, Nixon firmly told the press and the voters of California that he would not run for president in 1964 no matter what happened.

Another problem reared its head during 1962, and, as Nixon retold the matter in his books, the press flogged him with it all through the campaign. In the autumn, Nixon and Brown met in a televised debate. The publisher of the *Oceanside Blade Tribune* asked about a loan that the shady and phantomlike billionaire Howard Hughes made to Nixon's brother Donald. That issue first surfaced in 1960 but never amounted to much of a controversy and had little if any effect on the presidential campaign. Nixon's special nemesis Drew Pearson had reported that Hughes had lent Donald Nixon $205,000 in 1956. Hughes did a lot of business with the federal government and Pearson charged that the billionaire extracted favors from federal officials and agencies, including the Internal Revenue Service, after he made the loan. Hughes never asked for repayment and the loan was unsecured, which did nothing to dispel the clouds of suspicion. The story would not really go away, but neither did it balloon into a scandal as the fund story had in 1952.

Nixon suspected that the question had actually come from Governor Brown, since the questioner, Tom Braden, was a prominent liberal and a Brown appointee to the state board of education. Nixon explained that his brother was in serious financial trouble and had made arrangements with the Hughes Tool Company without consulting him. When Nixon got wind of the deal, he insisted that his brother do something to secure the loan. Consequently, the boys' widowed mother, Hannah Nixon, put up her farm property as security. Shortly afterward, Donald Nixon went bankrupt and Hannah Nixon lost her property to the Hughes Tool Company. If either or both Nixon brothers were trying to pull a fast one, they blew it.

Nixon told the television audience that in 1960 John F. Kennedy did not make an issue of the Hughes loan, and it was honorable of him to leave such irrelevancies out of the campaign, but now here was Governor Brown making an issue out of the misfortunes of Nixon's brother and mother. Nixon insisted that he had no part in the deal, and that he had not done Hughes any favors in return for Donald's loan. Brown and his "hatchet men" were saying that Nixon must have profited in some way, he complained, and that he must have done something wrong. "I have made mistakes, but I am an honest man." Nixon dared Brown to make the Hughes loan an issue. "All the people of California are listening on television. Governor Brown has a chance to stand up as a man and charge me with misconduct. Do it, sir!"

Nixon had taken command of the moment, and Brown retreated. The governor replied that he was not in fact trying to make the loan into a campaign issue. Nixon wrote in his memoirs that the Brown camp continued to raise it anyway, and the press clamped onto the Hughes loan and dogged him with questions about it for the remainder of the campaign. Nixon never appeared to consider that the press may have been asking legitimate questions, since the whole Hughes deal *did* look rather odd, if not shady.

The *Los Angeles Times*, Nixon's staunch ally in 1946 and 1950, gave the loan story prominent play. The paper had passed from the father, Norman Chandler, to the son, Otis. Just as a new king arose in Egypt and knew not Joseph, the new owner of the *Times* knew not Richard. Otis Chandler did not automatically support Nixon nor did he, as Ambrose and other historians have noted, obligingly ignore the Democratic opponent and devote pages and pages of favorable coverage to Nixon. Times had changed; in 1962 Southern California was no longer simply Nixon country, and the local press would not volunteer as his unpaid publicists. Otis Chandler wanted to make the *Times* into the West Coast's preeminent metropolitan newspaper, and he set out to guide his paper away from partisan hucksterism toward respectable journalism and intelligent editorial policies. He succeeded in making the *Times* into a major newspaper of national standing, but Nixon lost an important base of parochial support and identified yet another major enemy in the press.

Nixon had problems besides the Hughes loan and uncertain Republican unity. Hardly anyone believed that he would not run for president in 1964. Jonathan Aitken, the Nixon biographer who is himself a British politician, wrote that one would think voters would be proud to elect a governor who had a chance to become president. Aitken must have been thinking of the British system, wherein the prime minister continues to represent his constituency in Parliament while discharging the duties of his national office and so never needs to reassure his voters that he will not desert them for greater glory. American voters, however, generally look askance at a candidate they believe will not serve his full term but will use his office as a stepping-stone. Indeed, Californians may not have minded a governor of theirs becoming president later on, but the curious psychology of American voters dictates that a candidate must convince them that he intends to stick around, even if most of them will vote for him two years down the line when he does run for president.

That is a bit of classic self-deception on the voters' part. But one must play the game, and you will never hear a candidate say, "Of course I won't finish my term. I want to be president in two years." Nixon played the game, but the voters were unconvinced. Thus another Nixonian irony, since he was perfectly serious about not running against Kennedy again, having accurately assessed 1964 as a Democratic year.

But the reporters would not let up on those favorite themes, according to Nixon's complaint. At every press conference, he recalled, reporters asked about the Hughes loan, his plans for 1964, and whether or not he refused the John Birch Society's support. No one, Nixon lamented, was much interested in his program for running the state, his stands on crime, education, or improving conditions for business and investment in California. The majority of chroniclers do not agree with Nixon's assessment of the press's performance, though many of Nixon's campaign aides support his version of events. However, Nixon admitted there was some basis for reporters' skepticism, since he really was not terribly motivated to win the governorship.

Late in the campaign, too, Nixon, the political realist, understood that he was going to lose. His understanding turned into certainty when the Cuban missile crisis coincided with the campaign's final days.

Nixon blamed the press for a lot. Reporters and editors certainly gave him a hard time in the 1962 campaign, but, as noted, it is debatable whether or not they treated him unfairly. Equally questionable is how decisive a role they played in his defeat, if they played one at all. None of that was debatable as far as Nixon was concerned, and on the morning after the election, he decided to tell the press off, and his public display of temper has entered American political lore as the famous (or infamous, depending on one's point of view) "last press conference." That is a misnomer, since it was not a press conference in the classic sense. Nixon did not take questions from reporters; he lectured and scolded them, then left the building.

There are varying accounts of how the last press conference came about, and none strikes the author as any more reliable than another. Several hold that Nixon was drunk or at least severely hungover; Nixon's own account, of course, makes no mention of being either. John Ehrlichman described Nixon as "hungover, trembling, and red-eyed," but alert and in strong voice. Nixon described himself as simply angry.

Nixon's own version of the events leading up to the confrontation is pretty earthy, one of those instances of his periodic and quirky candor. Brown won by 297,000 votes out of just under six million, a massive turnout for California voters by any standards. Nixon did not feel like facing the reporters in the lobby of the Beverly Hilton Hotel, where he had spent election night. His aide Herbert Klein went down to read Nixon's concession statement. Nixon wrote that the reporters harassed Klein and demanded the vanquished candidate's presence. That actually was not so unreasonable, since losing candidates routinely face reporters and take the time to address and thank their own hardworking supporters. That is political etiquette and the supporters, at least, have a right to expect it.

But Nixon was thinking only about the reporters. When Klein came to him with their demand that he appear, he reacted with "the anger and frustration, the disappointment and fatigue struggling inside me...." Nixon told Klein, "Screw them. I'm not going to do it. I don't have to and I'm not going to." He again told Klein to read his concession statement to the reporters and, if they asked, to tell them that he had gone home to be with his wife and daughters. Klein went back downstairs, and Nixon watched the ensuing scene on television. The reporters again demanded to see Nixon, as if, Nixon felt, he was somehow required to appear before them. He decided to go down and face them. He had not shaven and he recalled that he "felt terrible" and "looked worse." When Nixon took the podium he gave what may stand as the strangest performance of his career.

"Good morning, gentlemen," he began. "Now that Mr. Klein has made his statement, and now that all the members of the press are so delighted that I have lost, I'd like to make a statement of my own." He imagined that the opening disappointed the press, since it "didn't sound like the abject performance they had been hoping for." That opening could hardly have disappointed the reporters, since its naked hostility promised a juicy rant to follow. Nixon did not let them down.

"I appreciate the press coverage of this campaign. I think each of you covered it the way you saw it. You had to write it according to your belief on how it would go. I don't believe publishers should tell reporters to write one way or another. . . . I have no complaints about the press coverage." Nixon congratulated Governor Brown and wished him well, but then abruptly abandoned his good loser's grace. "I believe Governor Brown has a heart, even though he believes I do not. I believe he is a good American, even though he feels I am not." Then he repeated his usual line about never having doubted his opponent's patriotism. He said that in 1946 about Jerry Voorhis and again in 1950 about Helen Gahagan Douglas. Now he claimed actually to have "defended my opponent's patriotism." The press did not report that, Nixon chided, but he was proud that he had done it. Nixon was proud that he "defended the fact that" Brown "was a man of good motive, a man that I disagreed with very strongly, but a man of good motive.

"I want that—for once, gentlemen—I would appreciate if you would write what I say, in that respect. I think it's very important that you write it—in the lead—in the lead." Nixon did not mean that every single reporter inaccurately quoted him. One reporter, *Los Angeles Times* correspondent Carl Greenberg, "wrote every word that I said," and he did so "fairly" and "objectively." Nixon did not mean "that others didn't have a right to do it differently. But Carl, despite whatever feelings he had, felt that he had an obligation to report the facts as he saw them."

Nixon thanked his volunteers, and he congratulated Republicans who had won office across the country, such as Governor Nelson Rockefeller in New York and Governor-elect George Romney in Michigan. He saw these victories as signs that the Republican party would revitalize itself for 1964. Nixon said he was proud to have run for governor of California and bore no one any hard feelings for the loss. Then he zeroed in on his real topic, the hard feelings he bore the press.

"One last thing. At the outset I said a couple of things with regard to the press that I noticed some of you looked a little irritated about. And my philosophy with regard to the press has never really gotten through. And I want to get it through.

"This cannot be said for any other political figure today, I guess. Never in my sixteen years of campaigning have I complained to a publisher, to an editor, about the coverage of a reporter. I believe a reporter has got a right to write it as he feels it. I believe if a reporter believes that one man ought to win rather than the other, whether it's on television or radio or the like, he ought to say so. I will say to the reporter sometimes that I think, well, look, I wish you'd give my opponent the same going-over that you give me.

"And as I leave the press, all I can say is this: For sixteen years, ever since the Hiss case, you've had a lot of—a lot of fun—that you've had an opportunity to attack me and I think I've given as good as I've taken. It was carried right up to the last day." Nixon compared press coverage of some of the gaffes and slips of the tongue that both candidates made during the campaign and concluded that the press gave him the short end of things, playing up his "flubs" and not covering Brown's. He singled out his former supporter, the *Los Angeles Times*, for a little special scolding for that last example of mistreatment, then added: "I think it's time that our great newspapers have at least the same objectivity, the same fullness of coverage, that television has. And I can only say thank God for television and radio for keeping the newspapers a little more honest." He would not talk that way about radio and television after he became president.

"Now," he continued, "some newspapers don't fall into that category... but I can only say that the great metropolitan newspapers in this field, they have a right to take every position they want on the editorial page, but on the news page they also have a right to have reporters cover men who have strong feelings whether they're for or against a candidate. But the responsibility also is to put a few Greenbergs on, on the candidates they happen to be against, whether they're against him on the editorial page or just philosophically deep down, a fellow who at least will report what the man says.... I leave you gentlemen now and you will now write it. You will interpret it. That's your right. But as I leave you, I want you to know—just think how much you're going to be missing."

Now came the most famous moment of Nixon's plaint. "You won't have Nixon to kick around anymore, because, gentlemen, this is my last press conference, and it will be one in which I have welcomed the opportunity to test wits with you. I have always respected you. I have sometimes disagreed with you. But unlike some people, I've never canceled a subscription to a paper and also I never will.

"I believe in reading what my opponents say, and I hope that what I have said today will at least make television, radio, and the press first recognize the great responsibility they have to report all the news and, second, recognize that they have a right and

211

responsibility, if they're against a candidate, to give him the shaft, but also to recognize if they give him the shaft, put one lonely reporter on the campaign who will report what the candidate says now and then.

"Thank you, gentlemen, and good day."

It was extraordinary. The author remembers watching it on the evening news and being amazed that a famous grown-up would talk that way in public. Many reporters apparently shared the author's sentiment. Governor Brown commented that the press would never let Nixon forget that outburst. Actually, the press never really exploited the last press conference in the way that Nixon supporters would have expected.

Just as the Checkers speech was unprecedented, so was the last news conference. Some of Nixon's defenders, and some historians who try only to be fair, judge Nixon's outburst as quite coherent and point out that in 1968, the Democrats actually could find no part of the last press conference to use against Nixon in the presidential campaign. The author disagrees; Nixon's speech was by no means entirely coherent. He rambled, his tortured syntax resembled Eisenhower's, and the paranoia in his words is obvious to the point of being painful. It was a public tantrum, all the more unseemly because the tantrum-thrower was a former vice president of the United States. If the Democrats could not use any footage of this sad play, that probably was only because Nixon's ramblings failed to arrange themselves in manageable sound bites. It was a disgraceful performance that dogged him for the rest of his life, although he always claimed to be proud of it.

John Ehrlichman, who was present, later commented on how the press treated the last press conference. Ehrlichman claimed that Nixon was badly hungover, and he believed that the reporters there who knew Nixon best, or sat or stood closest to him, must have perceived his allegedly hungover condition. Yet no one reported that anything seemed wrong with Nixon. For that matter, according to Ehrlichman, the press treated Nixon's statement as "bitter . . . but rational." Few if any commentaries appeared in the major papers or on the major network news shows to denounce or ridicule Nixon for throwing a tantrum, nor was there any consensus that Nixon had behaved paranoically or that he simply had lost his mind. Ehrlichman's opinion was that the press "cleaned up" the story.

That may be true, but the press did not let Nixon get by entirely unscathed, and shortly thereafter ABC News broadcast the documentary, *The Political Obituary of Richard Nixon*, described in this book's introduction. ABC invited comment from a number of Nixon's past adversaries, including Alger Hiss—which provoked a lot of angry letters and phone calls from viewers.

That ABC called the program a political obituary left no question but that the show's creators considered Nixon politically dead. So, it seems, did nearly everyone else.

THE PRESIDENT AND THE PRESS:
BEFORE WATERGATE

✶　✶　✶

When Richard Nixon decided to run for president, the 1962 California campaign and all its bitterness were recent memories—for Nixon and the press. From the outset, he expected press coverage to be unfavorable or downright hostile. A few years in the wilderness had not gentled him or eased the sting of the California defeat or his conviction that the press helped cause it. For that matter, Nixon still smarted over the Hiss case and clung to his cherished complaint that the liberal establishment—and specifically its powerful arm, the press—never forgave him for proving them wrong about Hiss. Nixon liked to repeat what a friendly reporter once told him, that the worst thing you can do to a newspaperman is prove him wrong about a major issue. Nixon believed he had proven all his enemies wrong about many things, beyond the Hiss case. Just being around to run for president proved them wrong.

As Nixon recalled in his memoirs, after the Hiss case, the fund crisis, and the "flagrant media favoritism" shown John F. Kennedy in the 1960 campaign, by 1968 he long since had come to consider the press part of his political opposition. His relationship with the press somehow differed from other politicians', even those whom reporters disliked. Nixon was, he wrote, prepared to "do combat" with the press in order to get his ideas and programs across to the voters. The power of the presidency would not alone accomplish that; he believed the press more powerful than the presidency in its capability to inform the public and shape popular opinion. The media, Nixon wrote, always have the last word.

Nixon entered the White House carrying decades of resentments and dubious expectations of human relations. More than one of his associates has commented that Nixon pretty much assumed that most people would not like him. Eisenhower once told a friend he found it odd that a professional politician of Nixon's age (that was during the 1950s) would have so few, if any, close friends. Years later, President Nixon commented to an acquaintance that he never was "one of the personality boys." Nixon ascribed some of his press troubles to that, in addition to his lifelong war with the liberal establishment. The press, of course, loved the personality boys. Nixon hated "the way the Kennedys played politics and the way the media let them get away with it." That left him "angry and frustrated." Nixon identified a lot of personality boys as liberals. Some were. Franklin Roosevelt and the Kennedy brothers were definitely personality boys. So, in his own way, was Adlai Stevenson.

Ironically, in his own way, so was Richard Nixon. The man possessed some charisma, and the author has known a number of people over the years who met Nixon individually or in small groups. All of them expressed surprise at how charming and magnetic he could be in such circumstances. According to legend, and to several of his associates and underlings, Nixon was uncomfortable talking to *anyone* other than large audiences. But Nixon could be articulate, fascinating, and, yes, charismatic, in any number of public and private circumstances. In his post-presidential interviews, he often appeared relaxed and chatty, and displayed a definite magnetism. He is fascinating to listen to, a good storyteller. The acting abilities that earned him praise in his student days show up in those interviews as Nixon shifts voices and accents to portray characters from his past.

But it is true that Nixon was not a "star" personality in the sense that the Kennedys and some others were, and it is true that stars appeal to the press and public in ways that the Richard Nixons of this world do not. The press treated the Kennedys differently, for the most part, than Nixon, but it still can be argued that Nixon's attitude toward the press had all the essential ingredients of a persecution complex. That perspective was not limited to his relations with the media. It was part of the way he saw the world and undoubtedly partly governed his thoughts and actions toward the press. Even the personality boys, after all, had their problems with media, including the much-admired Franklin Roosevelt. Nixon's belief that the liberals literally controlled the press and that the press was particularly hostile toward him denies or ignores that reporters typically have an adversarial relationship with politicians in general—and presidents in particular. Nixon seemed to understand that reality to an extent, but only when he was not seething over his own treatment at reporters' hands.

Such feelings harken to his undergraduate days, when he helped start the open-shirted social club at Whittier College. The other club's members, the personality boys with money, the ones who wore ties and tuxedoes, called themselves the Franklins. Nixon's club called themselves the Orthogonians—the squares. In that time and place, "square" did not have the precise slang meaning it has now. "Be square with me" meant "Be honest with me; give me the truth."

It is difficult to resist engaging in amateur psychoanalysis, so the author shall surrender to the armchair's siren call. Most of Nixon's biographers have made much of Nixon's lifelong Orthogonian versus Franklin outlook. It is interesting that so many of the men Nixon fought would have been Franklins at Whittier: Jerry Voorhis came from a wealthy family; Dean Acheson epitomized the Eastern establishment with his aristocratic appearance and speech; Alger Hiss, cut from the same cloth as Dean Acheson, was among the Washington glitterati until Chambers, Nixon, and HUAC laid him low; and the Kennedys, of course, defined the image of a new sort of aristocracy.

JFK was polished and cool and greatly appealed to the middle-class generation that came of age in the 1950s and 1960s. President Kennedy and his beautiful wife and beautiful children acted as ersatz American royalty; Jacqueline Kennedy gave the legend its name shortly after the assassination when, talking to Kennedy biographer Theodore White, she first invoked the famous Camelot metaphor.

Nixon always contrasted himself with such people and felt that fortune smiled on them in a way it never smiled on him. To continue the armchair psychoanalysis, it is worth noting that Nixon apparently felt a sort of kinship with and sympathy for Whittaker Chambers for the way the Washington snobs, the liberals, and the press heaped their scorn on him. Nixon chafed when Hiss treated Chambers and the HUAC members and staffers with effete disdain. Chambers was a subspecies of Orthogonian. He was not a personality boy. He was an outsider. Nixon in later years liked to hold forth on how the press and liberal intellectuals roasted Chambers at every opportunity. He lacked many social graces—something equally true of Nixon, although he was by conventional standards considerably more polished and presentable than Chambers. When one reads what Nixon wrote about Chambers in several of his books, it is striking how similar much of it is to what others said and wrote about Nixon.

Tom Wicker, among others, observed that Nixon often appeared withdrawn, graceless, and uncomfortable in public and even in private. Nixon often has been contrasted to other politicians in that respect; he was ill at ease among people, according to those descriptions, whereas the Kennedys or the Roosevelts, or whomever, reveled in others' attention. Many have commented on Nixon's physical awkwardness and standoffishness, comparing these traits unfavorably to the easy sociability of other political stars.

Both Nixon and Chambers fit many definitions of the outsider, although Nixon was the outsider who fought for acceptance and, for a time, achieved dominance. If he did not win his adversaries' love, he won their grudging respect. As for reporters, by and large they either were Franklins or worshiped the Franklins of the liberal establishment and worked to serve their purposes. They and Nixon lived in different worlds and held sharply disparate views of the world at large.

Nixon was as elusive and contradictory in this as he was about so much else in his thinking. He denied that the Orthogonian-Franklin competition at Whittier had anything to do with social class, although it is difficult to see what else it could have been about. He never identified his later enmities with the college clubs, even though he often criticized the upper classes in that distinct way of his: expressing resentment while simultaneously denying that he felt any. Nixon's class hostility was always obvious and he always denied it absolutely. So it was with the press: At times he praised them, at times he criticized them in a gentlemanly fashion, and at times he revealed his hatred for all to see. Usually, he did the latter unknowingly, or, as in the last press conference, indulged the illusion that his outburst was perfectly reasonable and fair.

When he took office as president in January 1969, he expected, in John Ehrlichman's words, "to exercise the fullest possible influence over what the press said about him and his administration." Nixon and his top aide, H.R. Haldeman, created a system to feed news to the White House press corps while simultaneously directly serving small newspapers and broadcasters outside the prime metropolitan areas. "For the first time, the White House would systematically propagandize the general public." Reporters were to be controlled, news was to be managed, the White House staff was to present a united front against the press and take their cues from the president himself. Nixon expected his closest aides to coordinate the war effort. The press will be out to get us, he told them repeatedly. The press is the enemy. The press is to be treated accordingly.

As part and parcel of his mania for managing the news, Nixon was a madman on the subject of leaks. The administration would be a tight ship. When leaks sprang, the Nixon White House formed a special unit of plumbers to plug them. The only one in the Nixon administration with the right or authority to leak anything to the press was Nixon himself. Administrations past and present have utilized the authorized leak as a tool of press relations and to help shape public opinion, but unauthorized leaks typically plague presidents and other administration figures. They drove Nixon to distraction.

His determination to control them, as well as his general hatred of the press, figured among the major factors that led to the Watergate scandal and ended his presidency. Nixon's horror at unauthorized leaks brought about such misadventures as burglarizing a psychiatrist's office and bugging the Democratic National Committee's telephones. Some of the president's men even considered firebombing a research institution. There are allegations that the president himself may have been privy to the firebombing idea. Whether that is true or not, Nixon rarely blinked at the commission or contemplation of these crimes and defended them in his memoirs.

Ehrlichman summed it all up quite succinctly in his memoirs, *Witness to Power: The Nixon Years*, wherein he quotes Nixon as frequently complaining, "They hate me because I have beaten them so often." Ehrlichman noted, "He had nailed Alger Hiss, whom Nixon saw to be the darling of the press Establishment. The Checkers speech had frustrated their effort to sink him. He'd come back from his 1962 California defeat in spite of the media's universal political obituaries. In simplest terms, he believed that they were liberal and he was conservative, and most of the people out there in the country believed him and not them. The press couldn't stand that, and so they were his sworn enemies."

Ehrlichman's last point, that average Americans "believed with him and not them" was central to Nixon's view of his press relations. The press served the elite; Nixon communicated with the people, the great masses who were not academics, nor rich liberals, nor reporters, nor Democratic senators. Later in his first term he coined an unforgettable name for his loyal, conservative masses: the silent majority. He believed these people mistrusted the press as much as he did. In that, he very likely was correct.

President Nixon had a knack for managing the press. Ehrlichman called him "a talented media manipulator" who could plan how "he or his spokesmen would dominate the evening news," grab headlines, and get on the front pages of all the major newspapers. Nixon, wrote Ehrlichman, thought like an editor. He knew how to cultivate columnists, most of whom were more conservative than reporters, and he knew how to manage prime-time appearances on network television so as to "speak to the people over the heads of the press and the commentators, commanding huge audiences, which sometimes could find nothing but Richard Nixon" on their television screens. His plans for controlling the news media were successful much of the time during his early years as president.

But, according to Ehrlichman, Nixon firmly believed that most journalists, even the columnists, would treat him unfairly "if left to their own devices." Consequently, the White House sought ways to prevent hostile commentators from "airing their biases." Nixon dealt with this problem by creating "visuals and photo opportunities," so that a film or videotape record of events could be shown on the evening news and circumvent straight commentary.

Nixon also figured that many reporters would content themselves with White House handouts rather than do a lot of legwork if they did not have to. Therefore, by the president's reckoning, the White House should hand out extremely detailed press releases, full of research and background, and create easy photo opportunities. The term *sound bite* did not yet exist, but Nixon thought of providing those, too. He assumed that many jaded Washington reporters would let the White House do their job for them and thus allow the administration to manage the news. A passive press would be a tame press. Finally, any reporter Nixon thought hostile was to be frozen out.

Amazingly, President Nixon could show a genuine respect for the White House press corps and at times responded to their professionalism. He always thoroughly prepared for press conferences and held his temper even under rowdy questioning, at least until Watergate. Unlike previous presidents, according to William Safire, he read daily press summaries that ran to fifty or more pages and which, in Safire's description, "displayed the entire range of coverage and opinion in the big networks and little magazines." Besides the summaries, Nixon carefully perused the *Los Angeles Times*, the *New York Times*, the *Washington Post*, and the *Washington Star* every day, giving those hated papers what Safire called a "grim reading."

The president's press policies ranged from manipulation to frontal assault. Ehrlichman reminisced about the many times he watched Nixon designing White House press releases or timing White House events and policy announcements so that they would dominate the evening news shows, but he and other Nixon underlings were on hand when the brainstorming sessions turned into war councils. Nixon not only wanted to control the news, he sought to punish and avenge. He treated reporters whom he disliked in similar ways to how he treated political opponents. He tried to get government agencies, such as the FBI and the IRS, to harass or spy on them, or put Justice Department lawyers or White House staffers to work digging up dirt on them.

When these schemes, some barely legal and some clearly illegal, did not work, which was usually the case, he often resorted to more drastic tactics. Nixon targeted individual reporters for various sorts of reprisals for unfavorable coverage. One of the most famous instances was the search for dirt on Daniel Schorr, a CBS correspondent who frequently drew the president's wrath. In 1973, Nixon ordered federal agencies to investigate Schorr, run a complete background check, and interview his friends, family, and associates, all in an effort to find anything questionable or incriminating in his life history. When questioned about the open and obvious inquiry, the White House claimed to be considering Schorr for a position in the administration.

Most of Nixon's measures to manipulate and harass the press were, past a certain point, unsuccessful. He could control the news to an extent by freezing reporters out of important stories and events. He could intimidate individual reporters and frighten publishers, but in the end, the press, collectively, neither feared nor obeyed him, and once the myriad scandals that rocked his administration broke into the open, he lost any ability to manage the news. Journalists responded to the administration's manipulations and attacks by turning into the implacable enemy Nixon always imagined them to be. The war between president and press contained a distinct element of self-fulfilling prophecy.

While Nixon raged to the end of his life about how the news media mistreated him, a dispassionate look at the record suggests that they treated Nixon no better or worse than most presidents in modern times. The amateur psychoanalyst again must suggest that an element of paranoia informed much of Nixon's thinking. He generally regarded himself as having been singled out by one Goliath or another, although his worldview allowed for a genuine and, at times, intense compassion for others he believed mistreated by the same enemies he faced. As noted, despite his belief that the press loved the Kennedys, he warned Edward Kennedy to beware of the press after Chappaquiddick. In Nixon's view, the press loved a story more than it loved a Kennedy, or anything else.

Nixon has been described as egocentric by many who knew him, at least in professional relationships. Others have noted that one of his more endearing traits was a genuine sympathy for people he considered downtrodden, put-upon, or despondent. Nixon apparently had a special affinity for Lyndon Johnson, and, when the former president visited the White House, Nixon listened sympathetically as Johnson held forth at considerable length about his own perceived mistreatment by Washington reporters. In a later filmed interview, Nixon said that he believed Johnson got a bad deal—he did not specify if he meant from the press—and added that he thought it superficial and petty to harass a president simply because one did not like his accent or for other silly reasons based on snobbery and prejudice.

Johnson spoke like the Texan he was, and many liberal Easterners made fun of him. His earthiness offended middle-class sensibilities; when he pulled up his shirt to show his surgical scar on national television, many pundits thought that American civilization had collapsed. According to LBJ's brother, Sam Houston Johnson, many of President Kennedy's circle ridiculed the vice president as "Uncle Cornpone," and the elite's regional prejudices rained down on Johnson throughout his presidency. In writings and interviews, Nixon often referred to Johnson's problems in ways that suggested intense empathy.

Nixon had friendly relations with individual reporters and columnists, of course, a few of whom played important roles in his life and career. Ralph de Toledano, a *Newsweek* correspondent, did favors for Nixon during the House and Senate campaigns, and could be relied upon to write friendly pieces for him. De Toledano coauthored one of the first major books on the Hiss case, and it depicted Nixon in a favorable light. Earl Mazo, another reporter, wrote one of the first major biographies of Nixon, which Nixon always considered a fair portrayal. Mazo's biography was no campaign tract; it was critical when appropriate and gave credit where credit was due. *Los Angeles Times* reporter Carl Greenberg, as mentioned, earned Nixon's respect during the 1962 California gubernatorial campaign.

There were others, and Nixon listed their names in *In the Arena*, but his relations with that happy few starkly contrasted with his view of the press in general. He wrote that he did not list all the reporters he liked because he thought that it would hurt their standing with their colleagues were it known that Nixon considered them fair and honorable. During the 1988 presidential campaign, Nixon liked to joke that the best way he could help the Republican nominee, Vice President George Bush, would be to sign on as Democratic nominee Michael Dukakis's press secretary.

In retirement, Nixon the elder statesman tried to give reporters their due. He thought that print reporters for the most part were more intelligent and thoughtful than broadcast reporters. He found many journalists more interesting as human beings than many politicians, and commented that an informal bull session with a group of reporters could be more fascinating and rewarding than one with congressmen. He credited reporters for being fair and supportive when covering him on foreign trips, specifically those who were with him in South America in 1958, regardless of how partisan they were at home. There is an old saying that in the United States politics stops at the water's edge. Nixon wrote that he found that truer for reporters than politicians.

But Nixon had many more bad things to say about the press, some of which, were he criticizing an ethnic group in exactly the same terms, would qualify as gross bigotry. Much of what he wrote and said on the subject was simplistic and even childish. "The press used to consider itself part of the fabric of society," Nixon wrote in one such critique, "with a shared stake in America's prosperity, the health of its institutions, and the success of its initiatives around the world. When they had to criticize, they did so as part of the team. But today the media consider themselves outside of and above society at large, looking down haughtily as they fire their thunderbolts at the rest of us. Frequently it appears that the media's excesses are weakening the fabric of society rather than strengthening it."

Late in 1969, Nixon made one of his more famous speeches just after the antiwar movement held its October 15 Moratorium march on Washington, and that speech heralded a new phase of his war against the press. In the process, the White House opened new fronts in its efforts to discredit the antiwar movement and, by extension, Nixon increasingly indulged his overall class resentments against the Eastern liberal establishment, which he saw as the greater enemy that encompassed the press and the antiwar protesters.

Press secretary Ronald Ziegler on October 13 announced that Nixon would make a major policy address on November 3. Many antiwar activists and more than a few reporters suspected that Ziegler's announcement was timed to undercut the planned protest, which Nixon denied in his memoirs. Nixon had other reasons for a November 3 speech; that date would be two days after a deadline the president secretly gave the North Vietnamese to achieve a breakthrough in the peace negotiations or face intensified American military action. When the president issued his ultimatum, antiwar leaders had not yet announced the October 15 Moratorium.

The day before the moratorium, a Radio Hanoi broadcast praised the American antiwar movement and encouraged full participation in the Moratorium Day protests. Nixon took that as a signal that the North Vietnamese would ignore the November 1 deadline. In reply, Vice President Spiro Agnew, under orders from the president, held a press conference to blast the North Vietnamese intrusion into American domestic affairs. Agnew called on the antiwar activists to repudiate the North Vietnamese. To Nixon's fury, a reporter asked Agnew if the news conference itself were not simply an attempt to undercut the moratorium.

On November 3, the president addressed the nation. "I have chosen a plan for peace. I believe it will succeed. If it does succeed, what the critics say now won't matter. If it does not succeed, anything I say then won't matter. . . . And so tonight, to you, the great silent majority of my fellow Americans, I ask for your support. . . . Let us be united for peace. Let us also be united against defeat. Because let us understand: North Vietnam cannot defeat or humiliate the United States. Only Americans can do that."

The silent majority speech was a hit, and Nixon's approval ratings shot up to 68 percent. Next came a White House public relations offensive to rally support for Nixon's Vietnam policies and derail the antiwar movement. Once that was rolling, inevitably, the campaign involved a nearly naked attempt to cow the press into supporting, or at least not opposing, the administration's policies. The White House called into service the very willing vice president.

Spiro Theodore Agnew was for a time one of Nixon's main weapons in the war against the press. Agnew launched a series of clownish attacks on several of the administration's designated enemies during 1969 and 1970, delivering speeches usually written by future presidential candidate and CNN commentator

Patrick Buchanan, with help from William Safire. Idiotic as Agnew's performances usually were, they played well with conservative audiences and had some real effect. For one, they scared the press.

Agnew as good as accused the press of un-American activities for daring to criticize the administration. He indicted reporters for trying to influence public opinion—in the wrong direction—by which he seemed to mean almost anything short of blind support for the president's policies. His attacks on the television networks were especially unsettling, since the Federal Communications Commission regulates television and radio, and much of what Agnew said contained the implicit threat of regulating broadcast news.

The threat of regulation was not idle and did not originate with Agnew, nor with Buchanan and Safire. Prior to Nixon's silent majority speech, White House aides—notably Chief of Staff H.R. Haldeman and Jeb Magruder, then a White House communications aide—were trading memoranda between them exploring ways to expedite the president's desires to control the news and intimidate the media. Among the ideas they bandied about, and which they undoubtedly discussed with Nixon, were having the FCC monitor network news shows for "fairness" in their coverage of and commentary on Nixon and his policies, as well as a plan to have the IRS check the tax records of unfriendly reporters, editors, and news producers.

The White House set Agnew loose for a time after the silent majority speech and then again during the 1970 midterm campaign. Since hardly anyone thought him very dignified anyway, he could hit the hustings and say things that would sound unseemly coming from the president. The vice president made a handy mouthpiece for Buchanan's assaults on the liberal media and the antiwar protesters, although, contrary to popular belief, he actually came up with some of his own memorable rhetoric. Ultimately, the law of diminishing returns set in, prompting the White House to rein him in.

The decision to unleash Agnew came when Republican voters

reacted favorably to a speech the vice president delivered in New Orleans. Agnew's rampage combined attacks on the press with attacks on the liberal establishment itself, which Agnew, reaching a bit, labeled the "radic-lib" establishment in later speeches. The New Orleans speech, delivered on October 19, 1969, at a high-powered banquet, described "a spirit of national masochism" perpetuated and encouraged by "an effete corps of snobs" who called themselves intellectuals. The blurring of liberalism and radicalism was by no means accidental and it smacked of old-fashioned Red-baiting. Safire considered the later "radic-lib" uncomfortably close to the old "com-symp" of the 1950s, a contraction of "Communist sympathizer." The Nixon administration reverted to the old practice of attacking critics' patriotism, and Agnew enthusiastically enlisted as a shock trooper.

Much of the youth protest movement did in fact renounce loyalty to the United States, overtly supported the North Vietnamese, openly condemned the American system, and advocated violent revolution. But it is highly unlikely that this youthful rebellion posed any serious threat to American society and it is debatable whether or not it had any real effect turning the public against the war. Agnew's traveling circus act did not constitute a reasoned critique or any sort of coherent answer to the radical position, and to blur radicalism with liberalism deliberately confused the issues and played the politics of division.

Agnew had been seeking an active role in the administration for some time, having grown thoroughly bored presiding over the Senate and being kept out of the way by skittish White House staffers. His antics and blunders during the 1968 campaign earned him a reputation for ineptitude and made him a liability. But by the time he began his memorable assault on the major network news, some of Nixon's aides recognized that he could prove useful in unexpected ways. He delivered his most famous speech on November 13, 1969, in Des Moines at the Midwest Republican Conference. Buchanan wrote it with Safire's assistance, and Nixon himself put in a few sharp sentences. Agnew criticized network correspondents for their hostility to the president's speech on Vietnam earlier that month. He complained that a television reporter did not even have to say anything disapproving to get his message across; a "raised eyebrow, an inflection of the voice, a caustic remark dropped in the middle of a broadcast can raise doubts in a million minds about the veracity of a public official or the wisdom of a government policy."

The correspondents were "a little group of men who not only enjoy a right of instant rebuttal to every presidential address but, more importantly, wield a free hand in selecting, presenting, and interpreting the great issues of our nation." Working in the "intellectual confines" of Washington and New York City, network correspondents as a group are unrepresentative of the nation at large and influence public opinion way out of proportion to their own numbers or the composition of their ranks. "We should never trust such power over public opinion in the hands of an elected government—it is time we questioned it in the hands of a small and unelected elite. The great networks have dominated America's airwaves for decades; the people are entitled to a full accounting of their stewardship."

After Des Moines, there was heavy demand for Agnew to speak at Republican dinners all over the country, and Republican audiences, never friends of the press, loved his attacks on the likes of David Brinkley, whom the vice president had specifically named in Des Moines. For Agnew to be utilized effectively, the White House had to keep him under tight supervision, hence the advent of Buchanan, who normally worked as one of Nixon's own speechwriters. Agnew could not be left to his own devices; among his graceless blunders back in 1968 was his reference to a photographer as a "fat Jap." Clearly, he needed a leash.

Under Buchanan and Safire's tutelage, Agnew hit new heights of pedantic and alliterative invective, berating the "nattering nabobs of negativity" in one speech after another, in front of wildly appreciative Republican audiences. Agnew the buffoon transformed into Agnew the fire-eater. The press criticized him but showed a measure of new respect for this new and formidable adversary.

But that strange honeymoon did not last, for Agnew proved too much even for some Republicans. As the vice president launched attack after attack on the administration's favorite bugaboos, mostly antiwar demonstrators and reporters, some Republicans—including the party's national chairman, Rogers Morton—feared that Agnew's hostile polemics were beginning to alienate potential Republican voters. Extremism could not be the party's central position, no matter how much Agnew's act pleased the White House. The media and the antiwar movement were not such easy targets, after all.

Agnew next hit the front lines during the midterm election campaign of 1970, and both Buchanan and Safire again contributed to the vice president's alliterative career. Buchanan put into Agnew's now-legendary mouth such choice phrases as "pusillanimous pussyfooters," which much have taken some rehearsal, and Safire gleefully admitted to coming up with "vicars of vacillation." Safire also contributed the famous "nattering nabobs of negativity," and the less memorable "hopeless, hysterical hypochondriacs of history." Agnew came up with "radic-lib" on his own, to Safire's dismay, as noted. Agnew, Buchanan, and Safire did in fact have their tongues planted partly in their cheeks and had a lot of fun brainstorming alliterations. Initially, the press enjoyed much of the spectacle, but the divisive consequences of Agnew's rampage were serious. Here was a top administration spokesman calling for the heads of Nixon's enemies and whipping up the mob to bay for blood. It was a bit much, even for the Nixon administration.

The presidential party traditionally loses congressional seats in midterm elections, but Nixon, wisely or unwisely, decided not to involve himself in the 1970 campaign, at least not at first. He counted on Agnew to rally the Republican faithful and perhaps appeal to conservative Democrats as well. The whole tone of the White House's campaign was inflammatory and divisive, and late in the campaign, the *Christian Science Monitor* ran a headline proclaiming that Nixon continued to sound the alarm bells as the Reichstag refused to burn—an unflattering reference to

Adolf Hitler's campaign against dissidents after an unexplained fire destroyed the Reichstag, the home of the German Chamber of Deputies in Berlin. That a respected national newspaper like the *Monitor* employed such terms indicated how intense the hostility between the press and the president had become.

By the time of the *Monitor*'s bilious headline, the president had jumped into the fray and the vice president no longer bore the administration's standard against the Democrats, the antiwar movement, the intellectuals, the liberal establishment, and whoever else failed to line up behind Nixon's policies and programs. The most notable result of Nixon's late participation was one of his worst political mistakes. Among the results of his blunder was the instant elevation of a formidable challenger for the 1972 presidential election and panic in the White House. The chain of events began in San Jose, California, during Nixon's national tour to speak on behalf of Republican candidates.

The president had finished a speech in the Municipal Auditorium and, as he walked to his limousine, saw protesters just a few hundred feet away, uncertainly restrained by police barriers. They were in a furious mood and shouted obscenities. Nixon was seized by an urge to fire back, to show that he did not respect what he termed their mindless, childish rantings. He climbed onto the car's hood and gave the crowd his famous double V-sign, which at the time was widely imitated and ridiculed by professional and amateur impressionists. His gesture inflamed the crowd, and in seconds, rocks, eggs, vegetables, and other missiles rained down on the president of the United States. Nixon ducked into the car and the Secret Service agents immediately activated emergency-evacuation procedures.

Nixon decided to tackle the subject of dissent in his next scheduled campaign speech in Phoenix. Addressing an enthusiastically cheering crowd there two days later, the president referred to protesters as terrorists and thugs, and said they would not make the president of the United States a prisoner in the White House. His hyperbole may have been understandable, considering that he had just been attacked by a mob in California, but the speech was inflammatory. Unfortunately for him, serious technical problems made a bad situation worse, and the speech ended up seeming even more inflammatory than it actually was.

The problem was the videotape of the speech. It was wretched. The picture looked ragged and the sound track was at times muffled and at other times shrill. Nixon came across a rabble-rouser. No one informed the president that the tape was unusable, and so it played on a national Republican campaign broadcast. Millions of viewers watched President Nixon as he seemed literally to shriek and bray about terrorists and violence. It was so bad that Nixon and everyone else in the White House knew, as they watched the broadcast, that they had blundered horrendously.

The speech in many ways was perfectly in keeping with the general Republican campaign, painting the Democrats as unpatriotic coddlers of criminals and rioting thugs. Shortly thereafter, Senator Edmund Muskie of Maine appeared on national television to speak for the Democrats. It was a masterful performance. He sat in an easy chair in a cozy den or living room and spoke to the nation in calm, measured tones. He came across as statesmanlike, dignified, and, more than one journalist declared, presidential. Several analysts called him Lincolnesque. He spoke of moderation and sanity. His speech contrasted Nixon's exhibition in many glaring ways, not the least of which was that he, a Democratic senator, called for unity and thoughtful, moderate action, while the Republican president had screeched about terrorists in our midst. As a result, Muskie was the instant front-runner for the Democratic nomination two years hence. The press declared that to be so the very next day, and the nation's newspapers and magazines gushed praise for the dignified Muskie and decried the president's crude histrionics. One editorialist commented that Nixon had "reverted to type."

His favorable press notices meant that Muskie would be the most formidable Democrat Nixon could face, and Nixon and his men quickly assessed that South Dakota senator George McGovern would be the weakest.

McGovern was already a prospect for the 1972 nomination but widely considered an unlikely choice since his stance against the Vietnam War marked him as a one-issue candidate. Like Eugene McCarthy before him, he stood as the quixotic crusader in a lost cause, but, also like McCarthy, he was about to surprise everybody. He had thrown his hat in the ring late in 1968, after Robert Kennedy's assassination, but his candidacy did not amount to much that year. In 1970, hardly anyone thought his 1972 candidacy would amount to anything, either.

The Nixon White House targeted Muskie for sabotage; their strategy was to do everything possible to defeat him and, once they assessed the range of candidates, they tried to eliminate other Democrats they believed would be stronger than George McGovern. But long before the public became aware that the White House was out to destroy Muskie, another battle with the press intervened, which had consequences beyond anyone's immediate comprehension.

That incident, which brought out the Nixon administration's worst in the war against the press, involved a leak that did not directly concern the administration at all, although it was probably the greatest leak in history. The gusher in question, known to history as the Pentagon Papers, was a collection of classified documents that held damning information about Lyndon Johnson's escalation of the Vietnam War. A former Defense Department analyst named Daniel Ellsberg leaked them to the *New York Times* in June 1971.

When the *Times* broke the story and published excerpts of the classified documents, a major scandal erupted and the Nixon administration considered prosecuting the *Times* and other papers that reprinted the excerpts for possession and publication of classified federal documents, or under espionage laws, or any other statutes that might apply. The White House never followed through on that; the constitutional issues would have been intricate, and a good result for the administration could not be taken for granted. The White House initially secured a court order to bar any further publication of material from the

Pentagon Papers, but shortly thereafter the Supreme Court set the order aside as violating the First Amendment.

Within days, the leaker's name was out; a reporter angered the journalistic community by publicly revealing Ellsberg as the source. Nixon ordered the Justice Department to indict Ellsberg, and in due course he went on trial for theft and espionage. But the president also wanted Ellsberg discredited, and subsequently a secret group of burglars, put together by the White House, headed by G. Gordon Liddy and E. Howard Hunt, and known in the administration as the "plumbers," broke into the office of Ellsberg's psychiatrist, Dr. Lewis Fielding. The burglary eventually led to the prosecution and imprisonment not only of the two head burglars, but of Haldeman and Ehrlichman, Nixon's two closest aides.

Some close observers, such as Ehrlichman, thought that Nixon went a little crazy over the Pentagon Papers. As a consequence, the administration resorted to the series of illegal activities that led right to Watergate. The plumbers were formed to "plug" unauthorized leaks, and one method was to intimidate leakers. Finding dirt on Ellsberg in his therapist's files looked like a marvelously effective way to discredit him and discourage potential leakers.

The only trouble was that Dr. Fielding was one step ahead and kept Ellsberg's file under a false name. The plumbers ransacked the office to create the impression of a normal burglary and left empty-handed. When the burglary became public knowledge as part of the Watergate revelations during 1973 and 1974, that killed any chance of convicting Ellsberg. The judge had no choice but to declare a mistrial since the very government that was prosecuting Ellsberg had committed crimes in order to discredit him.

That was not the only instance of White House interference in the Ellsberg case. While the trial was still in progress, Ehrlichman met with the presiding judge, Matthew Byrne, to tell him that the president was considering him for the post of FBI director. Byrne saw nothing improper about the conference, expressed interest, and was glad to go to San Clemente to meet President Nixon personally. Whether or not the meeting was improper, it *appeared* so to many, including, on later reflection, Judge Byrne. He included the meeting among the reasons for declaring a mistrial.

Some of the same burglars who broke into Dr. Fielding's office later were caught red-handed in the Democratic National Committee's offices in the Watergate complex. Their activities were part of a string of crimes that Attorney General John Mitchell, himself heavily involved in some of them, later called the "White House horrors," a label many Washington reporters and columnists picked up and used extensively, including a few who previously had been pro-Nixon. The horrors were extensive and far-reaching. Among the criminal acts that Nixon and his aides contemplated, but never implemented, was firebombing the Brookings Institution in New York. A friend of Ellsberg had given the institution sensitive materials related to the Pentagon Papers, and Nixon wanted them retrieved. He did not want classified documents floating around in New York, much less in a liberal think tank that might do God only knew what with them.

He also wanted to look at them himself, as they may have contained information about President Johnson's decision to halt bombing in Vietnam in 1968; Nixon frankly admitted that knowledge of the processes behind that decision might give him political leverage against members of the Johnson administration who now were attacking his own Vietnam policies. The president meant to retrieve the papers by means of another burglary, if necessary—something he admitted in his memoirs. Several of his close aides have since claimed that they and Nixon considered the firebombing idea, and one or two former aides asserted that it originated with the president.

Years later, in various writings, Nixon bitterly lamented that men like Ehrlichman and Haldeman went to prison while Ellsberg went free. He took no note of the fact that Ellsberg went free because the administration's own illegal acts forced Judge Byrne to declare a mistrial, and that Haldeman and Ehrlichman went to prison for specific federal offenses. He also never fully admitted knowing anything about the burglary in advance, although various White House staffers, including Ehrlichman, later insisted that he had. The most Nixon ever said about the burglary was that he did not *think* he knew about it ahead of time but, given "the temper of the times," had he been asked about it, he may not have quashed the plan. Whatever Nixon did or did not directly order, had the administration not committed crimes and other improprieties, there would have been no grounds for mistrial and the Ellsberg case would have proceeded on its merits. Nixon's sabotage backfired, but that did not stop him from complaining about the results.

Nixon viewed the Pentagon Papers as a horrendous misdeed, and perhaps it was. Nixon thought the press horribly irresponsible to publish the papers, and perhaps he was correct. He felt justified in conducting an ongoing campaign to control and intimidate the press in retaliation for the papers and to prevent any similar leaks in the future. In this he was terribly wrong and in the process violated the Constitution of the United States.

Several Nixon advisers tried to persuade him to ignore the Pentagon Papers and simply let the situation run its course. After all, they argued, their release only hurts the Democrats. If anything, it made Nixon look good; the chronicle of Democratic blunders and purposeful misdeeds could create the impression that Nixon was the sane, capable leader who cleaned up the mess that Lyndon Johnson and his idiot Democrats made of things in Vietnam. Among the many embarrassing revelations in the Pentagon Papers was the suggestion that the Johnson administration faked the incident that led to the initial escalation in Vietnam.

During the summer of 1964, President Johnson reported that North Vietnamese PT boats had attacked two American destroyers in the Gulf of Tonkin. In retaliation, Johnson ordered direct air attacks on North Vietnam. Congress promptly passed the Gulf of Tonkin Resolution, which, in effect, gave the president a blank check in Vietnam by authorizing "all necessary measures to repel any armed attack against the forces of the United States and to prevent further aggression." Johnson told Congress that he had no intention to escalate the conflict, but Oregon senator Wayne Morse, one of the only two senators to vote against the resolution (Ernest Gruening of Alaska was the other), called the resolution a virtual declaration of war.

The Pentagon Papers suggested that the event was a lie, that North Vietnamese PT boats never attacked any American ships, that the Johnson administration had pulled one of the all-time scams on the Congress of the United States. All of that is far from certain, despite the fact that it has entered American folklore as received truth, and in his memoirs Nixon stated his opinion that the attacks indeed took place, as Johnson had reported to Congress. However, the impression that LBJ lied his way into escalating the war quickly took root across the country and, many of Nixon's men told him, that could only benefit Nixon.

But Nixon did not see it that way, and he was probably correct. He undoubtedly did not shy from damning a Democratic predecessor, but he knew that the Pentagon Papers' effects reached far beyond simple public relations or political gamesmanship. The credibility of the United States was at stake in the world community. A government that could not keep its secrets, that could let something like the Pentagon Papers slip by, was a government that could not fully govern, could not implement foreign policy, and therefore negotiated from weakness rather than strength. The Pentagon Papers case had to be prosecuted in the courts, and the Nixon administration had to make it clear to the American people and to the world that such leaks would not be tolerated and that United States foreign policy was credible, workable, and foreign governments could trust America to keep its word and guard the secrets that international relations entailed. Were the administration simply to exploit the Pentagon Papers in order to humiliate the Democrats, Nixon realized, it would backfire on him.

Nixon's views were all well-reasoned and valid, but the steps his administration chose to take were misguided, destructive, and thoroughly illegal. Nixon's reaction to the Pentagon Papers brings us back to the old cliché of the two Nixons: The statesman adeptly assessed the problems that the Pentagon Papers posed, but the scoundrel could only think of shady, clandestine, and vengeful ways to deal with those problems. The administration went to war against two enemies: Daniel Ellsberg and the press. Both were ill-chosen, and the war was a losing one.

Nixon did not see it at the time, but his presidency was at stake. He put it on the line the moment he authorized forming the plumbers, the clandestine unit that existed to break laws. Its very existence broke the law; the White House is not authorized to create and fund its own agencies without consulting Congress. Once the Oval Office went into the business of domestic spying and covert operations, it took upon itself functions that were neither constitutional nor legal.

In the 1972 campaign, Nixon quickly became convinced that reporters favored the Democratic nominee, South Dakota senator George McGovern, just as they had favored John F. Kennedy in 1960. McGovern, in Nixon's opinion, was an inept campaigner and a one-issue candidate, and the liberal news establishment collaborated in cleaning up his image to help him appear more effective and intelligent than he was. In his later writings, Nixon refers on several occasions to McGovern "having his newspapers" print such and such an item, as if the senator exercised actual control over the media. Nixon ignored the fact that most of the major newspapers endorsed him for reelection and that much of the coverage of McGovern concentrated on his inept campaigning and the weaknesses of many of his arguments and positions.

The *New York Times*, a notable exception, endorsed McGovern and condemned Nixon for presiding over a "sinister" system of domestic spying and for attempts to stifle opposition through intimidation. By the time of that endorsement, the Watergate break-in had occurred and the nation was slowly becoming aware of the plumbers and the administration's other clandes-

SENATOR GEORGE MCGOVERN, 1972.

tine activities. However, all that had little, if any, effect on the public-opinion polls; people simply seemed not to care about Watergate, and the *Times* spoke in a lonely voice.

As far as Nixon was concerned, McGovern was another favored Democrat, and Nixon was sure the Kennedy machine backed him. That kind of support meant that the liberal media and mighty East Coast liberal elite would rally their considerable forces to promote McGovern. The president groused that those glittering liberals had gotten us into Vietnam in the first place, but now they blamed Nixon for trying to win the war they started, and had chosen a champion to bring him down. Regardless of Nixon's commanding lead in every significant public-opinion poll, the White House followed the dictates of its siege mentality and determined to counteract and preempt the attacks of Nixon's powerful enemies.

Nixon's fear of McGovern's supposed power over the press was especially absurd since McGovern was the candidate Nixon wanted to run against. After all, he had figured that McGovern would be far weaker than Senator Hubert Humphrey, who nearly beat Nixon in 1968, or the White House's most feared opponent, Muskie, who ran for vice president in 1968 and made that Lincolnesque speech in 1970. By the 1972 primary season, Nixon's men already had been at work for quite some time finding ways to weaken Muskie and derail his campaign for the Democratic nomination. White House operatives planted unflattering comments and stories in the press about Muskie and spread rumors that Muskie was racist and sexist.

The most memorable public result of these efforts came during the New Hampshire primary campaign, when operatives spread a rumor that Muskie had used the word "Canuck" to speak detrimentally of Canadians. At an outdoor press conference in New Hampshire, Muskie vehemently denied the canard, and for a moment burst into tears. On film, Muskie's brief fit does not look very serious, but word of mouth played it up as an intemperate emotional outburst. It never does a candidate good to lose his composure in public, even momentarily. The press had been successfully manipulated, and so had Muskie.

Whatever the actual effect of the story, Muskie won the primary with only 46 percent of the vote. McGovern won 37 percent. That turned the Democratic race on its head; McGovern had done to Muskie what Senator Eugene McCarthy did to President Lyndon Johnson in 1968, when McCarthy won 40 percent of the New Hampshire vote and thus showed Johnson's weakness. Muskie in February 1972 was the overwhelming Democratic favorite, and many pundits considered his nomination inevitable. Many also had him pegged as the next president, for he was nearly even with Nixon in the opinion polls, and hardly anyone took McGovern seriously. Muskie had a lot to lose in New Hampshire and, with his small margin of victory and McGovern's impressive showing, he lost it. Muskie's campaign never got back on track, and McGovern soon emerged as the front-runner.

In many ways, McGovern had Nixon to thank for the Democratic nomination, although the South Dakotan did in fact run an effective and energetic campaign against his Democratic rivals. His run for the nomination was as brilliant as his actual presidential campaign was incompetent. Once McGovern won the nomination, his inept efforts and terrible mistakes should have reassured Nixon that he was about to win reelection in a walk, but, years later, in several of his books, Nixon insisted that the liberal press promoted McGovern and, he implied, that made McGovern a formidable opponent. At the same time, in another classic Nixonian contradiction, he fully appreciated the Democratic campaign's sheer incompetence.

The McGovern campaign was wrecked before it properly began. At the Democratic convention, after the McGovern forces brilliantly dominated the action and virtually monopolized the floor, on the last day, everything essentially fell apart. McGovern delivered his acceptance speech at almost 1:00 A.M. Eastern time, thus losing most of the television audience. The delegates had squandered the prime-time hours with endless symbolic, quarrelsome, and ultimately meaningless motions and debates on the convention floor. The sorry spectacle gave the impression of a chaotic Democratic party and a presidential nominee who could not exert control and restore order. A campaign in that condition was not likely to exercise any coordinated control over any large or small news agencies. But no one could convince Nixon of that.

When the campaign was under way, McGovern suffered a devastating blow that in and of itself may have proved fatal, even if the rest of his campaign were not inept and the Nixon campaign so masterful and ruthless. Early in the campaign season, the story broke in the supposedly pro-McGovern press that his vice presidential running mate, Senator Tom Eagleton, suffered a breakdown some years earlier, and while hospitalized received shock treatments and medication. The story made national headlines and appeared on all the network news shows. The question hung heavily in the air: Was a former mental patient fit for the vice presidency?

What followed was painful. Under questioning from the press,

Eagleton said that he had learned to deal with stress by pacing himself. That came across poorly; it sounded anemic and unconvincing from a candidate for high national office. He was perfectly sane and stable, but he seemed to plead for understanding rather than assert his competence and mental good health. Once a candidate is on the defensive, the battle usually has been lost.

McGovern made matters worse. First he claimed to back Eagleton completely, then over the next few days publicly wavered and, finally, Eagleton resigned from the ticket, and the Democrats replaced him with R. Sargent Shriver, brother-in-law of the Kennedys and the first director of the Peace Corps during John F. Kennedy's presidency. Democratic National Chairman Lawrence O'Brien said publicly that the campaign was off to a bad start, which stated the obvious and delivered a rather pessimistic message to the party faithful. The press thoroughly covered all these damaging developments.

The press reaction to the Eagleton affair should have convinced Nixon that reporters were not conducting any coordinated efforts to unseat him and elect McGovern. Nixon, of course, simply assumed that reporters loved a story more than anything, including McGovern.

For Nixon, the whole mess sounded ugly echoes of his own experience in 1952, and he felt a real empathy for Eagleton and his family, just as he had felt genuinely sorry for Edward Kennedy immediately after Chappaquiddick. He took the trouble to write a long letter to Eagleton's young son, telling him that he should be proud of his father for acting so well during such a critical time. Privately, Nixon criticized McGovern for not supporting his own people.

McGovern's campaign never recovered from the Eagleton affair, and McGovern essentially hanged himself by campaigning primarily on the Vietnam issue. The few times he made any significant statements about other issues, particularly social ones, he performed so ineptly that he left himself open to devastating attacks by the Republicans. Nixon personally concocted many of the Republican answers to McGovern's proposed programs, and they were employed to devastating effect. For instance, the Republicans successfully portrayed McGovern's vague ideas for welfare reform as a plan to pay out a thousand dollars to every single American, a pretty outrageous idea from nearly any viewpoint.

Nixon considered McGovern a political radical, and fretted and raged that the press obscured his extremism. Nixon maintained that the public for the most part failed to see the truth because the news media portrayed McGovern as more moderate and reasonable than he was. Many reporters, Nixon insisted, believed most of what McGovern believed. They were a bunch of radicals, too. But, Nixon noted years later, there were exceptions. The *Christian Science Monitor*, by no means consistently friendly to Nixon, editorialized about the "love affair" between McGovern and many of the reporters covering the campaign. The *Monitor* asserted that these reporters gave McGovern a "free ride." Nixon could not have agreed more.

Nixon's victory over McGovern was overwhelming. The Democrat carried only Massachusetts and the District of Columbia; not even South Dakota could rouse itself to support its native son. A combination of Democratic ineptitude, Republican ruthlessness, and Nixon's record of real achievement doomed the Democratic nominee to crash and burn that November. Nixon should have felt on top of the world, but he did not. Some of his discomfort was due to an agonizing dental condition that he had no time to have treated before Election Day. But it also was because of Nixon's character; as many of his biographers have noted, he was magnificent in defeat but at his worst in victory.

Nixon did not wait until the final victory to revert to his worst. During the summer of 1972, months before the election, White House burglars broke into the Democratic National Committee's offices in the Watergate complex twice. Initially they went in to bug the telephones; the second time, they went in to inspect and repair a few bugs that were not working. On that second caper, they were caught and hauled off to jail by the Washington Metropolitan police.

PART III
NIXON AND THE DEMOCRATS

★ ★ ★ ★ ★ ★ ★ ★

1960:

"I WANT TO SAVE THE COUNTRY FROM HIM"

Richard Nixon's 1960 presidential campaign against John F. Kennedy destroyed a friendship and created one of the epic enmities of American political history. It may not have been a beautiful friendship, but, prior to 1960, Nixon held John Kennedy in high regard, and Kennedy appeared to reciprocate. Their rivalry for the White House made them bitter competitors and enemies thereafter, despite continued public cordiality between them and even the considerable compassion Nixon showed President Kennedy after the Bay of Pigs fiasco. Nixon and others have argued that Kennedy initially turned on Nixon. That may be true, or partly true, but one must bear in mind that Nixon had a way of converting political rivals into personal foes.

Richard Nixon and John F. Kennedy both entered the House of Representatives in 1947; Kennedy represented a mostly blue-collar district in Cambridge, Massachusetts. Kennedy's father, Joseph Kennedy, Sr., was a famous business tycoon, later head of the Securities and Exchange Commission, then President Franklin Roosevelt's ambassador to Great Britain. His father's position gave young John an unusual view of history in the making, with a ringside seat at the start of World War II. John Kennedy put that remarkable experience to good use for his Harvard University master's thesis, a study of England's lack of preparedness for war. He later published it as a book, *Why England Slept.*

Like Nixon, Kennedy served in the Pacific as a naval officer. Unlike Nixon, Kennedy wound up being lionized as a war hero after a Japanese destroyer rammed and sank the PT boat that he commanded. Two crewmen were killed, and in the dead of night the survivors swam for an atoll several miles away. One injured crewman could not swim; Kennedy took the man's life jacket cord in his teeth and towed him. Kennedy and his crew spent several hellish days on the atoll; Kennedy and another crewman swam out to sea nightly to watch for friendly craft they could signal. Ultimately, they were rescued.

As the son of the famous Ambassador Joseph Kennedy, JFK the war hero made good news copy, and the press duly publicized the story of *PT 109.* That boosted Kennedy's postwar political ambitions and, following his father's plan, he won a House seat in 1946. Congressman John F. Kennedy began the famous love affair between the working classes and the aristocratic Kennedy family, thus joining that American tradition of upper-class social activists, often charismatic leaders, with large blue-collar followings. Theodore, Franklin, and Eleanor Roosevelt all belong to that tradition, but they came from an older American aristocracy. The Kennedys carried the affinity of their immigrant Irish roots.

Though members of opposing parties, the two freshmen representatives held a number of similar positions. Both were moderately liberal on most social issues, both supported civil rights (although Nixon was the more outspoken, and years later, Senator Kennedy voted against a civil rights bill that Vice President Nixon supported), and both voted for the Marshall Plan and American participation in NATO. They found each other personally congenial and served together on the House Education and Labor Committee.

In those early years, Nixon outshined Kennedy. The young Democrat, for all his charisma and wealth, conducted a fairly routine congressional career, as his future rival gained national attention for his part in the Hiss-Chambers case. When Nixon ran for the Senate in 1950, Joseph Kennedy, Sr., sent a thousand-dollar contribution through his son. In 1952, Kennedy moved into the Senate by defeating the incumbent from Massachusetts, Henry Cabot Lodge, Nixon's future vice presidential running mate and later, President Kennedy's ambassador to South Vietnam. When Kennedy was elected senator, Nixon was elected vice president.

The senator's health problems were far worse than the public knew, until after his death. Besides suffering the debilitating effects of Addison's disease, his recurring back problems crippled him periodically during his Senate career. In 1954, Kennedy underwent back surgery and came so close to death that he received last rites from a Catholic priest. Nixon, in private with a Secret Service agent, burst into tears at the thought of Kennedy's impending demise. Afterward, when Kennedy could only walk with crutches, Vice President Nixon made some of his own office space available to his friend to spare him the agonizing and exhausting trip between the Senate chamber and his office.

Kennedy recovered, and sought the Democratic vice presidential nomination in 1956, but lost to Senator Estes Kefauver, who in turn was defeated with Adlai Stevenson at the hands of Eisenhower and Nixon. After that, his presidential ambitions were out in the open, and relations between Kennedy and Nixon started to change.

When Nixon realized that Kennedy might stand in the way of his own presidential ambitions, his competitive impulses kicked in, and his ever-present class hostility showed itself. At a 1958 banquet, both men made graceful speeches in praise of the guest of honor, and Kennedy, speaking first, employed a few Latin phrases. According to Christopher Matthews, author of *Kennedy and Nixon*, when it came Nixon's turn to speak, he took a shot at his erudite colleague. "I might have used a Latin phrase, but I didn't go to Harvard." Matthews recorded a comment by Charles Colson, the future Watergate figure, who was present as an aide to another senator. "I recognized . . . his resentment against the whole Kennedy–Harvard monied establishment. It came out as a joke, but in the humor was the truth."

Kennedy won the 1960 Democratic nomination against tough competition from Senate Majority Leader Lyndon Johnson and Minnesota senator Hubert Humphrey. Nixon faced no real competition for the Republican nomination, despite the fact that Eisenhower, during his second term, expressed doubts about his vice president's fitness to succeed him and tried to encourage one or two others to seek the nomination. Both rivals had obstacles, therefore, in 1960. Nixon faced uncertain Republican unity and unsteady White House support. Kennedy had to contend with anti-Catholic prejudice, rumors that his father "bought" him the nomination, and doubts about his maturity.

Nixon, at forty-seven, was not much older, but he was more experienced in many areas, including world affairs, and could at least claim that he had served at Eisenhower's right hand for the past eight years. Nixon supporters did indeed make much of Nixon's experience compared with Kennedy's, often portraying the senator as a happy-go-lucky playboy, an absentee senator, and an indifferent public servant. The Kennedy people countered by portraying their man as an agent of change, a leader who would invigorate the nation after eight years of Eisenhower's gray, sepulchral gerontocracy.

For Nixon, the 1960 presidential campaign was a distinct departure from his earlier duels. The public's appetite for Red-baiting had subsided considerably, a fact driven home to Nixon and other Republicans by the disastrous 1958 midterm election results. In 1960, McCarthy had been dead three years, and public attention was focused more on the Soviet threat than on domestic subversives. In the South, the growing civil rights movement would rise to prominence during the campaign season. Kennedy succeeded in taking the high ground in both civil rights and the cold war, as Nixon faltered on both counts.

Nixon found himself in the position that vice presidents typically face when seeking the presidency: He could not run entirely as his own man. On the one hand, he could bask in Ike's reflected glory, but on the other, he had to bear the burden of any voter dissatisfaction with the incumbent administration.

The people still gave Eisenhower high ratings, but after the recent economic downturn, they would likely saddle Vice President Nixon with their dissatisfaction and restlessness. After eight years as Ike's boy, Nixon himself looked rather stodgy. He also was the first sitting vice president to run for president since 1860, so he and his analysts were exploring new territory, and for all intents and purposes had to blaze new trails. They did this with uneven results.

Kennedy had to blaze new trails, too, owing to his relative youth and his religion. Only one other Roman Catholic had ever run for president as a major party's nominee: Democrat Alfred Smith, governor of New York, lost to Republican Herbert Hoover by a landslide in 1928. That was not encouraging. But Kennedy appeared confident and, to Nixon's sorrowful surprise, he knew how to act like a winner. With his fashionable wardrobe and athlete's grace, Kennedy looked very much like a movie star running for president. Only a few knew that his apparent physicality hid dangerously poor health. He billed himself as an agent of change, as the man who would get America moving again— assuming that the country spent the Eisenhower years frozen in some gray stasis. Kennedy accused the administration of botching the cold war, and put himself on the side of civil rights.

Nixon did none of these things. His position prevented him from doing the first, he had no inclination to do the second, and a terrible error of judgment and perhaps uncharacteristic political cowardice prevented him from doing the third at a crucial moment.

In October 1960, Dr. Martin Luther King, Jr., was arrested and jailed following civil rights protests in Atlanta. Kennedy called King's pregnant young wife to express his sympathy and offered to help in any way he could. Around the same time, his brother Robert, serving as his campaign manager, talked an Atlanta judge into releasing King on bail. Coretta Scott King subsequently told the press of Senator Kennedy's call, and coolly noted that Vice President Nixon had been "very quiet" during the crisis. Nixon in fact had a chance to act and decided against it for fear of alienating Southern white voters.

The white South had been solidly Democratic since Reconstruction, but Eisenhower had made inroads among white Southern voters, and Nixon considered them crucial in what was shaping up as a close presidential contest. But the vice president was going against his own political record. Nixon knew King personally and as vice president had a laudable record of backing civil rights legislation, as well as outspoken support of racial equality and integration. He was way ahead of the socially conservative Eisenhower, who found black civil rights activism troubling.

Baseball legend Jackie Robinson, a previously cordial Nixon acquaintance, called on Nixon and asked him to intervene for King in Georgia. Robinson and other prominent black leaders had no reason to think that Nixon would balk at helping King, but they were in for a shock. Reportedly, Robinson left the meeting in tears and told reporters that Nixon "doesn't understand."

Nixon's failure to support King alienated many African-American voters, and his good reputation among them was forever lost. Kennedy usurped Nixon's role as the civil rights advocate, even though three years earlier Senator Kennedy voted against civil rights legislation that Vice President Nixon supported. Nixon and Martin Luther King, Jr., had even regarded each other as political allies, but now the situation permanently changed. The Reverend Martin Luther King, Sr., pastor of an Atlanta church, told the press that he originally intended not to vote for Kennedy because he was Catholic, but since Kennedy had helped his son, the reverend would deliver a "suitcase" of votes into the senator's lap.

On the cold war front, Nixon found himself in the most unfamiliar position of his career, as Kennedy and the Democrats got some of their own back after years of Republican Red-baiting. Kennedy implied that the Eisenhower administration was soft on communism. He blamed the administration for a decline of America's international prestige, and criticized the president for botching the summit with Khrushchev earlier that year, when the Soviet leader stormed out, roaring with rage over the U-2 incident. Kennedy attacked Eisenhower's defense spending as insufficient and spoke of a "missile gap" between the United States and the Soviet Union. Those charges were unfair, although Eisenhower was far from a defense spendthrift, to the chagrin of the Pentagon. Additionally, the so-called "missile gap" did not exist.

For the first time, Nixon had to argue that he was just as tough as his opponent when it came to fighting communism. Helen Gahagan Douglas tried to turn that table on Nixon in 1950, with farcical results. Kennedy was a far more effective campaigner than Douglas, however, and his charges hurt. That Fidel Castro established a Communist government in Cuba barely a year earlier did not help Nixon, either, even though he had figured out that Castro was a Communist before Eisenhower did. Kennedy made much of the Communist presence ninety miles from Florida, and Nixon was in the unenviable position of having to argue that Castro's triumph was not Eisenhower's fault. While Kennedy never adopted the shrill, accusatory tones of the past, the state of affairs still harked back to 1949, when the Republicans lambasted the Democrats for "losing" China. Now the Republicans had "lost" Cuba.

All of this came into play when, for the first time in American history, two presidential candidates met to debate. American college students frequently identify the Lincoln-Douglas debates as the first presidential debates, but they are wrong. Lincoln and Douglas were competing for the Senate in 1858, and Douglas, the incumbent, won, two years before Lincoln beat him for the presidency. So Nixon and Kennedy were pioneers, and the debates define the 1960 campaign for many Americans.

The first debate was a disaster for Nixon. Just out of the hospital after suffering a serious knee infection, he looked pale and drawn and, on the way into the studio, bumped his bad knee. He was in terrible pain and refused to wear makeup, so in the harsh studio lights his face looked like something off a post office wanted poster.

Kennedy, by contrast, looked tan and rested, healthier and fitter than he actually was. Kennedy simply outperformed Nixon, and the Democratic campaign got a wonderful boost. Reportedly,

UPI CORBIS-BETTMANN

SENATOR JOHN KENNEDY AND
VICE PRESIDENT RICHARD NIXON, 1960.

Nixon's running mate, Henry Cabot Lodge, watched the debate
on television and blurted out, "That son of a bitch just lost the
election for us." Whichever son of a bitch he meant, the point was
the same.

Many have asked why Nixon agreed to the debates in the
first place, but others, including Nixon himself, have argued that
he could not credibly refuse. The networks suggested the
debates; Kennedy was willing and eager, and Nixon thought that
if he refused, both Kennedy and the hostile news media would
make an issue of his refusal. He had more to lose than Kennedy
did; he was the more famous and familiar of the two and his position as vice president automatically placed him on the defensive
since Kennedy, effectively the challenger, was free to attack the
administration while Nixon would have to defend Eisenhower
and himself, without much room to maneuver.

But Nixon did not walk into the debates with a sense of
impending doom or defeat. He was confident that he would
outdo his rival. The vice president was a formal debater in high

school and college, was comfortable speaking to large audiences, and had much more experience playing on the national and international stage than Kennedy had. He grew still less reluctant after observing Kennedy's speaking style. Again contrary to popular memory, Kennedy was not consistently a good speaker. He was capable of riveting performances—but not always. Many of his speeches were dull and his delivery often halting. Several of his appearances on interview shows were unimpressive, and his acceptance speech at the Democratic convention failed to ring the rafters, save for his call for a "new frontier." Nixon was not looking at the charismatic JFK of legend; he sized up the living, far from flawless Senator John F. Kennedy of Massachusetts.

The second and third debates came out more evenly as far as audience responses were concerned. Nixon, more presentable and healthier than in the first go-round, performed with considerably more strength and polish, and Kennedy was not so clearly ahead, despite today's popular memories. In the fourth debate, as Nixon tells the story, a cruel twist of fate stuck him with having to argue *against* a policy in which he believed and that he knew was secretly in effect. Additionally, Nixon felt a special sense of betrayal, since he was sure that Kennedy had received a foreign policy briefing from the CIA prior to the fourth debate.

The fourth debate took place on October 21, in New York. Kennedy advocated aiding a rebel insurgency against Fidel Castro's Communist regime in Cuba. What Nixon knew and the voters did not was that the Bay of Pigs operation was in the planning stages. The Eisenhower administration had for some time trained, funded, and supplied Cuban exiles for an assault on Cuba that, they hoped, would bring on a popular uprising against Castro once the exiles hit the Cuban shores. Nixon was sure that Kennedy knew this and had taken his position knowing that Nixon could not reveal what he knew. If that is true, then Kennedy stole Nixon's thunder and posed as the more militant cold warrior.

Nixon took evasive action. According to his later account,

he felt compelled to argue against Kennedy's position, which was his own and the administration's position. In order to guard the plan's secrecy, Nixon pretended that he thought it irresponsible to advocate overt intervention in Cuba. He described his ruse as "the most uncomfortable and ironic duty" he ever had to carry out during a campaign. He bemoaned the fact that Kennedy managed to appear "tougher on Castro and communism than I was."

A question arises: Why did Nixon feel compelled to offer a strong argument against intervention in Cuba? He could have suggested a certain restraint without creating the impression that the very thought horrified him. He could have offered a ringing denunciation of Castro and the Communists and pledged that a Nixon administration would do everything in its power, would take every responsible action, to bring freedom to the Cuban people. Why Nixon felt he had to represent himself as thinking the exact opposite of what he actually thought puzzles many chroniclers, not just this author.

The day after, the *Washington Post* praised Nixon for his restraint on Cuba, which Nixon took as a dubious honor. Kennedy actually backed off from his interventionist stance after a certain amount of negative reaction from reporters and columnists, but he had made a lasting impression on the television audience. However, as Nixon later noted, the election was so close that it is impossible to determine how much any one or all of the debates affected the vote. On Election Day, the opinion polls showed the candidates almost dead even, separated by less than a percentage point.

The transformation of Nixon and Kennedy's relationship into mutual enmity completed itself long before Election Day. Kennedy said privately on several occasions that he had an awesome responsibility, since he was all that stood between Dick Nixon and the White House. Nixon waged a restrained and fairly responsible campaign, possibly his first, but resented what he considered Kennedy's dirty tactics and the press's love affair with Young Jack, his beautiful and pregnant wife, Jackie, and their adorable little daughter, Caroline. Nixon had a beautiful family, too, but the press concentrated on the future denizens of Camelot.

Kennedy's private criticisms of Nixon turned personal and, it must be said, sounded much like upper-class snobbery. Kennedy ridiculed Nixon's lack of style and told people that Nixon had no taste. He recalled his father's 1950 thousand-dollar contribution to Nixon and told friends and supporters that delivering it was the "biggest damn fool mistake" he ever made. Only days before the election, Kennedy told *Time*, "When I first began this campaign, I just wanted to beat Nixon. Now I want to save the country from him."

Nixon conducted himself with restraint in public and never made his feelings about Kennedy's tactics a campaign issue. Overall, Nixon treated his opponent respectfully, a radical departure for him. Nixon hardly attacked Kennedy at all, and the attacks he did launch were models of restraint. He even defended Kennedy on occasion, strenuously explaining that he did not doubt Kennedy's honesty and patriotism. Here was a new Nixon. Unfortunately for him, he faced a new Kennedy.

Significantly more unfortunate for Nixon, President Eisenhower was not much help and even did some damage. Early in the campaign, Eisenhower was finishing a press conference when a reporter asked him if his vice president had contributed any major ideas to the administration during the past eight years. In one of the most wondrous political gaffes of the twentieth century, the president irritably replied, "If you give me a week, I might think of one." Eisenhower afterward apologized to Nixon and explained that his thought had come out wrong. Nixon's interpretation was that Eisenhower, tired and cranky after all the questions, misspoke and meant something more like, "Ask me at the next press conference."

That may sound like wishful thinking, until one recalls that the president had suffered a major heart attack and a serious stroke and was in unsteady health. Some have argued that Eisenhower consciously or unconsciously sought to undermine Nixon, and there is the fact that Eisenhower previously expressed doubts about Nixon's fitness for the presidency. On the other hand, the episode could as easily be read as the tired reaction of a sick old man who never fully recovered from his stroke and was grouchy when reporters would not cease their questioning once the press conference had officially ended. It was not generally known at the time, but after his stroke Eisenhower had difficulty finding the words to express his thoughts. Nixon wrote of that in his memoirs, describing how painful it was for him to watch the president grow frustrated as he groped for words in private conversations.

Nixon later claimed that a worried Mamie Eisenhower asked Nixon to discourage the president from actively participating in the campaign. She asked him never to tell Eisenhower of her request, and, as Nixon recorded it years later, the president was visibly bewildered when he offered to dive into the campaign and Nixon talked him out of it. Several Nixon biographers have expressed skepticism about this story.

The election result was the closest since 1888, when Democratic incumbent Grover Cleveland won a close popular vote but lost the electoral vote, and the presidency, to Republican Benjamin Harrison. Kennedy won 34,221,463 votes, which counted for 49.7 percent; Nixon won 34,108,582, or 49.6 percent of the popular vote. The margin was an agonizingly close 112,881 votes. Kennedy won the electoral vote 303 to 219.

There were allegations that Democrats committed voter fraud in Illinois and Texas, and the evidence was strong enough that people around Nixon urged him to demand a recount. He decided otherwise, for reasons both responsible and political. To tie up the election results would bring the presidency to a standstill and paralyze foreign policy. Politically, Nixon would look like the all-time sore loser, especially if the votes proved legitimate. When the president-elect and the outgoing vice president met face-to-face shortly after the election, Kennedy said that the outcome looked in doubt. Nixon responded, "No, you are the winner."

With the 1960 campaign over, the landscape of Nixon's life was forever changed. The following January, for the first time in fourteen years, he held no elective office. He carried into private life a great and festering bitterness. Though he refused to press for a recount, he never shook the nagging suspicion that the Democrats stole the election. He believed the Kennedy campaign resorted to foul tactics, though he never wrote a coherent account of what he thought those tactics were. He resented the way the press covered the campaign and felt certain that Washington reporters placed themselves at Kennedy's beck and call. He resented Kennedy. They had been friends, and once upon a time Nixon wept when he thought Kennedy was about to die.

Nixon sharply criticized President Kennedy's foreign policies as naive and ineffective, and blamed Kennedy for a decline in American prestige among foreign leaders. Not long after the 1963 overthrow and murder of the Diem brothers in South Vietnam, Pakistani leader Ayub Khan told Nixon that to be a friend of the United States was dangerous. Nixon understood Khan's attitude and blamed Kennedy's misguided policies for creating that impression. Still, after the 1961 Bay of Pigs invasion failed, Kennedy summoned Nixon to the White House; and the former vice president sought to reassure and comfort his adversary. Afterward, he decided to refrain from criticizing the president for a time, and tried to persuade other Republicans to do the same.

The Kennedys made the transition that so many others in Nixon's life had made—the transformation from mere political opponents to enemies. It overstates and distorts the case to portray, as dramatists have, a drunk President Nixon speaking to a portrait of John F. Kennedy in the White House, or forever expressing bewilderment as to why people loved JFK but hated him. The Kennedys haunted Nixon in another way, as the sacrosanct leaders of the hated liberal elite. They were the liberal trendsetters and preeminent manipulators of the news media. They were his rivals and tormentors. He believed that for the rest of his life.

THE PRESIDENT AND CONGRESS:
BEFORE WATERGATE

⋆ ⋆ ⋆

After Nixon lost his California gubernatorial race in 1962, he had plenty of time over the next few years to reflect on his life, career, and the harm his enemies had done him. He used the time constructively and destructively. He plotted strategy, educated himself further on world affairs, and brought his formidable intellect to bear on weighty political issues, all with the intention of preparing himself for the presidency. Whether one likes or dislikes Nixon, it must be acknowledged that he was one of our most experienced and capable presidents. His intelligence and self-discipline had everything to do with that, and he achieved a great deal. What one may think of those achievements is another matter.

On the destructive side of the ledger, he stewed and simmered in his resentments. Nixon thought often during those wilderness years of his enemies: the Democrats, the Kennedys, the press, and the entire East Coast liberal establishment. When the IRS audited his taxes, he took it as a spiteful shot from the Kennedy administration. When he lost the election for governor of California, he threw his famous tantrum at the last press conference. When he occupied the White House, he was among the most vengeful and politically aggressive of presidents.

He had plenty of enemies waiting. Congress was solidly in Democratic hands. Nixon liked to observe that he was the first incoming president to face opposition majorities in both congressional houses since Zachary Taylor took office in 1849. Taylor, a Whig, did not have to endure the congressional Democrats' hostility for very long, as he died in 1850; Nixon lived and had to deal with Congress far longer.

Congress had to deal with him, too. Stephen E. Ambrose described the situation as one of remarkable personal hatred between Nixon in the White House and the Democrats on the Hill. It was beyond anything any living American had seen; president and Congress went at each other with a ferocity unknown since the 1860s, when the House impeached President Andrew Johnson after a long, acrimonious struggle between the executive and legislative branches. The Senate vote fell only one short of the two-thirds majority necessary to remove Johnson from office. The animus between Nixon and Congress was not equaled again until the Clinton years, if then.

A more or less adversarial relationship between president and Congress is inherent in our constitutional system, regardless of party affiliations. Congress and the president often have different agendas. Every member of Congress, in both houses, answers to a localized constituency; senators represent their states and representatives their districts. The president is the only elected official in the federal government who answers to a national constituency. Even when the president's own party controls Congress, trouble often arises. The best of intentions on both sides, the determination of both sides to work together constructively, will not altogether vitiate the inherent conflicts.

In January 1969, it is not unfair to say, the new president and the new Congress had little use for each other. As much as Nixon liked to refer back to Zachary Taylor's dilemma, the situation in 1969 was rare and possibly unprecedented. The new Congress and the new president were instant, intractable enemies. Nixon's personality and political history had as much if not more than anything else to do with that state of affairs. Here was a man who, first, had been nursing his animosities against Democrats and liberals for years and, second, believed in a powerful presidency that should function largely unfettered by congressional interference.

Nixon was not always so insistent on presidential power. When he was a member of Congress, he believed that Harry Truman exercised undue authority in certain areas. There is yet another irony in that, since, during the Hiss case, Congressman Nixon held that the president issued executive orders specifically to interfere with HUAC's investigation. Nixon also tangled with the Justice Department and the federal grand jury over whether he, as a legislator, could withhold evidence so that HUAC could examine it first. Now, as president, Nixon viewed executive prerogatives as sacrosanct, and he was not about to let Congress get in the way of his progressive leadership, especially in foreign policy.

Nixon's disposition toward the Democratic Congress was not sweetened any by the fact that, no sooner was he installed in the Oval Office, than the Democrats and the press were touting Senator Edward Kennedy as president-in-waiting. It seemed that way to Nixon, and it seemed that way to others, too. The last Kennedy brother was the designated anti-Nixon during the president's first year, and at times it seemed the entire Washington press corps, as well as the congressional Democrats, simply took it for granted that Kennedy would win the Democratic nomination in 1972 and subsequently defeat Nixon. Nixon, therefore, would be a one-term president, in office by way of a quirk in the nation's political climate, meanwhile keeping the seat warm for Teddy.

One can argue that Nixon's discomfort and siege mentality were not wholly off base, although the author considers it a stretch to argue that Nixon's responses were fully justified. His operatives took actions toward Kennedy that Nixon afterward argued were politics as usual, and perhaps they were, but they were still sleazy. White House spies watched Kennedy and photographed him in the company of women other than his wife.

Nixon wrote of one particular picture that his people took of the senator with a woman in Paris; he was pleased with it and not at all reluctant to use it if a fitting occasion arose. Had Kennedy not destroyed his own presidential chances on the bridge at Chappaquiddick in the accident that tragically ended the life of young Mary Jo Kopechne, the 1972 campaign may have been dirtier than the mudslinging contests to which Americans have grown accustomed in the eighties and nineties. Nixon, true to form, complained that had anyone except a Kennedy driven off that bridge, the media would have run him out of politics altogether.

Nixon's problems with Congress were not purely political. In many ways, his positions did not drastically diverge from those of his adversaries. The radical antiwar movement had not made significant inroads in Congress, and few if any on Capitol Hill echoed the movement's call for immediate withdrawal from Vietnam. Peace talks began under Johnson and would continue under Nixon. On the domestic front, Nixon was not nearly as conservative as many other Republicans and announced no intentions to dismantle government agencies or eradicate Social Security or abolish welfare. Nixon did not even set out to destroy Johnson's Great Society, though he tried to rein in spending. When he impounded Great Society funds, he faced the wrath of congressional Democrats. Nonetheless, liberals had no need to fear that the new administration would seek a drastic reversion to the days of Calvin Coolidge.

Nixon got into his massive struggles with Congress because he was Nixon. Again, every president and every Congress will grapple and disagree. Lyndon Johnson once said that in all his years in Washington, he saw that sooner or later every Congress took the measure of the president with whom it dealt. But in Nixon's case, both sides were loaded for bear from the start. Tom Wicker commented that no Republican could unite the Democrats the way Nixon did. He stood ready to do battle with Congress because he was Nixon, and Congress stood ready to do battle with Nixon because he was Nixon.

As Nixon remembered it years later, he had a definite domestic agenda in mind, including progressive welfare reform (although Stanley Kutler turned up a taped conversation wherein Nixon said he hoped that Congress never actually would pass his welfare proposals, which they did not), but, he wrote in his memoirs, after referring yet again to Zachary Taylor, "enthusiasm and determination" could not erase the fact that the opposing party controlled Congress. Nixon wrote that he sent more than forty domestic proposals to Congress during his first year as president, including a major tax reform plan, a reorganization of foreign aid, a message on population control—the first ever from a president to Congress—and proposals concerning pornography, drugs, and crime. Congress only passed those concerning military draft reform and Nixon's tax bill. Nixon saw these numerous rebuffs as the shape of things to come.

But it was a two-way street. Nixon packed his White House staff with men who knew little or nothing of Congress and about whom Congress knew little or nothing. Many incoming presidents, including Eisenhower, made sure that their staffers knew how Congress worked and were themselves known on the Hill. Many House and Senate members, from both parties, saw Nixon's staffing policies as an expression of his own contempt for Congress, since his men acted as if they considered Congress irrelevant.

Although his disregard for Congress proved ill-advised in both the short and long runs, Nixon's determination to conduct a strong presidency was not in itself out of keeping with recent history. The twentieth century has seen a drastic expansion of presidential power and a series of harsh congressional reactions to that expansion. Since Franklin Roosevelt, all presidents, including the avowedly conservative ones, have either helped expand presidential power or at least made full use of the power that their immediate predecessors bequeathed to them. Eisenhower, not the liberal Roosevelt or Truman, first used the term *executive privilege*. Nixon, taking his cue from the man he served as vice president, employed that very term when he wished to circumvent Congress.

Nixon had his own views on what historian Arthur Schlesinger called the "imperial presidency." He believed it did not exist. Nixon saw so many restraints on presidential power, some official and some de facto, that he judged "the periodic talk about the 'imperial presidency' . . . ludicrous." Nixon saw many disparate factors limiting presidential powers, from Congress's power to confirm or deny presidential appointments to the news media's power over public opinion. As usual, he detected a liberal double standard and asserted that many who complained about excessive presidential power voiced no such objections when a liberal occupied the Oval Office. They worried about the imperial presidency, Nixon wrote in *In the Arena*, "when a conservative president who disagreed with their political views came into office."

Disputes over political philosophies are well and good, but Nixon and Congress fought many of their fiercest battles over money, specifically over the impoundment of funds. Impoundment was one of the great sticking points between the executive and legislative branches dating back to the days of Thomas Jefferson. The term refers to a president's refusal to spend congressionally appropriated funds. It was not a common practice of presidents, between Jefferson and Nixon, but it was not rare, either. Congress on occasion acquiesced when presidents impounded funds and at other times showed anger and restiveness when presidents thwarted congressional will in this way. On some occasions, Congress passed resolutions authorizing presidential impoundments of specified amounts, as happened during Nixon's first term. Congress authorized Nixon to impound 6 billion dollars during his first year as president. The trouble started in 1970, when Congress did not renew its authorization, but Nixon sat on 13 billion dollars anyway.

When Nixon analyzed the impoundment issue in his later writings, he conceded that the Constitution's framers "wisely" limited presidential power and gave Congress the discretion to "decide what money can be spent." Congress passes the federal budget, but, starting with Jefferson, "presidents impounded funds

the Congress appropriated that would have busted the budget."
Nixon impounded funds, he explained in his retirement, to
restrain wild spending by the Great Society programs he inherited from Johnson. That drove the Democratic Congress crazy,
Nixon wrote with obvious glee, but they could do nothing about
it until Nixon's power eroded during the Watergate crisis, when
Congress passed the 1974 Budget Control Impoundment Act.
Nixon wrote that by doing so, Congress assured itself the right to
spend irresponsibly without fear of presidential interference.

Nixon had strong doubts about the Impoundment Act's con-
stitutionality; he was certain that the War Powers Act of 1973 was
unconstitutional. The still-controversial War Powers Act limits a
president's power to wage undeclared war by requiring the president to notify Congress within forty-eight hours of initiating
armed actions and to withdraw armed forces from action within
sixty days, unless the president obtains an extension from
Congress. Nixon and all of his successors have been unhappy with
the War Powers Act, but it has not been constitutionally tested.

Nixon described both the War Powers Act and the Impoundment Act as part of the "congressional power grabs" entailed in
the backlash against presidential power following the Vietnam
War and the Watergate scandal. There is a long history of congressional backlashes after extended periods of strong presidential leadership: Andrew Johnson's impeachment, for instance,
was partly a backlash against the near-dictatorial presidency of
Abraham Lincoln. So, in the Nixon era's waning days, when
Watergate had drained his strength, Congress accordingly limited future presidents' powers to determine spending and to
wage war. Those developments horrified Nixon. The War Powers
Act passed over his veto.

Nixon continually resented Congress for thwarting his will
with what he interpreted as interference in presidential business
or blocking legitimate presidential prerogatives. When Congress
rejected his first two Supreme Court nominees, that struck him
as congressional arrogance, and he accused the liberal Democrats on Capitol Hill of refusing to allow any Southerners on the

Supreme Court. Nixon missed two important points on this question. First, the two nominees, Clement Haynesworth and Harold Carswell, were problematic. Carswell was a particularly ill-advised choice and any number of legal advisers could have foreseen his rejection. Second, Nixon confused a presidential right of nomination with an independent right of appointment. The Constitution uses the word *appointment* but clearly requires congressional approval of a Supreme Court appointment, and appointments to other posts in the executive branch. Whatever the merits of the two nominees, it was the constitutional role of Congress to confirm or reject them, and failure to rubber-stamp presidential appointments hardly qualifies as interfering with a president's legitimate authority.

Judge Clement Haynesworth was rejected largely on partisan grounds. He was an avowedly conservative Southerner, and congressional Democrats feared that Nixon nominated him as part of his plan to dismantle the liberal majority on the activist Warren court. In 1968, candidate Nixon condemned the Supreme Court's liberal activism and accused the Court of making law instead of interpreting it. That complaint had long been a favorite right-wing cause; since the middle 1950s, "Impeach Earl Warren" billboards dotted Southern and Southwestern landscapes, so Nixon's anti-court rhetoric was a blatant pitch for right-wing votes. The fact that Nixon's first nomination was a conservative Southerner set off alarm bells in the Capitol dome.

Soon after the White House announced Haynesworth's nomination in August 1969, civil rights groups protested that the South Carolinian was a segregationist, and several major labor leaders criticized his record on labor issues. According to Nixon, a "pack mentality" set in, and special-interest groups mounted a major anti-Haynesworth effort in Washington. The press, according to Nixon, provided heavily biased coverage to the liberal campaign to defeat Nixon's nomination and preserve the Supreme Court's liberal majority. Democratic senators made what Nixon thought were false or overblown charges against Haynesworth involving alleged conflict of interest in cases on which he ruled as a judge. Nixon ignored Republican suggestions to withdraw the nomination, and the Senate rejected Haynesworth on November 21 by a vote of fifty-five to forty-five, with seventeen Republicans voting to reject. When Nixon saw Haynesworth shortly after the Senate vote, he thought the judge appeared "dazed" by what had happened to him.

Judge Harold Carswell was a decidedly poor nomination; he had an undistinguished legal record and gave every appearance of mediocrity or worse. After opponents criticized his mediocrity a few times, Nebraska senator Roman Hruska said that mediocre people deserved representation on the Supreme Court, and thus supplied the proceedings their one moment of surreal and unintentional levity. A few of Nixon's biographers have hinted, and at least one or two have said outright, that they suspected Nixon nominated Carswell in revenge for Haynesworth's rejection, as if to say, "Since you rejected a reasonable prospect and called him a poor nomination, here's a *really* poor one."

That, of course, is pure speculation. Nixon submitted the Carswell nomination in January 1970, and almost immediately a report surfaced that, as a candidate for state office in Georgia in 1948, Carswell had endorsed racial segregation. According to Nixon, Carswell had long since renounced segregation, but the revelation fatally hurt the nomination. Congress rejected Carswell fifty-one to forty-five the following April. The president issued an angry statement chastising the Senate for refusing to allow Southerners on the Supreme Court and calling the Senate hypocritical for attacking his nominees' records. Nixon argued that the liberals really objected to adhering to a strict view of the Constitution's original intent. *Original intent* is a loaded term under nearly any political circumstances, and it sounded especially strange coming from the champion of executive privilege.

Nixon's four remaining Supreme Court nominations were confirmed. Warren E. Burger replaced Earl Warren as Chief Justice in 1969; Harry A. Blackmun, appointed in 1970, still sits on the Court; Lewis F. Powell, Jr., served from 1971 to 1987; and William H. Rehnquist, appointed in 1971, became Chief Justice in 1986.

In his retirement, Nixon still brooded over the Haynesworth and Carswell defeats and regarded them as another fatheaded way in which Congress blocked his legitimate exercise of presidential power. Whatever the merits of the two respected nominees, Nixon never abandoned his feeling that Congress simply should have ratified his will without objection. He never reconciled himself to the idea that if the Constitution assigns specific powers and functions to a governmental branch, it hardly qualifies as harassment or unfair interference when that branch uses those powers. Nixon believed in executive privilege but had no corresponding brief with legislative privilege.

PART IV
NIXON AND WATERGATE

★ ★ ★ ★ ★ ★ ★ ★

THE BUTCHER'S TALE

✹   ✹   ✹

The story of Watergate may not be as commonly known as it was only a short time ago, given the world's tendency to move on, but there remain extant so many books, television documentaries, and dramatizations of the subject that the author has decided to make no attempt to produce yet another recounting of the sorry epic of Nixon's ruin. Instead, and more in keeping with this book's focus and character, we will examine Nixon's own relationship to Watergate, although we will fill in blanks here and there as necessary. For extensive analytical narratives of Watergate, the author strongly recommends two books: *Watergate,* by Fred Emery, and *The Wars of Watergate,* by Stanley Kutler. Both are fascinating, extremely well-written, and wonderfully readable, and both will tell the reader more about Watergate than anyone could possibly think to ask. Emery and Kutler supplied many of the more enjoyable moments for this author during this book's research phase.

The old adage, "character is destiny," decidedly applies to Richard Nixon. He created a presidency, staffed his White House, and conducted his relations with Congress all in such a way that made Watergate as inevitable as anything can be in the course of human events. Nixon got into the Watergate mess because he was Nixon. He claimed to the end that it was politics as usual, and probably some of it was, but a lot of it carried Nixon's special blend of paranoia and hubris. Nixon participated in a criminal conspiracy to obstruct justice. He lost his presidency for that; he was not driven from office by partisan spite, although such spite was abundantly present. He defended Watergate to the end, but in standard Nixonian fashion, he justified and minimized it, and protested that he did not deserve to lose office for it, and to the end proclaimed himself a man more sinned against than sinning.

Historian Joan Hoff commented that the Watergate tapes indicated that Nixon could not tell right from wrong. When reading Nixon's accounts of Watergate in his later writings, particularly in his memoirs and *In the Arena*, one sees Hoff's point. Something is missing. Nixon did not grasp some central truth; something eluded his basic understanding. He insisted it was politics as usual, and never seemed to ask himself why a court of law should care whether or not politicians usually play the game that way. "Politics as usual" is not a license for abetting criminals and committing crimes.

The basic facts of the case are as follows. On June 17, 1972, Washington police arrested a group of burglars in the Democratic National Committee offices in the Watergate complex. They all turned out to be connected to the Committee to Re-elect the President, known to Nixon supporters as the CRP and to the rest of the world as CREEP. One, James McCord, was a former CIA agent and CREEP's security chief. They had broken in to repair telephone bugs they planted in a previous break-in. McCord later testified that they also intended to photograph DNC documents.

The White House immediately took action to cover up its connection to the CREEP burglars, but in time, it came out that Attorney General John Mitchell had personally approved the break-in. That led to questions as to whether or not the president was involved. While it is still questionable as to whether he had prior knowledge of the break-in, it became clear in time that Nixon participated in the cover-up. Beyond that, the scandal brought out the fact that the Nixon White House engaged in a number of clandestine, illegal activities. Nixon knew and approved of the overall program, whether or not he involved himself in many of the specifics. Ultimately, the scandal led to his resignation.

While vacationing in Key Biscayne, Nixon read of the arrests in the *Miami Herald*. His reaction was, in his own words, completely pragmatic. "If it was also cynical," he wrote, "it was a cynicism born of experience." He had seen a lot of dirty tricks during his many years in politics and figured that reaction to the break-in probably would not amount to much. By his account, he did not fear for his presidency that sunny morning in Key Biscayne. The Democrats might proclaim their horror and outrage, and no doubt would, but they were politicians, too, and tapping opponents' phones was old news. Nixon recalled that an Adlai Stevenson operative admitted that during the 1960 race for the Democratic nomination, he tapped John F. Kennedy's phone lines at the convention. Barry Goldwater suspected that Johnson's people bugged him in 1964. J. Edgar Hoover told Nixon that President Johnson wanted Nixon's campaign plane bugged in 1968. Nixon claimed that McGovern operatives tried to break into a CREEP office.

Nixon recalled that he was distressed at CREEP's stupidity rather than by legal questions. It made no sense, Nixon wrote, to bug the DNC, since a party's campaign headquarters is never the place to go for a campaign's real inside information. Bugging the DNC was a colossal waste of time and a bunch of CREEPs got themselves arrested for no good purpose. So, if Nixon is to be believed, he was annoyed rather than worried, and did not anticipate that a crisis would grow out of the Watergate break-in.

Things took a scary turn only two days later, on June 20, when the *Washington Post* ran a front-page story tying Howard Hunt, another former CIA agent, to the break-in. Hunt was a White House consultant working with Charles Colson, one of Nixon's close advisers, which the *Post* noted. Seeing Colson's name in the story, Nixon wrote, gave him his first real jolt in the matter. Nixon liked the way Colson played hardball, but now he feared that things had gone too far. Before the day was out, Nixon's deputy director of communication, Kenneth Clawson, warned him that "a hell of a barrage" was on the way. Clawson, a former *Post* reporter, had been to lunch with some *Post* employees.

By the next day, Nixon was worried and angry. He grumbled about the double standard at work here: The *Post*, the *New York Times*, and other major newspapers printed the Pentagon Papers, that collection of illegally obtained classified documents, but he was sure they would piously condemn this muddled break-in at the Watergate. Nixon told an aide that someone should recommend the Watergate burglars for a Pulitzer Prize, since the *Times* got one for the Pentagon Papers story. Colson predicted that the Democrats and the media would become obsessed with Watergate, so the administration had to take care not to become obsessed as well. Nixon told Colson that the break-in would not affect the election. He was absolutely right.

Since four of the five burglars were Cubans, Nixon thought of portraying the break-in as the product of Cuban exiles' fear of McGovern. With that angle, Nixon reasoned, the break-in might actually work in the White House's favor: A group of overly zealous Cubans in CREEP's employ, but working without CREEP's authorization, broke into the DNC because they feared a McGovern victory would deflect the United States from its strong opposition to the Castro regime. They sought to ensure Nixon's reelection, since the president's tried and true anticommunism meant that America would not abandon the exiles' cause as long as he remained president.

Nixon told Colson that his "understanding was that" the White House would "leave the matter where it was, with the Cubans." Nixon hit on the idea of calling his friend Bebe Rebozo to get anti-McGovern Cubans in Florida to start a bail fund for the Cuban burglars. Rebozo and his people, Nixon thought, could attract media attention and remind everyone about the Democrats' Bay of Pigs fiasco.

On June 21, according to Nixon's memoirs, Haldeman told him that G. Gordon Liddy, the finance committee counsel for

CREEP, was responsible for the break-in, not James McCord, the former CIA agent and current CREEP security chief arrested on the scene. Ehrlichman suggested that Liddy confess, since that would "establish guilt at a low level" and discourage the press from searching for guilt higher up the White House chain of command. All of the arrested burglars thought Liddy was in charge anyway, so if he took the rap, the others would present no problem for the White House. Nixon, apparently not thinking about what McCord probably knew, endorsed Ehrlichman's idea. He also agreed with press secretary Ronald Ziegler's characterization of the break-in as a "third-rate burglary," and said he planned to characterize it as a "third-rate *attempt* at a burglary" (Nixon's italics). Nixon's only worry at this juncture was whether or not anyone could implicate Attorney General John Mitchell.

At the meeting's end, Nixon complained to Haldeman about the double standard, one of his favorite topics. The Democrats had done this sort of thing to Republicans for years, Nixon said, but no one ever caught them at it. Haldeman agreed with the president and commented that the press never went after the Democrats the way it went after Republicans. Later that day, Nixon fumed that "every time the Democrats accuse us of bugging, we should charge that we were being bugged and maybe even plant a bug and find it ourselves!" Nixon later characterized that as a bitter joke, but one wonders.

A day later, the president rejoiced at the good news that the FBI still had nothing on Hunt. The White House knew that he was present at the Watergate break-in, but the FBI did not. More good news followed that day: The FBI could not trace the money they found on the burglars. That pleased Nixon because following the money would connect CREEP directly to the break-in.

At this point in Nixon's account, a reader may ask if he understood that he was describing an obstruction of justice. He had, after all, endorsed withholding evidence of Hunt's presence at the Watergate and of CREEP's monetary connection to the burglary. Those two acts qualify as felony offenses, and Nixon described them in his memoirs almost matter-of-factly, by implication dismissing their inherent criminality. In further discussion on handling the Watergate problem, Nixon told Haldeman to "play it tough," which is how, he said, the Democrats always played things, and "that's the way we are going to play it." After Liddy did indeed offer to take the rap, Nixon wrote that he hoped "some Cuban motive could be retained in our explanations.... I said the story had to be true to some extent."

Throughout his writings, Nixon complained about double standards, overreactions, and unjustified outcries over Watergate and other deeds and misdeeds during his career. But here, in his memoirs, he described, step-by-step, a conscious progression of untruths and obstructions aimed at deceiving and obstructing a legitimate FBI investigation of a crime. He justified these actions with the politics-as-usual argument time and again, as if politics existed in an extralegal vacuum, answering to no authority other than its own internal rules of engagement. When he returned to the topic in *In the Arena*, published many years later, in 1990, Nixon's essential public stance on the cover-up remained unchanged. Joan Hoff's observation again comes to mind: In some basic way, Nixon could not tell right from wrong. As a consequence, he saw no good reason for losing his presidency, and attributed Watergate's results to his enemies' political vengeance. Nixon's White House was a world unto itself.

Meanwhile, he had a presidential campaign to conduct. Nixon thought poorly of George McGovern but considered him dangerous. Though he knew little of McGovern personally, he deplored the man's politics. Nixon thought it "critically important" to America's future that McGovern's "radical ideas" did not prevail in the 1972 election. Nixon noted in his diary that right-wing extremists, of the Goldwater type, prefer to lose on their principles rather than win by compromising their principles, but leftists routinely compromise their principles to win power. That is why, Nixon continued, Communists usually defeat rightists, since rightists "always" fight for their principles, but Communists willingly compromise or hide their intentions and, once in power, crush the opposition.

Nixon may not have meant to equate McGovern with Stalin; after all, he generally regarded his Democratic opponent as politically inept and ineffective. Rather, it seems that Nixon saw McGovern's candidacy as representing a terrible leftist threat to the United States, although one wonders if Nixon *really* feared a McGovern victory would open the floodgates to ultimate subversion. Nixon differed from his predecessor, Lyndon Johnson, who believed that the real threat to America came from the right, not the left. America was strong enough to withstand its cold war adversaries, the Soviet Union and the Chinese, and those whom Johnson called the "pissants on the campuses" posed no real threat. It was the right wing, not the left, that could undermine American democracy from within.

Nixon, apparently, *did* see the campus radicals and the McGovernites as communism's domestic vanguard—or, if not the vanguard, then as the Communists' dupes. He insisted that foreign Communists must have been behind the antiwar movement at least to some extent, and he never abandoned that belief despite a complete absence of evidence. Whether conscious agents or not, in Nixon's view, they still were creatures of the left, who would, if permitted, open America to destruction. McGovern might not be Stalin or Lenin, but a dupe in the White House would do the job quite nicely.

But Nixon's reelection campaign was not a crusade to save the United States from McGovern and the left. It was a reelection campaign. Reelection and not the nation's final destiny was the priority. The White House engaged in dirty tricks throughout Nixon's first term, not just at election time. His politics-as-usual argument could not vitiate the fact that Nixon and his men spent an inordinate amount of time thinking up and implementing plans to screw their opponents. The Watergate investigations revealed much of these things to the world, and much of the world, including this author, finds it hard to believe that the Nixon administration's antics were entirely typical of White House operations under other presidents.

That is not to say that other presidents were squeakily

honest and above such deeds but rather that the intensity and extent of the Nixon White House dirty tricks reflected the obsessions and persistent enmities of Richard Nixon. It is simply difficult to imagine that many other presidents were like him. It is difficult to imagine that presidents normally spent huge chunks of time obsessively complaining about every imaginable enemy and endless hours brainstorming with their aides to plot their enemies' downfall. Not every president abuses presidential power and crosses the line to criminal conduct— at least, not to the point of creating unauthorized and clandestine agencies that commit felonious acts on no authority granted by constitutional or statutory law.

In the summer of 1972, Nixon held commanding leads over any possible Democratic nominee. McGovern entered the Democratic convention the undisputed front-runner, having eliminated Muskie and Humphrey, both of whom looked far stronger than McGovern going into the primaries. Once the nomination was assured, the McGovern campaign fell apart. Nixon sat back and watched his opponent start to destroy himself even before the Democratic convention ended.

McGovern showed a distinct tendency to back down when challenged, even when doing so meant betraying or abandoning people he had promised to support. According to Nixon, McGovern asked Lawrence O'Brien to remain as DNC chairman, then backed off from that when members of his staff objected. He promised to support a feminist challenge to the South Carolina delegation during the convention, then backed out of that one. He proposed Pierre Salinger, formerly President Kennedy's press secretary, for a DNC vice chairmanship, and backed away from that, too. Nixon saw McGovern's doom written all over these capitulations and betrayals, which makes one wonder why he did not feel sufficiently secure to let the campaign run its own course.

When the Eagleton affair broke in the news, Nixon predicted that McGovern, after reaffirming his support for his running mate, would dump him after all. McGovern's word was unreliable, Nixon assessed, and he expected that McGovern would "have his major newspapers" call for Eagleton's resignation. That is one of the more astonishing things that Nixon ever wrote. *McGovern would "have his major newspapers" call for Eagleton's resignation.* With or without the help of "his" newspapers, McGovern accepted Eagleton's resignation, and the Democrats nominated the frenetic Sargent Shriver.

Nixon also predicted, or at least he wrote that he predicted, that the Democrats would use the Watergate story to divert attention from McGovern's obvious flaws and deficiencies. Nixon never really understood that Watergate was a legitimate news story, and he always saw the intensive press coverage as part of the Democratic campaign against him. In the same vein, he thought the continuing Watergate coverage after the election was another part of the liberal crusade to bring him down.

The trouble with Nixon's assessment is that he indeed was guilty of criminal wrongdoing and abuse of presidential power. He committed some of his more notable abuses during the 1972 campaign, when he sought to discredit the Democrats through clandestine means. Nixon probably would have done well to listen to Johnson's advice, relayed through their mutual friend, the minister Billy Graham. "Ignore McGovern, and get out with the people. But stay above the campaign, like I did with Goldwater. Go to ball games and factories. And don't worry. The McGovern people are going to defeat themselves." Graham told Nixon that he asked Johnson about Watergate. Johnson replied that Watergate would not hurt Nixon at all, which was true regarding the election.

Nixon would not ignore the opposition. He wanted to get federal agencies to dig up dirt on the Democrats. To justify this to posterity, Nixon wrote in his memoirs that the Democrats were doing it to him. On August 16, for instance, Nixon was annoyed because McGovern was telling the press he believed Nixon responsible for bugging the DNC. He irked Nixon further by comparing such tactics to "the kind of thing you expect under someone like Hitler." Democrats made charges about Nixon's campaign contributors, claiming that CREEP received funds laundered through Mexico, and criticized the Nixon campaign for having so many anonymous donors. According to Nixon, many of those anonymous donors were Democrats who would be embarrassed to be named publicly. Nixon denied receiving any illegal funds, laundered or otherwise.

In his memoirs, Nixon argued that his improper use of government agencies came about as a defense against charges like the preceding. Nixon wrote that he wanted to fight back and saw no reason for McGovern and other Democrats to be spared the sorts of attacks they were launching on him. He regarded access to government information on political opponents as one of the perks of incumbency and claimed that Democratic administrations used that perk flagrantly, such as when the IRS audited Nixon himself during John F. Kennedy's term.

Nixon wrote in his diary that not to investigate the Democrats would be a "failure," and that it was "ironic" that, when they had the presidency, they were always going after Republicans, and now, out of office, they were still going after Republicans. That, Nixon reasoned, was because all the lower-ranking federal bureaucrats were old New Deal Democrats who gave the McGovern forces access to inside information. Anticipating a triumphant reelection, enjoying a huge lead in the polls, President Nixon still portrayed himself as a victim of the mighty liberal forces and insisted that his crimes were slingshots against the Goliaths who sought to crush him and all he stood for.

Nixon wanted Haldeman and Ehrlichman to pressure the IRS to check up on McGovern's main staffers and contributors. If any "shady dealings" were discovered, that information should be given to the media. If nothing turned up, Nixon instructed them to drop the project, but he wanted the effort made. As far as he could tell, though, his two top aides had little or no success in getting the IRS to cooperate. Those same New Deal bureaucrats, Nixon believed, gummed up Haldeman and Ehrlichman's efforts to deploy the advantages of incumbency.

Meantime, the administration's Watergate disinformation

campaign was well under way. At an August 29 press conference, Nixon told a reporter that he thought a special prosecutor would be unnecessary, since the appropriate federal agencies were investigating the matter. John Dean, the White House counsel, was also on the case, Nixon told the press. Dean's investigation so far had found nothing to implicate anyone on the White House staff, and Nixon emphasized that no one on his staff was involved in "this very bizarre incident." These things happen, Nixon said, since in every campaign zealots go overboard and do improper things, but, "What really hurts is if you try to cover it up." Nixon, of course, was trying to cover it up.

In those early days, the cover-up seemed to be working. The initial indictments of mid-September only went as high as Hunt and Liddy, along with McCord and the other four burglars caught at the scene. Nixon complimented Dean for his work containing the scandal and two days later noted in his diary that he was "enormously impressed" with Dean. The polls showed Nixon heading for a massive landslide victory over McGovern and, in Nixon's opinion, the Democrat's campaign grew more desperate and shrill as Election Day drew nearer. Vice presidential candidate Shriver revived the old "Tricky Dick" epithet, blasted Nixon for the Vietnam War, impugned his sanity, and called him power-mad. Nixon considered the attacks vicious and irresponsible.

Nixon's November victory was a foregone conclusion. The White House dirty-tricks campaign was almost certainly unnecessary to ensure Nixon's victory. The antiwar movement had not cut into the president's popular support, nor had it enhanced McGovern's political strength. Two months before the election, a Harris poll showed 55 percent approval for the ongoing heavy bombing of North Vietnam. When Nixon later ordered the mining of Haiphong Harbor, approval ratings were even higher. Nixon was correct in asserting that McGovern and the antiwar movement did not represent mainstream American opinion. Nixon two years earlier identified the silent majority and spoke to them, and now they were about to reelect him by a record margin. On Election Day 1972, few voters expected Watergate to turn into a major scandal. Even then, many of us—perhaps most of us—did not realize it would drive Nixon from office.

The Watergate revelations confirmed the suspicions that Nixon's enemies held for years. Many of the anti-Nixon crowd, this author included, were not the least surprised when it was revealed that the Nixon administration routinely engaged in domestic espionage and dirty tricks. What shocked or surprised many of us was that so many other people were shocked and surprised. When we heard of the enemies list and the Huston Plan, we simply shook our heads and told each other that we knew it. Cries of horrified disbelief did not emanate from the anti-Nixon camps across the nation. Those anguished sounds came from people who supported Nixon and believed in him.

The American public first heard of the fabled enemies list during John Dean's testimony before Senator Sam Ervin's special Watergate committee. Dean, under questioning by Connecticut Republican Lowell Weicker, revealed that "in my possession is a . . . memorandum that was requested of me, to prepare a means to attack the enemies of the White House. There was also maintained what was called an enemies list, which was rather extensive and continually being updated."

According to Dean's Watergate memoirs, *Blind Ambition*, the enemies-list revelation caused a "press frenzy," and being on it immediately became a status symbol. The list occasioned both horrified gasps and sardonic jokes. Dean told the committee that Charles Colson's office prepared the list. Colson, according to Dean's memoirs, "defended himself with a statement that the list was nothing more than a compilation of names of people to be banned from White House functions." That, according to Dean, was true, but he reported that Haldeman designated about twenty names from the list for IRS harassment.

Nixon, naturally enough, minimized the enemies list in his later writings. Dean, too, thought the media frenzy unjustified and explained that, in the final analysis, the list never really was anything more than a list. Daniel Patrick Moynihan also thought the fuss a little silly. Moynihan, a Democrat, had for a time served

JOHN DEAN, 1973.

as one of Nixon's domestic advisers and was Nixon's favorite liberal. Nixon spoke and wrote highly of Moynihan for the rest of his life. Despite their political differences, the Republican president and his liberal Democratic adviser got on famously, often talked for long hours, and found each other fascinating. During the Watergate crisis, Moynihan told an interviewer that Nixon's first term was an exercise in "damn good government," and asked what was the big deal about the enemies list. It was nothing more, said the future New York senator, than a list of people not to invite to dinner.

That may be true, but what was shocking about the list was the mentality that called it into being, irrespective of the fact that little or no effective action came of it. Dean himself had written a memo about the list that Stephen E. Ambrose quoted in *Nixon: Ruin and Recovery, 1973-1990*: "We can use the available federal machinery to screw our political enemies."

The enemies list immediately entered the nation's political folklore, but the lesser-known Huston Plan was potentially far more sinister and dangerous. Several of Nixon's biographers employed the same metaphor to describe it—they called it a time bomb ticking in the administration's files. Their image is apt, for the Huston Plan's revelation was a giant nail in Nixon's political coffin. It conveyed the image of an administration bent on establishing a national police state, on its own authority without consulting Congress, and no amount of minimizing or dismissive remarks could eradicate that impression.

The Huston Plan, named for White House staffer Tom Huston, who at least partly originated it, provided for gathering domestic intelligence by means of wiretapping, burglary, and other methods deemed necessary. Huston was to oversee the plan, but, according to Dean, it was scotched when FBI director Hoover objected to the White House implementing such a program. Dean said Hoover had "lost his guts." Others involved thought Hoover viewed it as a White House encroachment on FBI territory. Hoover himself said that there was too great a risk of public exposure. Whatever the case, Hoover had Nixon's ear on the matter and the plan never went forward. But the documents describing it sat in the White House files, waiting for the right whistle to blow. The whistle blew during the Watergate hearings.

In his memoirs, Nixon described how he withdrew his approval of the Huston Plan after Hoover objected. The next year saw a spate of bombings and shootouts involving members of the Weather Underground and the Black Panther Party; Nixon wrote that he regretted discarding the Huston Plan and wondered if some of the death and destruction could have been avoided had it been implemented. That seems to beg the question, since the FBI and other agencies have the legitimate function of keeping an eye on potential federal lawbreakers and investigating terrorist acts.

Other evidence supports the idea that Nixon's main interest in the Huston Plan was political. In Stanley Kutler's collection of White House taped conversations, *Abuse of Power*, Nixon referred to the Huston Plan when discussing with Haldeman and national security adviser Henry Kissinger the classified documents in the Brookings Institution. Nixon said to Haldeman, "Bob? Now do you remember Huston's plan? Implement it." Kissinger interjected, "Now Brookings has no right to have classified documents." Nixon went on, "I want it implemented. . . . Goddamnit, get in and get those files. Blow the safe and get them." Nowhere did Nixon suggest or consider pursuing the Brookings matter through legal means. He took an insular view; the Brookings matter was for the White House to resolve in its own way.

While the Huston Plan was officially defunct, Nixon conceded in his memoirs that to an extent some its provisions were carried out. Others argue that, officially or not, to a *great* extent its provisions were carried out. In light of the activities of the plumbers and the CREEPs, arguing over the extent is merely arguing over words. Nixon's own account of the Huston Plan, like his accounts of many other topics, tended to be self-serving and not overly reliable.

The revelations of domestic espionage contributed to Nixon's fall in the public's esteem and added momentum to the Watergate hearings and the eventual House Judiciary Committee hearings to consider articles of impeachment.

Nixon liked to invoke William Ewart Gladstone, a major figure in nineteenth-century history and one of the greatest British prime ministers. Gladstone said, as Nixon paraphrased, the first requisite of a prime minister is to be a good butcher. Nixon added that the first requisite was also the most difficult. "A president must sometimes fire people. . . . It is never pleasant. . . . If he is unable or unwilling to lower the boom personally, he must have a chief of staff who will do it for him." He had H.R. Haldeman, who called himself "Nixon's son of a bitch." In later years, Nixon several times returned to Gladstone's aphorism and criticized himself for not being a good butcher. There are those, including to an extent Haldeman, who would disagree with Nixon's self-assessment.

In his first book, *The Ends of Power*, much of which he later disavowed after getting back on good terms with Nixon, Haldeman offered many interesting displays of what he and others called Nixon's dark side. Haldeman wrote that his boss

ARCHIVE PHOTOS

H.R. Haldeman, 1973.

was "both the statesman extraordinaire . . . and Tricky Dick . . . who was essential . . ." to realizing the statesman's dreams. Haldeman recalled Nixon ranting about cabinet appointments, that he wanted "none of them in the cabinet, do you understand, none of those Harvard bastards!" Nixon, wrote Haldeman, saw enemies everywhere, "most of them real."

Haldeman also addressed Nixon's claim not to be a good butcher and sought to correct that impression. In the famous David Frost interview, as Haldeman saw it, Nixon said he himself was responsible for Watergate, but then told the story in such a way so as to have the onus fall on Haldeman and Ehrlichman. It was a classic Nixonian maneuver.

Haldeman described the moment: "May 4, 1977. The ex-president perspiring, as David Frost pressed him to say one word . . . 'guilty.' Instead, he received an emotional Nixon performance whose impact on the American public was that Nixon's only real guilt in Watergate was his failure to fire those two arch villains, Haldeman and Ehrlichman, who ran the cover-up, earlier than he did. He just couldn't be a butcher, Nixon said." Haldeman was having none of it.

But Haldeman, like Nixon, was a creature of contradictions. Only a few pages before recounting the Frost interview, Haldeman explained that Nixon *should* have cared only for his own survival since, as president, he was indispensable, whereas a president's underlings are dispensable. In the same passage, Haldeman buttressed his argument by criticizing President Carter for riskily standing by Bert Lance, his scandal-ridden budget director. To Haldeman, that was irresponsible; Carter should have been willing to jettison Lance, as Nixon had Haldeman and Ehrlichman. One wonders if Haldeman actually believed that. Still, his resentment at being sacrificed—or butchered—manifests itself even as he explains that Nixon was right to put his own survival above that of his aides.

Like many leaders, Nixon, at least to an extent, surrounded himself with men who told him what he wanted to hear. Haldeman was his most loyal retainer for many years. Charles Colson wrote in his own Watergate memoirs that he and Nixon encouraged each other's dark sides, an opinion supported by many who knew about Nixon and Colson's relationship. Dean, during one taped conversation prior to the 1972 election, described the prospect of using federal agencies against political enemies as "exciting."

Haldeman wrote that Nixon's dark side caused problems, which is obvious. In the same passage, Haldeman wrote that he was not drawn to serving the presidency, nor the man Richard Nixon, but rather what drew him was the combination *President Nixon.*

Haldeman may have been correct in a way other than he thought. The dynamics of the Nixon White House were made possible by the collection of the personalities there, and Nixon made that collection possible in the first place. Haldeman's explanation in some ways recalls Florence R. Miale and Michael Selzer's analysis of Albert Speer in *The Nuremberg Mind*, a psychological study of the Nuremberg war crimes defendants based on their answers to the standard Rorschach test. Speer wrote, "I would have sold my soul, like Faust." The authors argue that Speer's soul was for sale only to the devil, and only the devil would have wanted to buy such a soul. It is not a direct parallel—Speer and Hitler were very different from Haldeman and Nixon—but a similar dynamic seemed at work in that H.R. Haldeman would serve only President Nixon. Only a president capable of the Watergate cover-up and the other dark things that characterized Nixon's presidency could have drawn him.

It would be difficult to imagine Haldeman serving as chief of staff in an administration that did not commit and abet such acts. Nixon was no Hitler and Haldeman was no Speer, and the analogy may be harsh and inaccurate in terms of specific actions and personalities, but it illustrates a principle of dark power and its minions. Nixon was the sort of president he was because he was Nixon, and being Nixon, he gravitated toward underlings who made it possible for him to act as he did. Those underlings— Haldeman, Ehrlichman, Colson, Dean, and others—were drawn to him because he was what he was. They committed crimes because they saw their jobs, and the political world in which they functioned, in criminal terms.

The minions, running true to Haldeman's philosophy, were dispensable. First, the White House wanted to hang it all on G. Gordon Liddy. After trying for a time to protect John Mitchell, "the Big Enchilada," Nixon and his advisers willingly fed him to the prosecutors. As the crisis mounted, presidential counsel Dean felt the heat and feared for his own fate; even before he realized that Nixon wanted his resignation, he sang to the prosecutors. Dean implicated Colson, Haldeman, Ehrlichman, and the president himself. Eventually, Nixon asked Haldeman, Ehrlichman, and Dean to resign. By the time the Ervin committee opened its hearings, the Nixon administration was shaken to its foundations. After the firings and resignations, Nixon stood without the advisers who had been his coconspirators.

Alexander Butterfield's testimony before the Ervin committee opened the scandal's final phase that led directly to Nixon's resignation. Butterfield, a deputy to Haldeman, revealed the existence of the White House tapes. Once that was known, the clamor for them drove Nixon into a corner, and he reacted like a wounded predator. The infamous Saturday Night Massacre, for instance, was caused by Nixon's resistance to giving certain tapes to Archibald Cox, the first of the Watergate special prosecutors. Nixon handed tapes over in sections, as he lost one legal battle after another.

The tapes undid his presidency. They showed Nixon to the world: the paranoia, the anger, the obsessions. Nixon wants someone to break into the Brookings Institution. He talks scornfully of the Jew-boys in the Justice Department. He talks about hush money for the Watergate burglars. He hanged himself with the tapes. Knowing what was on them, he fought desperately to keep them from becoming public. He considered burning them. It never crossed his mind, before Watergate, that the tapes would or could serve any purpose other than preserving material for his eventual memoirs. When Butterfield blabbed, the game was over. The administration would end in the proverbial whimper, but a few bangs were on the way first.

As the crisis deepened, the White House's siege mentality intensified. Nixon saw the press and the congressional Democrats joining forces in their final crusade against him. He wrote in his diary in late March 1973 that he and his administration had previously assumed that Watergate was not a major issue to the nation, that it was only a real concern to the Washington–New York circles of politics and media. But now, in March, Watergate had grown into a major issue after all, and the media had given the story "an enormous assist." Nixon now understood that things were going to get worse.

Nixon's reverie was prompted by James McCord's cooperation with Ervin's Watergate committee. The committee's chief counsel, Samuel Dash, told a press conference that McCord had given him a "full and honest" account of the background of the Watergate break-in. The *Los Angeles Times* printed leaked reports that McCord told Ervin's investigators that John Dean and Jeb Magruder knew about plans for the break-in. Nixon noted in his diary that he heard that CBS reporter Roger Mudd "had positively gloated" while describing McCord's story on the evening news broadcast. A few days later, Nixon concluded that the media had essentially forgotten such major stories as Nixon's price controls and possible North Vietnamese cease-fire violations. Only Watergate commanded the press's attention.

Despite his realization that Watergate had spiraled out of control, Nixon still grasped at a few straws of hope. In early April, not long after Nixon met Judge Matthew Byrne, he mused that Watergate still would not do serious damage if other things went well for the administration. On the other hand, Nixon noted in his diary, should the economy decline, then Watergate not only would hurt more, but the scandal would add emphasis to other problems. That was why, Nixon believed, domestic programs were now so important—not only to divert attention away from Watergate but so that voters would not get the impression that the administration was falling apart. That, Nixon reminded himself, happened to the Truman administration, and he was determined that the same fate would not befall him.

Within a few days, Nixon realized that he hoped in vain. Colson told him he had reason to believe that Mitchell hoped to avert blame for the break-in by setting up Haldeman to take the rap. Nixon sadly concluded that "everyone is going into business for himself . . ." The situation was not under control, and concentrating on domestic policies would not divert the public's attention from the scandal. Nixon was losing control of his people, as Mitchell resisted the role of sacrificial lamb and went gunning for Haldeman, Nixon's very own son of a bitch. Nixon recalled what Dean told him only a couple of weeks before, that there was a cancer close to the presidency.

Haldeman and Ehrlichman resigned later that month, just after Nixon fired Dean. Nixon, on reflection, decided that he and his advisers had handled the scandal ineptly up to that point. His quarter-century-old political instincts, he wrote in his memoirs, told him that he now faced "no ordinary opposition." This was a war to the death. In his second term, he issued his challenge to the liberal establishment to join in "epic battle."

They had been fighting over presidential appointments, impoundments, and the federal budget, and Watergate "had exposed a cavernous weakness in my ranks." Nixon believed that, were he to admit or reveal anything about Watergate at that late date, his enemies would use the information to keep the scandal alive, making it impossible for Nixon to function in office or exert his authority or leadership as president of the United States. He thought the only sensible course to follow was to assert his innocence and conduct a shake-up of his administration. Consequently, he banished Haldeman, Ehrlichman, and Dean.

Haldeman and Ehrlichman did not go willingly or happily, despite Haldeman's later endorsement of Nixon's self-preservation instincts. Haldeman's later writings are in some ways as contradictory as Nixon's, with Haldeman praising Nixon and then resenting being scapegoated in the Frost interview. Ehrlichman, for his part, was just plain angry. Both men felt insulted when the first person to raise the issue of their resignations was not the president but Ronald Ziegler, who was only the lowly press secretary. Ehrlichman later wrote that he thought, "The presidency is in some lot of trouble . . . if Ron Ziegler has become Lord Chamberlain."

Ehrlichman believed that John Dean, working with the press, specifically targeted Haldeman and him. Ehrlichman also thought that Nixon was mistaken in giving in to the pressure, and he would be in more trouble with his two top aides gone from the White House than if they remained. Nixon thought otherwise, and his was the only opinion that counted. A furious Ehrlichman thought that if he had to leave because he was "under a cloud," then plenty of others should leave, too, including Ziegler. There were, Ehrlichman wrote, many clouds overhead. He prepared a memo listing the names of seventeen people, Ziegler's among them, whom Ehrlichman thought had committed actual crimes or at least had been accused in the media of serious improprieties.

When the two top aides met with the president to discuss the question of resigning, Haldeman commented, "Our resignation will be quite a headline." According to Ehrlichman, Nixon answered, "It would be good in that it will say I'm cleaning house." Haldeman disagreed. After more discussion, Ehrlichman knew the game was up and that he and Haldeman would indeed resign. Only a couple of days later, Ehrlichman and Haldeman went to Camp David, where Nixon met each one separately, and emotionally told them they had to resign. There is no way to know if, at that late date, with his two closest and most visible aides driven from office, Nixon thought he could still preserve his presidency.

One thing we do know, owing to Nixon's later writings, is that he accused the press and the Democrats of improper behavior during Watergate; however, he seemed to have forgotten how the scandal originated. There is a special sort of irony one feels when reading Nixon's complaints that Washington fell into a "convulsion" over Watergate, that "restraints" inherent in "professional and political conduct for decades" were cast aside by the press and other agents of Nixon's destruction. The FBI and the Justice Department, Nixon wrote, leaked confidential information, mostly grand jury testimony. In Congress, his enemies asserted anything they wished and made many outrageous accusations, justifying such conduct as "righteous indignation over Watergate." Nixon ridiculed the idea of "investigative journalism." He called it "rumor journalism" and denounced the practice as nothing more than printing leaks from government sources whose agenda was toppling the administration. Nixon thought all of it improper and, unlike his own improprieties, it was not politics as usual.

It is true, of course, that a certain amount of misreporting occurred. Misreporting is nothing new in the world and, while regrettable, it does not signify the deterioration of the American news media. There was a feeding frenzy as the Watergate scandal intensified, and certainly the press is accountable for excesses, avoidable errors, and printing unsubstantiated rumors. Responsible members of the press spoke out at the time. The press did not then, nor will it ever, achieve perfection. Objectivity is not a final product but an ongoing, disciplined effort, and some journalists try harder than others. What must not be forgotten is that the press did not cause Watergate, and if the scandal went unreported, Nixon and his administration no doubt would have continued to commit illegal acts and trample the Constitution by ignoring or bypassing Congress. The press reported a scandal that was real despite Nixon's hollow objections.

Nixon harbored equally hard feelings about Senator Ervin and his special committee. He compared the committee's tactics to McCarthyism, accused committee members and staff personnel of committing past misdeeds themselves, and called into question their moral right to judge him. Nixon recounted that special prosecutor Archibald Cox tried to talk Ervin out of holding public hearings for fear that the publicity would compromise chances for fair jury trials in the future, and that a *Times of London* reporter called Ervin's conduct "deplorable." Nixon quoted further from the reporter's article to shore up his by now traditional double-standards argument: ". . . the lack of any serious protest against [Ervin's] behavior is in itself a measure of the loss of nerve of . . . Americans in the press, the academic world, and politics itself, who would once, in similar circumstances, have been campaigning vigorously to bring him to heel. . . ."

The televised hearings garnered large audiences and for a time, Sam Ervin was a national hero, often called "Uncle Sam" by adoring fans. The hearings were quite a show, replete with dramatic confrontations, showstopping retorts, and comic relief. They were riveting and held the public's attention until the list of major witnesses was exhausted.

A few of the witnesses tried to justify Nixon's actions and their own. They were not all there to hang Nixon and save themselves. Haldeman and Ehrlichman each tried to save themselves and to do their former master one last service by stating the White House case. That effort led to one of the more memorable moments in television history when, in reference to the Huston Plan, the plumbers, and other related Nixonian phenomena, Georgia senator Herman Talmadge addressed Ehrlichman.

"Do you remember," Talmadge asked, or rather declared, "when we were in law school, we studied a famous principle of law that came from England and also is well known in this country, that no matter how humble a man's cottage is, that even the king of England cannot enter without his consent." Ehrlichman, not about to give an inch, responded, "I'm afraid that has been considerably eroded over the years, has it not?" Ehrlichman thus stated the White House case more openly, even nakedly, than anyone ever had in public.

Talmadge, like Joseph Welch before him, knew a dramatic cue when he heard one. He peered, owl-like, over his spectacles and said, "Down in my part of the country we still think it's a pretty legitimate principle of law." The gallery burst into applause and cheers before Talmadge finished speaking. The senator had, in a few succinct sentences, answered Nixon's challenge to "do epic battle." Nixon had challenged and lost.

To the end, Nixon insisted that the Ervin committee and his other enemies were out to get him. That was true, of course; what Nixon left out of his analysis was that they had good reasons to go after him. Nixon voiced his feelings directly to Senator Ervin in a telephone clash one morning when, unknown to Ervin, the president was suffering from pneumonia and it caused him considerable pain even to speak. After arguing about access to presidential files for the committee's investigation, Nixon, despite the pain in his chest, nearly shouted into the receiver, "Your attitude in the hearings was clear. There's no question who you're out to get." Ervin, unfazed, answered, "We are not out to get anything, Mr. President, except the truth."

Nixon stood firm and told Ervin that no committee staffer would be allowed to look through his files, but he would have a "man to man" meeting with Ervin. Nixon told Ervin he was cooperating as much as possible, but he had to think about the future of the presidency itself. Nixon reminded Ervin of the constitutional separation of powers. Ervin was wary and unsure that he and Nixon could work things out to their mutual satisfaction, but he told the president he would report their talk to the committee and assured him again that he was not out to get him.

On August 29, Federal District Judge John Sirica, before whom the original Watergate burglars appeared in June 1972, ruled that Nixon had to give up nine tapes that the special prosecutor demanded. However, Sirica ruled that he would listen to them himself, then rule on Nixon's privilege claims; he would give special prosecutor Cox whichever tapes Sirica judged not privileged and relevant to the Watergate case. Nixon believed the ruling violated the separation of powers and later wrote that he would have resisted Sirica's ruling, on the grounds that the judge had impinged on executive authority, had not Watergate's political realities precluded resistance. The president opted to appeal the ruling through the regular judicial process. The case made it to the Supreme Court; in an important ruling, the court acknowledged the existence of executive privilege but, concerning the tapes, decided against Nixon.

As for special prosecutor Cox, Nixon had nothing good to say about him. Cox was allegedly a Kennedy family favorite, a new frontier Democrat, and, in Nixon's phrase, a "partisan viper . . . in our bosom." Florida senator Edward Gurney, a Republican member of the Ervin committee, asked why a Republican president would appoint someone like Cox unless he had a gun held to his head. Nixon bridled when Cox happily told reporters that an ancestor of his worked on Andrew Johnson's impeachment case. As 1973 wore on and Nixon saw that he was losing the "media battle" and that Cox was one of the effective field commanders in the war against his presidency, Nixon determined that, somehow or another, Cox had to go. The eventual result was the infamous Saturday Night Massacre, which may be the incident that once and for all cost Nixon the public relations battle.

After Sirica ruled that Nixon had to hand the tapes over to the court, the president and Cox both appealed. Each wanted custody of the tapes and neither wanted the judge to parcel them out. In mid-September, the U.S. Court of Appeals tried a compromise. Rather than let any single judge have the tapes, the appeals court suggested that Nixon and Cox put together a special group, acceptable to both, to hear the tapes and make the necessary determinations. Cox may have been willing to accept that, but Nixon rejected the idea. Instead, he offered to make written summaries of pertinent information on the tapes. Predictably, the special prosecutor found that unacceptable.

As the case wound its way upward toward the Supreme Court, Nixon shocked many by saying he would comply with a *definitive* majority ruling against him. Observers took that to mean he would defy a decision that either was not unanimous or not passed by a sufficient majority, whatever *sufficient* might mean to Nixon.

Shocking as many Americans found his statement, Nixon's stance was not without historical precedent. In the twentieth century, Americans have grown accustomed to accepting the Supreme Court as the supreme arbiter whose decisions all must accept, including any president of the United States. During the nineteenth century, it was not unusual for a president to defy or ignore the court. Thomas Jefferson and Andrew Jackson were notorious for their combative attitudes toward the judicial branch, and Jackson argued that, as president, he, too, had a right to interpret the Constitution. But in the 1970s, many Americans found Nixon's stance unacceptable.

When the court ruled unanimously against him, Nixon complied and yet another constitutional crisis was averted—assuming that Nixon indeed would have defied a less "definitive" ruling. Considering his weakened position, his threat of defiance may have been idle.

A few other solutions were proposed; all came to naught. For a brief time that autumn, Vice President Agnew's unrelated scandal diverted public attention. Agnew resigned and pleaded no contest to a charge of receiving illegal kickbacks and bribes when he was governor of Maryland and even during his vice presidency. Public attention was not diverted for long, though, and by mid-October the Nixon–Cox battle for the tapes once again occupied the headlines. On the weekend of October 20, the president moved against Cox. After first trying to implement an order to Cox to restrict his judicial moves, Nixon ordered Attorney General Elliot Richardson to fire him. Richardson resigned rather than execute the order. Nixon next gave the order to Richardson's deputy, William Ruckelshaus. He resigned, too. Finally, Robert Bork, the number three man in the Justice Department, carried out the president's wishes and fired the special prosecutor.

The Saturday Night Massacre outraged a significant portion of the voting public and energized the drive against Nixon on Capitol Hill, not that it needed much energizing. Constitutional scholar Raoul Berger said on national television that by firing Cox, President Nixon committed an impeachable offense. Still, the mood in the White House was jubilant. The president and his men thought they had executed, in Fred Emery's words, "the big play." Emery himself, covering Watergate for the *Times of London*, was not so sure. In his superb history of the Watergate scandal, he wrote that Judge Sirica, following events through the news media, thought that Nixon must have "lost touch with reality." On Capitol Hill, the weekend's events sealed the Democratic leadership's resolve to have the House Judiciary Committee begin hearings to consider grounds for impeachment. The big play landed the White House back in its own end zone.

After the massacre came further damaging developments, as tapes were altered—one of which contained the famous eighteen-and-a-half-minute gap. The present volume will not follow each development of Watergate step-by-step; in the next few months, the president's position deteriorated rapidly and, by December, he realized how tenuous was his hold on his office. The tapes made him look very bad for a variety of reasons. They contained damaging material, although not the "smoking gun" that many people thought might materialize to link the president directly to the cover-up.

What was there was bad enough, though, as it showed Nixon discussing any number of unethical matters, using profane language, and teetering on the fine edge of illegality. Many wondered what could be on the tapes he had refused to hand over, since what had been released did plenty to erode his standing with the public. In particular, there was a good deal of pious horror over the profanity, as the presidential circle's word usage offended the ever-present puritan sensibilities of middle-class America.

Nixon was badly damaged, and two days before Christmas, he wrote on a notepad, "Last Christmas here?" He knew he faced possible impeachment or resignation. On New Year's Day 1974, he sat down for several sessions of thinking on paper. He wrote copious notes, arguing with himself whether to capitulate or fight. He resolved to fight.

Were he to resign, he wrote to himself, that would set a dangerous precedent for his successors, and it would be tantamount to admitting guilt. Resigning would let down his friends. To fight now would make possible for him a "future as a man of principle." He admonished himself to be strong in this "unprecedented adversity," and to avoid speaking or acting intemperately. Later in the day, he wrote another note. "Above all else: Dignity, command, faith, head high, no fear, build a new spirit, drive, act like a president, act like a winner. Opponents are savage destroyers, haters. Time to use full power of the president to fight overwhelming forces arrayed against us."

The forces were indeed overwhelming. The House Judiciary Committee's impeachment inquiry went forward, carrying a huge television audience with it. This was only the second time in history that the Judiciary Committee took up the question of impeaching a president. Nixon assessed the situation realistically. At the end of December, 54 percent of Americans polled did not favor Nixon's impeachment and removal, but 45 percent said they wanted him to resign. Nixon wrote that, early on, he thought the public would tire of Watergate and thus compel Congress and the press to drop the matter. Instead, the "congressional and media assault" and the tapes controversy made the public see Nixon as the villain and the main obstacle to moving past the Watergate morass. "Unless I could do something to stem this tide, it would sweep me out of office."

Haldeman wrote of the president's indispensability. Here, however, conditions fueled the opposite argument. By staying in office, President Nixon bogged down the presidency. He was so consumed with Watergate that it impaired his ability to execute his proper duties. The administration lost most of its real authority, policies were not implemented, orders were not executed, and other programs and operations were paralyzed. Secretary of State Henry Kissinger was largely on his own concerning foreign-policy questions. The presidency stopped working. Those favoring Nixon's resignation argued that he needed to leave so that the presidency could again function.

But, on that New Year's Day, Nixon resolved to fight, and more than half the coming year went by before he accepted the immutable fact that all hope was lost. He resigned only when he had to face the inescapable conclusion that the House was certain to impeach him and the Senate was certain to remove him from office. He left only when his back was to the wall. He prided himself for not being a quitter, but he had for some time put his own personal interests above the nation's. He paralyzed the presidency rather than resign in a timely fashion. He claimed, almost to the last, that he stayed on so as not to damage the presidency by setting destructive precedents, but he did more to damage the office, perhaps, than any other president.

The tapes, in the end, showed Nixon guilty of nearly everything for which he previously denied guilt. Eventually, Nixon had to release the most damaging tapes, one of which contained the "smoking gun" that was the June 23, 1973, conversation between Nixon and Haldeman in which the president complains that the FBI is not "under control," and, most damning, discusses the problems posed by the money trail leading to CREEP. Nixon tells Haldeman that, if anyone asks the people at CREEP what the money was for, they should lie and say that the Cubans solicited it. The conversation ranged over several topics, but it all added up to the president's conscious participation in the cover-up.

When Nixon gave up the smoking gun tapes, he shame-facedly told the nation that some of his earlier accounts were "at variance" with what the tapes actually contained. In other words, he had lied. This came at the most awkward of times, just after the House Judiciary Committee voted three articles of impeachment. Most of the Republican committee members voted with the Democratic majority, but a small group of die-hard Republicans voted against the articles and seemed ready to stand by their president to the death. After the smoking gun discharged, they recanted their support and called for his resignation. Nixon's already low public-opinion ratings plunged lower.

When Nixon told the nation of his intention to resign, he frankly admitted he had lost his "political base" in the Senate. The House was certain to accept the Judiciary Committee's articles and pass a bill of impeachment, and the smoking gun tapes killed any chance of surviving a Senate vote. Barry Goldwater told him as much shortly before, that Nixon could count on perhaps ten senators to vote in his favor. Goldwater did not indicate that he would be one of the ten.

Nixon addressed the nation on the night of August 8, 1974, to announce his resignation, to take effect the next day. He showed little emotion during that televised address. The next morning, as he bade farewell to the White House personnel in another nationally televised address, he showed considerably more feeling, laying bare the terrible wound he had sustained.

Nixon's White House address is often described as rambling and incoherent, but it was neither. He was perfectly coherent, did not ramble, and delivered a clear, well-prepared speech. His obviously strong emotions gave many viewers, more than a few of them prejudiced against him anyway, the impression that he was not all there. He was there, all right. Nixon spoke of his family, of his father's career and character, his mother's saintliness, his two brothers who died of tuberculosis. He quoted Theodore Roosevelt's memorial to his first wife: "And when my heart's dearest died, the light went from my life forever."

He spoke of coming back from seemingly hopeless defeats. "We think that when someone dear to us dies, we think that when we lose an election, we think that when we suffer a defeat,

that all is ended. We think, as TR said, that the light had left his life forever." That is not true, Nixon said. "It is only a beginning, always. . . . It must always sustain us, because the greatness comes not when things go always good for you, but the greatness comes and you are really tested when you take some knocks, some disappointments, when sadness comes, because only if you have been in the deepest valley can you ever know how magnificent it is to be on the highest mountain."

Nixon exhorted his listeners, both in the White House and in the television audience, always to give their best and never get discouraged. One must never be petty, he said, for, "always remember, others may hate you, but those who hate you don't win unless you hate them, and then you destroy yourself."

Nixon hated *them,* and he destroyed himself. For neither the first nor last time, he was that morning both wrenchingly honest and maddeningly disingenuous. Also, for neither the first nor last time, Nixon opened his emotions to the nation and the world. He grieved and invited us to grieve with him. Many did, even some who were glad to see him go.

After that painfully intimate speech to the White House

personnel, the nation, and the world, Nixon and his wife, Pat, walked across the White House lawn, over the red carpet that marked his path, to the waiting helicopter. He paused at the hatch, atop the ladder, and gave his victory salute to the crowd, the same signal that infuriated the mob in San Jose four years earlier. There was no spite intended now, but rather a sad attempt to show that he was down but not out. But, Nixon was beaten, and looked it.

On that morning of August 9, he began the journey home to California, disgrace, and exile—and resurrection.

PART V

NIXON AND HIS ENEMIES— THE SUNSET YEARS

★ ★ ★ ★ ★ ★ ★ ★

THE LONG GOOD-BYE

✭ ✭ ✭

During that first year in California, Richard Nixon endured widespread acrimonious reaction to his presidential pardon, a critical illness that nearly killed him, and months of crippling depression. He had delivered himself to ruin. For a time he lived as a disgraced recluse, perhaps the most despised man in the United States of America.

When Nixon left the presidency, he and his enemies were far from through with each other. The New York Bar Association disbarred him. He faced numerous lawsuits. His legal fees skyrocketed. Bebe Rebozo, Nixon's closest personal friend, had his own legal problems that were related to Nixon's. Nixon believed Rebozo was being punished for their friendship. These things passed, in time, but made life difficult for several years. Still, Nixon considered himself down but not out.

True to form, he came back, claimed the role of elder statesman, and lived out the last part of his life respected and in some quarters admired. He wrote books, contributed to the world's knowledge and perspective, and in many ways earned the status he wanted. Nevertheless, as discussed in this book's introduction, he never shed Watergate and never gained forgiveness for it.

He was allowed back into the public arena but only on an honorary basis. It was a sort of parole, and he had to stay within certain bounds. As one pundit commented after Nixon reemerged, "He still couldn't get elected dogcatcher."

That was all right; Nixon had no desire to be dogcatcher. He preferred to write his books, to give over a body of work that distilled the perspectives of a lifetime's experience in politics and diplomacy.

Just as the man himself was rife with paradoxes, so is his literary corpus. Nixon's books form a repository of wisdom, generosity, profundity, pettiness, and vengefulness. Probably without fully realizing how much he revealed, he left a written record of himself at his best and worst. No comparable body of work exists; no other president left writings so intensely personal and painfully honest even as they were self-serving and deceitful. Their historical value cannot be calculated; they will intrigue and educate scholars and students for as long as anyone studies American history. What they will tell future American generations not only about Nixon but about the United States of America, we can only guess.

More immediately and narrowly, Nixon's writings give us his final testament of his hatreds, resentments, and enmities. They are all there, alongside his assessments of the United States over the last two decades of his life, his views of the cold war's final years, his late perspectives on Watergate and his other political struggles. Nixon took it as his final task to warn, enlighten, educate, inform, and avenge.

For all of his wisdom, his profound insights into any number of international and national issues, Nixon to the end thought that his enemies treated him unfairly, sabotaged him, and conspired to bring him down. There is some truth to that, of course, since any leader is subject to concerted opposition. Nixon had real enemies, and they did work to bring him down. But Nixon never seemed to understand his own role in his downfall. He never acknowledged his own double standards, spitefulness, and vengefulness. He was a haunted, obsessed man, all the more so for not understanding that he was haunted and obsessed. At least, he gave no public indications of such understanding.

Even *Six Crises*, which he wrote just after leaving the vice presidency, while still comparatively young, contains broad hints of Nixon's dark outlook. In every book, no matter the main subject, Nixon got around to excoriating enemies, complaining about what they did to him, and expressing a certain profound pessimism about his country and his world, even as he included the politician's obligatory positive aphorisms. Nixon's darkness suffuses everything. His books have much to offer, but they will also show future readers the haunted byways of Nixon's labyrinthine mind.

Nixon intrigues us endlessly, because he is so unusual in American history. Other politicians just were not like him, and other presidents most certainly were not like him. Tom Wicker called his Nixon biography *One of Us*, but one wonders if Nixon *was* one of us—at least, one of us in the sense that Wicker seems to have meant. For all his "common" beginnings, for all his "ordinariness," Nixon was neither common nor ordinary. He was different.

Of course, we run into trouble here. What precisely is a common or ordinary American? The author has no desire to explore that complex and lengthy question but will venture the opinion that, whatever a common or ordinary American may be, Nixon was not one. He was a man of extraordinary talents and broad vision who was afflicted with equally extraordinary blindness and pettiness. Nixon in some ways approached greatness, but he was doomed to thwart himself time and again. The grand spirit of the statesman could neither suppress nor escape the stunted soul of the scoundrel. Character is destiny. Nixon's character raised him high, against formidable odds. Nixon's character laid him low, against formidable odds.

There is no telling what future generations will make of Richard Nixon, or anyone else. There is no definitive historical judgment, by historians or anyone else. As times change, perceptions of the past change.

I will venture one prediction: However future Americans regard Richard Nixon, and however many times their perceptions of him change with the shifting political winds of their ages, Americans will find him fascinating, compelling, and haunting, as long as people regard themselves as Americans, and as long as they care about their national past.

BIBLIOGRAPHY

Magazines and Newspapers

Many periodicals were consulted for *Nixon's Enemies*, among them: *The Atlantic Monthly, Time, Newsweek, U.S. News and World Report, The New Yorker, The New Republic*, the *New York Times*, the *Washington Post*, the *Washington Star*, the *Los Angeles Times*, the *San Francisco Chronicle*, the *San Francisco Examiner*, the *Newark Evening News*, and the *Newark Star-Ledger*, among others. Reports from the Associated Press and the United Press also proved useful.

Books

Acheson, Dean. *Present at the Creation*. New York: W.W. Norton, 1969.

Aitken, Jonathan. *Nixon: A Life*. Washington, D.C.: Regnery Publishing, 1993.

Ambrose, Stephen E. *Rise to Globalism*. New York: Penguin Books, 1985.

———. *Nixon: The Education of a Politician, 1913-1960*. New York: Simon and Schuster, 1987.

———. *Nixon: Ruin and Recovery, 1973-1990*. New York: Simon and Schuster, 1991.

Andrews, Bert. *Washington Witch Hunt*. New York: Random House, 1948.

Beschloss, Michael R. *The Crisis Years: Kennedy and Khrushchev, 1960-1963*. New York: Edward Burlingame Books, 1991.

Brodie, Fawn M. *Richard Nixon: The Shaping of His Character*. New York: W.W. Norton, 1981.

Buckley, William F., Jr., and L. Brent Bozell. *McCarthy and His Enemies: The Record and Its Meaning*. Chicago: Henry Regnery Company, 1954.

Bullock, Paul. *Jerry Voorhis: The Idealist as Politician*. New York: Vantage Press, 1978.

Caute, David. *The Great Fear: The Anti-Communist Purge Under Truman and Eisenhower*. New York: Simon and Schuster, 1978.

Chambers, Whittaker. *Witness*. New York: Random House, 1952.

Colodny, Len, and Robert Gettlin. *Silent Coup*. New York: St. Martin's Press, 1991.

Cook, Blanche Wiesen. *The Declassified Eisenhower*. New York: Penguin Books, 1984.

Cook, Fred J. *The Nightmare Decade: The Life and Times of Senator Joe McCarthy*. New York: Random House, 1971.

Cooke, Alistair. *A Generation on Trial: USA v. Alger Hiss*. New York: Alfred A. Knopf, 1950.

Crossman, Richard, ed. *The God That Failed*. New York: Harper, 1950.

Crowley, Monica. *Nixon Off the Record*. New York: Random House, 1996.

———. *Nixon in Winter*. New York: Random House, 1998.

Dallek, Robert. *The American Style of Foreign Policy*. New York: Oxford University Press, 1983.

———. *Lone Star Rising: Lyndon Johnson and His Times, 1908–1960*. New York: Oxford University Press, 1991.

———. *Hail to the Chief*. New York: Hyperion, 1996.

Dean, John. *Blind Ambition*. New York: Simon and Schuster, 1976.

De Toledano, Ralph, and Victor Lasky. *Seeds of Treason: The Strange Case of Alger Hiss*. New York: Secker and Warburg, 1950.

Douglas, Helen Gahagan. *A Full Life*. New York: Doubleday, 1982.

Draper, Theodore. *The Roots of American Communism*. Chicago: Elephant Paperbacks, 1985.

———. *American Communism and Soviet Russia: The Formative Period*. New York: Vintage Books, 1986.

Ehrlichman, John. *Witness to Power*. New York: Pocket Books, 1982.

Eisenhower, Julie Nixon. *Pat Nixon: The Untold Story*. New York: Simon and Schuster, 1986.

Emery, Fred. *Watergate*. New York: Simon and Schuster, 1994.

Evans, Rowland, Jr., and Robert D. Novak. *Nixon in the White House*. New York: Vintage Books, 1972.

Fromkin, David. *In the Time of the Americans*. New York: Vintage Books, 1995.

Gaddis, John Lewis. *Strategies of Containment*. New York: Oxford University Press, 1982.

Goldman, Eric F. *The Crucial Decade and After: America, 1945-1960*. New York: Vintage Books, 1960.

Goodman, Walter. *The Committee: The Extraordinary Career of the House Committee on Un-American Activities*. New York: Farrar, Straus, and Giroux, 1968.

Griffith, Robert. *The Politics of Fear: Joseph R. McCarthy and the Senate*. Rochelle Park, N.J.: Hayden Book Company, 1970.

Haldeman, H.R., with Joseph Di Mona. *The Ends of Power*. New York: Times Books, 1978.

Haldeman, H.R. *The Haldeman Diaries*. New York: G.P. Putnam's Sons, 1994.

Hamby, Alonzo L. *Beyond the New Deal: Harry S Truman and American Liberalism*. New York: Columbia University Press, 1973.

Harper, John Lamberton. *American Visions of Europe*. Cambridge, England: Cambridge University Press, 1994.

Hiss, Alger. *In the Court of Public Opinion*. New York: Alfred A. Knopf, 1957.

———. *Recollections of a Life*. New York: Seaver Books, 1988.

Hoff, Joan. *Nixon Reconsidered*. New York: Basic Books, 1994.

Hofstadter, Richard. *The Paranoid Style in American Politics*. New York: Alfred A. Knopf, 1966.

Hoover, J. Edgar. *Masters of Deceit: The Story of Communism in America and How to Fight it*. New York: Henry Holt and Company, 1958.

———. *A Study of Communism*. New York: Holt, Rinehart and Winston, 1962.

Isaacson, Walter, and Evan Thomas. *The Wise Men: Six Friends and the World They Made*. New York: Simon and Schuster, 1988.

Jaworski, Leon. *The Right and the Power*. New York: Reader's Digest Press, 1976.

Khrushchev, Sergei. *Khrushchev on Khrushchev*. Boston: Little, Brown, 1990.

Kissinger, Henry. *White House Years*. Boston: Little, Brown, 1979.

———. *Years of Upheaval*. Boston: Little, Brown, 1982.

———. *Diplomacy*. New York: Simon and Schuster, 1994.

Kleher, Harvey. *The Heyday of American Communism: The Depression Decade*. New York: Basic Books, 1984.

Kurz, Kenneth Franklin. *Franklin Roosevelt and the Gospel of Fear*. University of California, Los Angeles, dissertation, 1995.

Kutler, Stanley I. *The American Inquisition: Justice and Injustice in the Cold War*. New York: Hill and Wang, 1982.

———. *The Wars of Watergate*. New York: Alfred A. Knopf, 1990.

———. *Abuse of Power*. New York: The Free Press, 1997.

LaFeber, Walter. *America, Russia, and the Cold War, 1945-1984.* New York: Alfred A. Knopf, 1985.

Matthews, Christopher. *Kennedy and Nixon.* New York: Simon and Schuster, 1996.

Mazo, Earl. *Richard Nixon: A Political and Personal Portrait.* New York: Avon Books, 1960.

Mazo, Earl, and Stephen Hess. *Nixon: A Political Portrait.* New York: Popular Library, 1968.

Miale, Florence R., and Michael Selzer. *The Nuremberg Mind: The Psychology of the Nazi Leaders.* New York: Quadrangle Books, 1977.

Mitchell, Greg. *Tricky Dick and the Pink Lady.* New York: Random House, 1998.

Morris, Roger. *Richard Milhous Nixon: The Rise of an American Politician.* New York: Henry Holt and Company, 1990.

Nixon, Richard. *Six Crises.* Garden City, N.Y.: Doubleday, 1962.

———. *RN: The Memoirs of Richard Nixon.* New York: Simon and Schuster, 1978.

———. *The Real War.* Simon and Schuster, 1980.

———. *Leaders.* New York: Warner Books, 1982.

———. *No More Vietnams.* New York: Avon Books, 1985.

———. *1999: Victory without War.* New York: Pocket Books, 1989.

———. *In the Arena.* New York: Pocket Books, 1990.

———. *Seize the Moment.* New York: Simon and Schuster, 1992.

———. *Beyond Peace.* New York: Random House, 1994.

Oudes, Bruce, ed. *From: The President—Richard Nixon's Secret Files.* New York: Harper and Row, 1989.

Parmet, Herbert S. *Richard Nixon and His America.* New York: Konecky and Konecky, 1990.

Powers, Richard Gid. *Secrecy and Power: The Life of J. Edgar Hoover.* New York: The Free Press, 1987.

Reeves, Richard. *President Kennedy: A Profile of Power.* New York: Simon and Schuster, 1993.

Reeves, Thomas C. *The Life and Times of Joe McCarthy.* New York: Stein and Day, 1982.

Rovere, Richard. *Senator Joe McCarthy.* New York: Harcourt, Brace, 1959.

Safire, William. *Before the Fall.* Garden City, N.Y.: Doubleday, 1975.

Schwartz, Bernard. *A History of the Supreme Court.* New York: Oxford University Press, 1993.

Scobie, Ingrid W. *Center Stage: Helen Gahagan Douglas—A Life.* New York: Oxford University Press, 1992.

Sirica, John J. *To Set the Record Straight.* New York: W.W. Norton, 1979.

Smith, John Chabot. *Alger Hiss: The True Story*. New York: Holt, Rinehart and Winston, 1976.

Strober, Gerald S., and Deborah Hart. *Nixon: An Oral History of His Presidency*. New York: HarperCollins, 1994.

Talbott, Strobe, ed. *Khrushchev Remembers*. Boston: Bantam Books, 1971.

———. *Khrushchev Remembers: The Last Testament*. Boston: Bantam Books, 1976.

Tanenhaus, Sam. *Whittaker Chambers*. New York: Random House, 1997.

Tebbel, John, and Sarah Miles Watts. *The Press and the Presidency*. New York: Oxford University Press, 1985.

Trudeau, G. B. *Guilty, Guilty, Guilty!* New York: Holt, Rinehart and Winston, 1974.

Truman, Harry S. *Memoirs*. Garden City, New York: Doubleday, 1956.

Voorhis, Jerry. *Beyond Victory*. New York: Farrar and Rinehart, 1944.

———. *Confessions of a Congressman*. Garden City, New York: Doubleday, 1947.

———. *The Strange Case of Richard Milhous Nixon*. New York: Paul S. Eriksson, Inc., 1972.

Walsh, Kenneth T. *Feeding the Beast: The White House Versus the Press*. New York: Random House, 1996.

The *Washington Post*. *The Presidential Transcripts*. New York: Delacorte Press, 1974.

———. *The Fall of a President*. New York: Dell, 1974.

Weinstein, Allen. *Perjury: The Hiss-Chambers Case*. New York: Alfred A. Knopf, 1978.

White, Theodore H. *The Making of the President 1960*. New York: Atheneum, 1961.

———. *The Making of the President 1972*. New York: Atheneum, 1973.

———. *Breach of Faith: The Fall of Richard Nixon*. New York: Dell, 1975.

Wicker, Tom. *One of Us: Richard Nixon and the American Dream*. New York: Random House, 1991.

Wills, Garry. *Nixon Agonistes: The Crisis of the Self-Made Man*. Boston: Houghton Mifflin, 1970.

Zeligs, Meyer A. *Friendship and Fratricide: An Analysis of Whittaker Chambers and Alger Hiss*. New York: Viking Press, 1967.

INDEX